ENCYCLOPEDIA OF

FAMILY HEALTH

ENCYCLOPEDIA OF

FAMILY HEALTH

CONSULTANT

DAVID B. JACOBY, MD

JOHNS HOPKINS SCHOOL OF MEDICINE

VOLUME
3

CARTILAGE—DIAGNOSIS

MARSHALL CAVENDISH
NEW YORK · LONDON · TORONTO · SYDNEY

Marshall Cavendish Corporation
99 White Plains Road
Tarrytown, New York 10591-9001
© Marshall Cavendish Corporation, 1998
© Marshall Cavendish Limited 1998, 1991, 1988, 1986, 1983, 1982, 1971

Update by Brown Partworks
The material in this set was first published in the English language by
Marshall Cavendish Limited of 119 Wardour Street, London W1V 3TD, England.

Printed and bound in Italy

Library of Congress Cataloging-in-Publication Data

Encyclopedia of family health
17v. cm.
Includes index
1. Medicine, Popular–Encyclopedias. 2. Health–Encyclopedias. I. Marshall Cavendish Corporation.
RC81.A2M336 1998   96–49537
610'. 3–dc21   CIP
ISBN 0-7614-0625-5 (set)
ISBN 0-7614-0628-X (v.3)

INTRODUCTION

We Americans live under a constant bombardment of information (and misinformation) about the latest supposed threats to our health. We are taught to believe that disease is the result of not taking care of ourselves. Death becomes optional. Preventive medicine becomes a moral crusade, illness the punishment for the foolish excesses of the American lifestyle. It is not the intent of the authors of this encyclopedia to contribute to this atmosphere. While it is undoubtedly true that Americans could improve their health by smoking less, exercising more, and controlling their weight, this is already widely understood.

As Mencken put it, "It is not the aim of medicine to make men virtuous. The physician should not preach salvation, he should offer absolution." The aims of this encyclopedia are to present a summary of human biology, anatomy, and physiology, to outline the more common diseases, and to discuss, in a general way, the diagnosis and treatment of these diseases. This is not a do-it-yourself book. It will not be possible to treat most conditions based on the information presented here. But it will be possible to understand most diseases and their treatments. Informed in this way, you will be able to discuss your condition and its treatment with your physician. It is also hoped that this will alleviate some of the fears associated with diseases, doctors, and hospitals.

The authors of this encyclopedia have also attempted to present, in an open-minded way, alternative therapies. There is undoubtedly value to some of these. However, when dealing with serious diseases, they should not be viewed as a substitute for conventional treatment. The reason that conventional treatment is accepted is that it has been systematically tested, and because scientific evidence backs it up. It would be a tragedy to miss the opportunity for effective treatment while pursuing an ineffective alternative therapy.

Finally, it should be remembered that the word *doctor* is originally from the Latin word for "teacher." Applied to medicine, this should remind us that the doctor's duty is not only to diagnose and treat disease, but to help the patient to understand. If this encyclopedia can aid in this process, its authors will be gratified.

DAVID B. JACOBY, MD
JOHNS HOPKINS SCHOOL OF MEDICINE

CONTENTS

Cartilage

Q My toddler is always falling over but has never broken any bones. Is there a reason for this, or is she just lucky?

A A child's skeleton contains a great deal of cartilage. This is much tougher and more flexible than true bone and has more shock-absorbing power, which explains why your daughter—and most other children—can take countless falls without breaking any bones. Falling is also less damaging to the young because they weigh less than adults. Also the younger they are, the less fear they have, and therefore they do not get tense as they feel themselves falling. This is why you may occasionally hear of babies falling out of buildings several stories up and literally bouncing.

Q My brother had the cartilages taken out of his knee. How can he manage without them?

A The cartilages of the knee are part of the movement system of the joint. If the cartilages are removed, the joint is less efficient for a while, and then the muscles learn to compensate for the missing cartilage.

Q I am 63, and I recently discovered that I am 2 in (5 cm) shorter now than when I was a girl. Why is this?

A As the body ages, not only do the bones in the vertebral column get smaller, but the disks of cartilage between them get thinner and harder. This thinning makes the disks shrink in size and, together with the bone shrinkage, makes you shorter in stature.

Q My joints give a loud click whenever I bend down. Could there be something wrong with them?

A The reason your bones click when you bend down is because the movement releases a vacuum in the joint. A high-pitched clicking sound is nothing to worry about, but if the sound gets deeper and there is pain, it could mean that there is something wrong. If this occurs, see your doctor.

The different types of cartilage form a vital part of the body's framework. Among its many functions, it surrounds the bronchial tubes, supports the nose and ears, and lines bones and joints.

The different types of cartilage

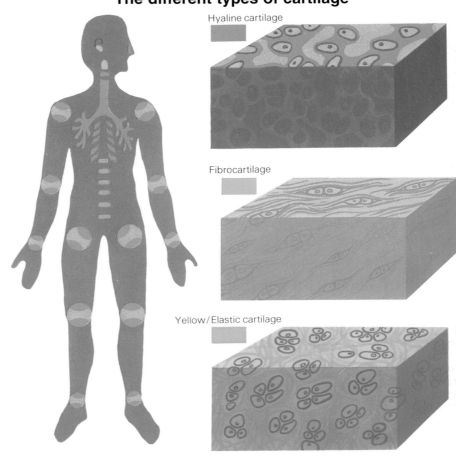

Hyaline cartilage

Fibrocartilage

Yellow/Elastic cartilage

Hyaline cartilage lines bones in joints and forms the respiratory tract. Fibrocartilage acts as a shock absorber in the backbone and other joints. Elastic cartilage is very flexible and forms the outer ear and the epiglottis in the throat.

Cartilage, or gristle, is a smooth, tough, but flexible, part of the body's skeletal system. In adults it is mainly found in joints and covering the ends of bones, but it forms the complete skeleton of a developing fetus. In it true bone is formed. Those cartilages that are subject to a great deal of wear and tear may cause problems, particularly in the spine and knees.

Nearly all the bones in the body begin as rods of cartilage, which are gradually hardened by deposits of calcium and other minerals. This process, called ossification, begins before birth, in the third or fourth month of the fetus's life. It is not complete until about the age of 21, since the cartilage not only forms the foundation for bone formation, but also allows the bones to grow. In adults cartilage remains at strategic points in the skeleton, where its toughness, smoothness, and flexibility are most needed.

Structure

The structure of cartilage is not the same throughout the skeleton. Its makeup varies according to the specific job it has to do. All cartilage is composed of a groundwork, or matrix, in which there are embedded cells plus fibers made up of substances called collagen and elastin. The consistency of the fibers varies according to the type of cartilage, but all cartilage is alike in that it contains no blood vessels. Instead it is nourished by nutrients that diffuse through the covering (perichondrium) of the cartilage, and lubricated by synovial fluid, which is made by membranes lining the joints. According to their different properties, cartilages are known as hyaline cartilage, fibrocartilage, and elastic cartilage.

Types of cartilage

Hyaline cartilage is a bluish-white, translucent tissue and, of the three types, has the fewest cells and fibers. What fibers there are all consist of collagen. This cartilage forms the fetal skeleton and is capable of the immense amount of growth that allows a baby to grow from about 18 in (45 cm) into a person up to 6 ft (1.8 m) tall or more. After growth is complete, hyaline cartilage remains in a very thin layer, only 0.04 in (1 mm) across, on the surface of the ends of the bones in the joints.

Hyaline cartilage is also found in the respiratory tract, where it forms the end of the nose and the stiff, but flexible, rings surrounding the windpipe and the larger tubes (bronchi) leading to the lungs. At the end of the ribs, bars of hyaline cartilage form the connections between the ribs and the breastbone and play their part in enabling the chest to expand and contract during breathing.

In the larynx, or voice box, hyaline cartilages not only help to support the structure, they are also involved in the production of the voice. As they move, they control the amount of air passing through the larynx, and therefore the pitch of the note that is emitted.

The second type, fibrocartilage, is composed of many bundles of the tough substance collagen, which makes it both resilient and able to withstand compression. Both these qualities are essential at the site in which fibrocartilage is most plentiful, namely between the bones of the vertebral column.

In the spine each bone or vertebra is separated from its neighbor by a disk of fibrocartilage. The disks cushion the spine against jarring and help make it possible for the human frame to remain upright. Each disk is made up of an outer coating of fibrocartilage that surrounds a thick, syrupy fluid. The cartilaginous part of the disk, which has a lubricated surface, prevents the bones from being worn away during movement, while the fluid acts as a sort of natural shock absorber.

Fibrocartilage also forms a tough connection between bones and ligaments; in the hip girdle it joins the two parts of the hips together at a joint known as the symphysis pubis. In women this cartilage is particularly important because it is softened by the hormones of pregnancy to allow the baby's head to pass through.

The third type of cartilage is known as elastic cartilage. It gets its name from the fibers of elastin that, with collagen, make

it up. The elastin fibers give elastic cartilage a distinctive yellow color. Strong but supple, elastic cartilage forms the flap of tissue called the epiglottis, which snaps down over the entrance to the airway as food is swallowed.

Elastic cartilage also makes up the springy part of the outer ear, and supports the walls of the canal leading to the middle ear and the eustachian tubes that link each ear with the back of the throat. Along with hyaline cartilage, elastic cartilage forms part of the supporting and voice-producing areas of the larynx.

Problems and treatment

The most vulnerable cartilages are those that have to withstand constant pressure in the knees and vertebral column. The knee joint contains a pair of cartilages shaped like half-moons, and it is these cartilages that are most likely to be damaged by strenuous sports, particularly sports in which the knee joint is frequently twisted. If one or both cartilages become torn, and then their frayed ends get caught between the surface of the joint, the knee will lock or give way.

In such injuries, which are 20 times more common in men and are a notorious problem for soccer players, the knee should be firmly bandaged. In severe cases a splint may be needed behind the knee. The doctor may try to manipulate the joint to move the torn ends of the cartilage away from the joint surface, and to remove some of the excess fluid that accumulates around the site of the injury.

Torn cartilages in the knee are a common problem for professional soccer players.

However, the only way to cure the complaint completely is by surgical removal of the offending cartilage. The surgeon makes an incision from the bony lump at the side of the knee to the base of the knee joint and takes out the cartilage. After surgery it is important to get the knee moving as soon as possible, and physiotherapy should be given.

A slipped disk is another very common cartilage problem. Strain or sudden twisting movements can tear the disks of cartilage between the vertebrae, making the pulpy center protrude, and pushing the whole disk out of shape. The protrusion can press on nerves, causing pain in the back and possibly in the buttocks, thighs, and one leg. Apart from rest in bed with a hard board under the mattress, the doctor may recommend traction, manipulation, or the wearing of a corsetlike belt. If none of these is successful in curing the trouble, surgery may be required.

In old age the joints become stiffer as the cartilage covering the ends of the bones loses its smoothness. This is quite normal, but in a condition called osteoarthritis, the cartilage and parts of the underlying bone actually degenerate. Osteoarthritis is not only a disease of old age: it can affect sportspeople and people who put excess strain on their joints by being overweight. Analgesics will relieve the pain, and physiotherapy and heat treatment might ease the joints.

Cataracts

Q My doctor says I have to wait for my cataract to "mature" before I can have it removed. What does this mean?

A The term *mature* simply means the cataract has developed to such a degree that surgery is necessary. A cataract can be removed at any stage, but this is not normally done unless vision is likely to be significantly improved by the operation. Your doctor will recommend surgery when it is necessary, but at the moment your eyesight has probably not deteriorated sufficiently.

Q My uncle just had cataracts removed. How can I avoid getting them?

A Don't worry, they are not hereditary or contagious. The only precaution you can take is to avoid ultraviolet sunlight; so wear sunglasses on bright days. Otherwise, cataracts are likely to be merely the result of advancing age.

Q I have had a successful cataract operation. Why is my vision still so poor?

A One of the reasons for your continued impaired vision is that the center of sight in the retina has been affected; once the cataract and the lens are removed, the ability to focus is lost. For this reason vision has to be corrected with spectacles, contact lenses, or implants. Ask your doctor which would best suit your condition; once you have been prescribed the correct visual aid, your sight should return to normal.

Q How can I tell whether someone has a cataract?

A In most cases, there is no obvious external indication. The opacity is in the internal lens behind the iris. If it is at the back of the lens, the appearance of the eye may be entirely normal. It is only if the opacity is dense and involves the front part of the lens that a whitish pupil is seen. It is a common mistake to confuse a cataract with a corneal scar from injury or disease, which may cause a milky film over the surface of the eye.

Cataracts are a common condition of the lens of the eye. If left untreated, they can lead to severe visual impairment, but modern surgical techniques are very effective in restoring good vision.

The term *cataract* dates from many centuries ago, when the appearance of whiteness was attributed by physicians to a kind of miniature waterfall descending from the brain to the eye.

The lens is a minor focusing part of the eye, situated in a capsule immediately behind the pupil; the bulk of the work is done by the cornea(see Cornea), which is itself a fixed-focus lens. A cataract—an opaque film like a snowflake—can form on the lens, dimming vision until only light and dark can be seen.

Eventually the cataract reaches a "mature" state and, if not surgically treated, the cataract can give rise to secondary effects that, in some cases, can damage the eye. Such complications are uncommon, however, and it is rare for cataracts to lead to a permanent loss of vision.

Causes

The most common cause of cataracts is old age, in which case the cataracts mostly affect the center of the lens first. Blindness is delayed for many years until eventually the whole lens is affected. Some cataracts are congenital—that is, people are born with them. Within the first few months of the human fetus's development, the cells of many organs, including the eye, can suffer injury from infections or drugs that can enter the mother's blood system during pregnancy. The most serious maternal infection of early pregnancy that can cause congenital cataracts is rubella (see Rubella). This can also cause congenital heart disease and other serious misfortunes. All young girls should be protected by rubella vaccination before there is he slightest risk of pregnancy.

Other, less severe, congenital cataracts consist only of a light filming of the eye that resembles powder, throughout the substance of the lens. Such cataracts rarely require any treatment at all, and vision is likely to remain good.

Diabetes is a rare cause of cataracts, but long-term diabetics will usually develop age-related cataracts at an earlier age than nondiabetics—up to 10 years earlier in some cases. Sometimes in the early stages of diabetes, usually in adolescence, the sudden changes in blood-sugar levels are associated with dense cataracts that come on in a matter of days. This is fortu-

Cataracts can be removed by ultrasound. Very small incisions are made in the eye, and the cataract is washed out—the water bath is shown below.

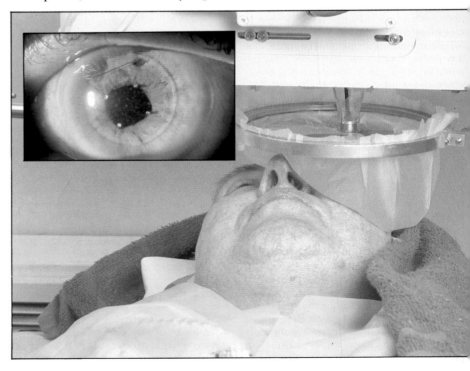

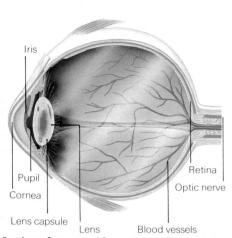

Section of an eye with a cataract. When a cataract affects only the center of the lens, dilation of the pupil with drops enables light to enter at the edges of the lens.

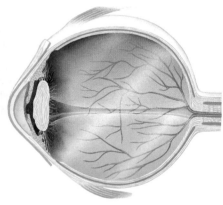

One surgical method of removing a cataract —the extracapsular—involves removing the lens fibers of which the cataract is formed, while leaving the lens capsule itself in place.

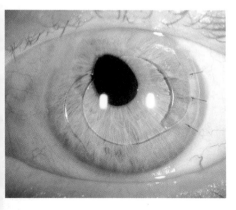

The most common way of getting rid of a cataract is to remove all opaque lens matter from within the capsule of the lens, and to replace it with a tiny plastic lens, held in place by springy plastic loops.

nately rare, and full vision can be restored by a simple operation. A genetic disorder known as galactosemia, which causes high blood levels of an abnormal sugar, can cause cataracts in babies. This can be prevented by giving a galactose-free diet.

Cataracts can form for other reasons too. A high concentration of drugs in the blood can have a toxic (poisonous) effect on the lens, while steroid drugs (see Steroids), taken either by mouth, in the eye (in the form of eyedrops), or by injection, may induce cataracts if given over a long period. Exposure to electromagnetic, cosmic, microwave, or infrared radiation can have a similar effect.

Cataracts can be formed as a result of accidents and industrial and play injuries. A blow to the eye will sometimes cause a cataract to develop several years later. A miniscule injury from a needle, thorn, or metal foreign body, if it involves the lens capsule or the lens itself, can lead to a similar problem—either immediately, or sometimes many years after the accident has occurred.

Symptoms
The most obvious symptom of cataracts is a loss of distinct vision, and sometimes the inability to see in bright light. Cataracts commonly alter the perception of colors so that everything seen may have a yellowish, or even reddish, tinge. This is often inapparent if both eyes are equally affected, but if the cataract is one-sided for a time, the effect may be more obvious when the vision in the two eyes is compared. After surgery, patients will commonly express surprise at the vividness of the color of blue objects or of the sky. This phenomenon is due to the greater absorption of light of long wavelength by the cataract.

Another symptom of maturing cataracts, with increasing density of the lens substance, is progressive short sight. This is called index myopia, and it is due to greater bending of light rays. The effect of index myopia is that a person who formerly required strong reading glasses may, for a time, be able to read without them. This advantage, however, is offset by poor distance vision, as is the case with all shortsighted people. Index myopia usually progresses fairly rapidly, and if glasses are obtained for distance vision, they are not likely to be suitable for more than a few months.

As the cataract matures, near vision is lost, and finally only light and dark can be distinguished. Usually one eye is affected before the other, but nearly always both will show signs of developing cataracts, and if treatment is not given, blindness may occur. The term *blindness* is used here to imply loss of useful vision. A

cataract does not cause blindness in the sense of total absence of the perception of light. However dense, a cataract will always allow the passage of diffuse light.

A person with cataracts who has no perception of light in the affected eye must have some other disorder, usually of the retina or optic nerve (see Optic nerve), that has caused his or her blindness. Regrettably, in such a case, vision cannot be restored by surgery, and operative treatment would be unwarranted.

Treatment
When cataracts affect only the center (nucleus) of the lens, drops containing drugs that dilate the pupil are helpful; they enable light to enter the eye at the outer edges of the lens. However, the majority of cataracts affect the entire lens, and for this reason the only effective treatment is surgery.

There are three basic surgical methods, depending upon a person's age and the type of cataract present. In children and young people, the lens matter remains soft, even after a cataract has developed, and can be fairly easily removed by one of several possible techniques.

The operation is done under general anesthesia, and drops are used to widen the pupil as fully as possible. The surgeon uses an operating microscope and very delicate instruments. Typically a tiny, oblique incision is made on either side of the cornea, and a sharp, hollow needle is passed through one of these and a fine, blunt tube through the other. A source of sterile salt solution, formulated to produce minimal irritation to the eye, is connected to the tube. The sharp needle is then used to perforate the front capsule of the lens, and as the solution is run into the eye to maintain its shape, the lens

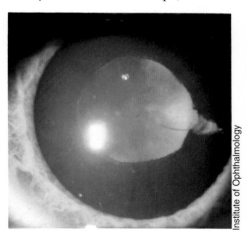

This close-up shows a congenital cataract; it is luckily an uncommon condition. It can be caused by an infection or drug in the mother's system during pregnancy.

matter is sucked out through the sharp needle. This procedure is continued until the pupil is completely clear. No stitches are required. After the operation the eye will, of course, be grossly unfocused, and an optical correction will be required. In young people this is best provided in the form of contact lenses. Some surgeons will, however, insert plastic implants into the eye at the time of the operation.

The second method of removal is by ultrasound (phacoemulsification). This advanced procedure combines the opening of the lens capsule and the washing out of the cataract, and can be used in the treatment of any age group. The advantage of this method is that only small incisions into the eye are necessary. The disadvantage is that a second operation is sometimes necessary later to produce better vision.

The third type of operation, used in patients over the age of 20, is the removal of the complete lens. In this method the eye is opened, and the front capsule of the lens is carefully cut away. The opaque nucleus of the lens is gently squeezed out of the capsule and removed from the eye. All residual opaque lens matter is now

A surgeon scans a microscope suspended over the patient while performing the delicate surgery required to remove a cataract from the patient's eye.

scrupulously removed by washing and suction. If any lens matter is left, vision will be impaired. The inside surface of the back capsule is also carefully cleared of lens matter by a delicate polishing technique. A tiny plastic lens of predetermined power and fitted with supporting loops is now inserted into the empty capsule, where it is automatically centered by the springy loops. The incision in the cornea is closed using a continuous zigzag stitch, using material finer than a human hair.

Healing of the incision takes about a month, and it is usually unnecessary to remove the stitch. The results of this operation, which is the routine procedure for adult cataracts, are usually excellent. Assuming the eye is otherwise healthy, there is no reason why full vision should not be restored.

Correction of vision
Although every effort is made to select the correct lens power, this is not always possible in practice. The normal optical methods of determining the power of the eye and the appropriate correction that will be required when the lens is removed cannot always be used before surgery takes place.

In an attempt to achieve accuracy, it is common to measure the internal axial length of the eyeball by means of an ultrasonic beam, produced by a specialized ophthalmic machine. The curvature of the cornea is also usually determined by another machine called a keratometer.

These data, together with prior information on the power of the glasses used before the cataract developed, will enable the surgeon to calculate the power of lens implant most likely to produce normal distance vision without glasses. If this is achieved, regular reading glasses will then be needed for close work. Sometimes the outcome is a minor degree of short sight, so that reading is possible without glasses. In this case glasses will be needed even for clear distance vision.

Outlook
A number of undetermined factors, including limitations in the accuracy of measurements, may, however, make either of these outcomes impossible. In addition slight variations in the tension of the stitch used to close the operation incision may induce some degree of astigmatism in the cornea. (*Astigmatism* means that the corneal curvature is flatter than normal along one meridian.) In such cases a spectacle correction (i.e., glasses) may be needed, both for distance and near vision.

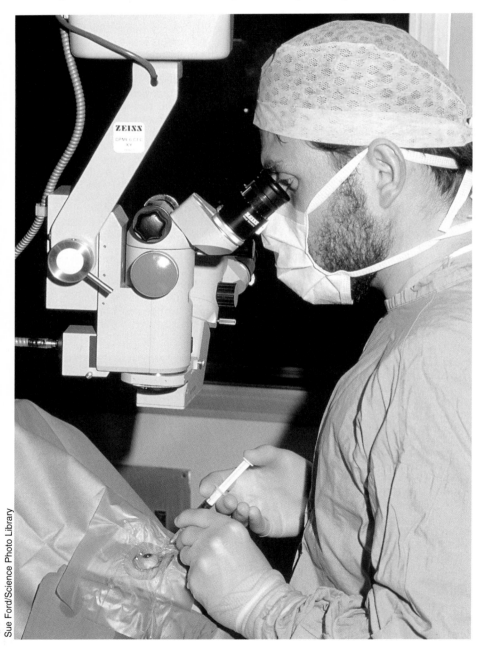

Sue Ford/Science Photo Library

Celiac disease

Celiac disease is an inability to tolerate gluten, a substance found in foods made from wheat, rye, barley, and oats. The condition is controlled by avoiding these foods.

Q My brother has celiac disease. Am I likely to develop it as well?

A Celiac disease does run in families, though it is not clear just how it is passed on from generation to generation, and not everybody with celiac disease has relatives who also suffer from it. There is a theory, though it is still controversial, that celiac disease can be brought on by feeding infants gluten-containing foods at too early an age, before their immune system knows how to cope with foreign proteins. So it may be due to a combination of hereditary and dietary factors.

Q How can I avoid eating gluten altogether?

A Gluten-free foods can be bought in stores or may be prescribed by a doctor. However, many of these are based on wheat and other gluten-rich cereals and still contain traces of gluten. Potato or soya flour can be bought from health food shops, and these are genuinely gluten-free. Following a gluten-free diet outside the home may be difficult. The best policy for eating in other people's homes is to tell them in advance that you cannot eat floury foods, and in restaurants you would be wise to avoid anything with pastry or a floury sauce unless you can be sure it is gluten-free.

Q My doctor has just diagnosed celiac disease. Has any permanent damage been done to my intestines?

A Probably not. If you avoid eating gluten, your intestines should return to normal within weeks. Celiac disease is like an allergy: if you keep away from the cause (the allergen), you will stay perfectly healthy.

Q How do I know if a food is gluten-free?

A Anything with wheat, rye, oats, or barley in it contains gluten unless the label says it is gluten-free. Some gluten-free products also carry the gluten-free symbol, a crossed-out ear of wheat.

Celiac (pronounced SEE-lee-ack) disease means disease of the belly. But the name is inaccurate, because the complaint is a disorder of the lining of the intestine, which prevents the body from absorbing fats, calcium, and other important nutrients from food. Sufferers have an intolerance (a form of allergy) to gluten, which is a natural protein found in wheat and other cereals. Celiac disease is not very common, affecting only one person in 500, but it is a permanent condition, and sufferers need to follow a gluten-free diet very carefully.

Causes

No one knows why gluten should damage the intestines of celiac sufferers. It could be due to an allergy, to the lack of an enzyme that is supposed to break down gluten, to an abnormality in the intestinal membrane, or to a combination of all these possible causes.

Symptoms

The main symptom is loss of weight, due to food not being properly absorbed. Other symptoms include diarrhea, a puffed-up, painful stomach, and the passing of pulpy, foul-smelling feces that are full of undigested fat.

Diagnosing the disease in babies is simple because the symptoms are obvious: they are sick and bloated, and fail to put on any weight.

A gluten-free diet
- Avoid all foods made from, or containing, gluten. This includes anything containing wheat, rye, barley, or oats
- When in doubt, check the ingredients listed on the label
- Some gluten-free products carry a special symbol: a circle containing a crossed-out ear of wheat
- Use gluten-free, not ordinary, varieties of the following foods:

Baby foods (cereals, vegetables, fruits)
Spaghetti and spaghetti loops
Macaroni
Semolina
Cookies
Flour
Bread (bread mix, canned white or brown bread)
Baking powder
Cakes
Crackers
Topping and cookie mixes
Bedtime drinks
Soup mixes
Soya bran

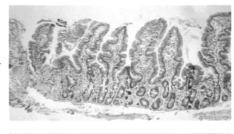

Dr. H. J. Brueton, Westminster Children's Hospital

These are microscopic views of the lining of the jejunum (part of the small intestine) when normal (above), and in a patient with celiac disease (below).

Tests for the disease are undertaken at gastroenterology clinics. The patient swallows a small capsule attached to a special tube. An X ray is taken, and a sample of the intestinal lining is then retrieved through the tube. In a healthy person the lining is covered with little fingerlike fronds called villi. In celiac sufferers these are destroyed.

Dangers

Celiac disease is only dangerous when it is not diagnosed. Chronic diarrhea, weight loss, anemia, and malnutrition can all result.

Treatment

The only effective treatment is a gluten-free diet. Once gluten is avoided, the villi grow back, but they will disappear again if gluten is eaten. Treatment is not a cure.

Outlook

Once gluten is excluded from the diet, the condition of sufferers improves in time. Avoiding gluten is not always very easy, but gluten-free products and alternatives are available.

Cells and chromosomes

Q Do the number of cells in a child's body increase as he or she grows up?

A Yes. A person has millions more cells as an adult than he or she had at birth. The increase in cell numbers is not, however, evenly distributed throughout the body. The number of cells in the brain, for example, increases much less as the body develops than those in the bones, skin, and muscles.

Q I am in my 50s and have heard that cells can be revitalized by utilizing certain creams. Will these really stop the aging process?

A No. There are no preparations that can stop the gradual deterioration and replacement of cells or reverse the changes that take place in cells as they age.

Q I have read that nuclear radiation can cause birth abnormalities. Why is this?

A Nuclear radiation has two great dangers: it can kill cells, and it can produce permanent changes in the chromosomes, the parts of the cell that carry hereditary instructions. If these changes, called mutations, affect the chromosomes of the eggs or sperm, which are brought together at the moment of fertilization to produce a new individual, then the result can be an abnormal baby. And if that baby manages to survive into adulthood, then he or she could well pass on the abnormality to future generations.

Q My twin girls are identical. Are their cells exactly the same, and if so, why?

A Identical twins are born when an egg from the mother splits in two after it has been fertilized by a sperm from the father; thus both members of the twin pair are always the same sex and always carry exactly the same genetic instructions. It is for this reason that identical twins are so fascinating to scientists, because all the differences that exist between them must be due to environmental factors.

Every part of the body is composed of millions of cells. Chromosomes are found in each cell and contain the genes that determine the characteristics we inherit.

The cells are the basic units of life, the microscopic building blocks from which the body is constructed. Within the cells are the chromosomes that contain the vast amount of information essential to the creation and maintenance of human life and an individual's personal characteristics.

Every adult body contains more than a hundred million cells, microscopic structures averaging only a hundredth of a millimeter in diameter. No one cell is capable of surviving on its own outside the body unless it is cultured (artificially bred) in special conditions, but when grouped together into tissues, organs, and systems of the body, the cells work together in harmony to sustain life.

Types

The body cells vary greatly in shape, size, and detailed structure according to the jobs they have to do. Muscle cells, for example, are long and thin and contain fibers that can contract and relax, thus allowing the body to move. Many nerve cells are also long and thin, but they are designed to transmit electrical impulses that compose the nerve messages. The hexagonal cells of the liver are equipped to carry out a multitude of vital chemical processes, the doughnut-shaped red blood cells transport oxygen and carbon dioxide around the body, while spherical cells in the pancreas make and replace the hormone insulin.

Structure

Despite these variations, all body cells are constructed according to the same basic pattern. Around the outside of every cell is a boundary wall or cell membrane enclosing a jellylike substance, the cytoplasm. Embedded in this is the nucleus that houses the genetic instructions in the form of chromosomes.

The cytoplasm, although between 70 and 85 percent water, is far from inactive. Many chemical reactions take place between substances dissolved in this water, and the cytoplasm also contains many tiny structures called organelles, each with an important and specific task.

The cell membrane also has a definite structure: it is porous, and it is rather like a sandwich of protein and fat with the fat as the filling. As substances pass into or out of the cell, they are either dissolved in the fat or passed through the porous, semipermeable membrane.

Some cells have hairlike projections called cilia on their membranes. In the nose, for example, the cilia are used to trap dust particles. These hairs can also move in unison to waft substances along in a particular direction.

The cytoplasm of all cells contains microscopic, sausage-shaped organs called mitochondria, which convert oxygen and nutrients into the energy needed for all the other actions of the cells. These powerhouses work through the action of

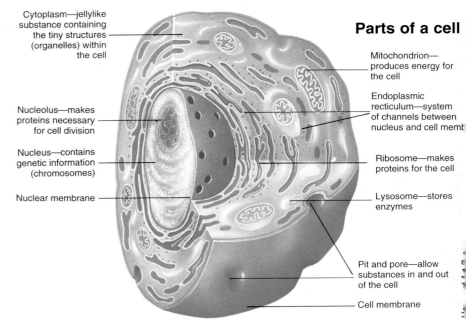

Cytoplasm—jellylike substance containing the tiny structures (organelles) within the cell

Parts of a cell

Mitochondrion—produces energy for the cell

Endoplasmic recticulum—system of channels between nucleus and cell memb

Nucleolus—makes proteins necessary for cell division

Nucleus—contains genetic information (chromosomes)

Nuclear membrane

Ribosome—makes proteins for the cell

Lysosome—stores enzymes

Pit and pore—allow substances in and out of the cell

Cell membrane

Different types of cells in the body

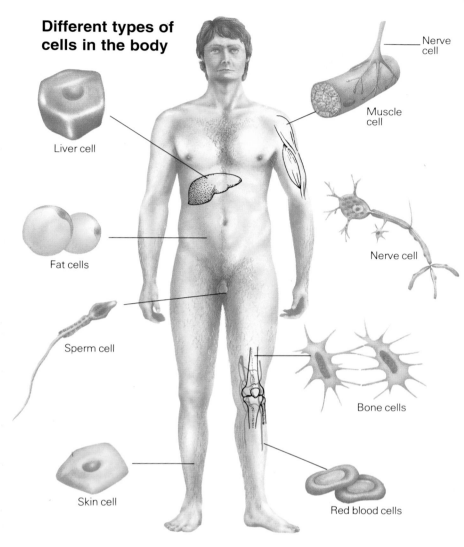

Liver cell

Fat cells

Sperm cell

Skin cell

Nerve cell

Muscle cell

Nerve cell

Bone cells

Red blood cells

Apart from mature red blood cells, which lose their chromosomes in the final stages of their formation, and the eggs and sperm (the sex cells), which contain half the usual number of chromosomes, every body cell contains 46 chromosomes, arranged in 23 pairs. One of each pair comes from the mother and one from the father. The eggs and sperm have only half that number, so that when an egg is fertilized by a sperm, the new individual is assured of having the correct number of chromosomes.

At the moment of fertilization, the genes start issuing instructions for the molding of a new human being. The father's chromosomes are responsible for sex determination. These chromosomes are called X or Y, depending on their shape. In women both the chromosomes in the pair are X, but in men there is one X and one Y chromosome. If an X-containing sperm fertilizes an egg, the baby will be a girl, but if a Y sperm fertilizes the egg, then the baby will be a boy.

How a cell divides

In addition to being packed with information, the DNA of the chromosomes also has the ability to reproduce itself; without this the cells could not duplicate themselves, nor could they pass on information from one generation to another.

The process of cell division in which the cell duplicates itself is called mitosis; this is the type of division that takes place when a fertilized egg grows first into a baby and then into an adult, and when worn-out cells are replaced.

When the cell is not dividing, the chromosomes are not visible in the nucleus, but when the cell is about to divide, the chromosomes become shorter and thicker, and can be seen to split in half along their length. These double chromosomes then pull apart and move to opposite ends of the cell. Finally the cytoplasm is halved and new walls form around the two new cells, each of which has the normal number of 46 chromosomes.

Every day a huge number of cells die and are replaced by mitosis; some cells are more efficient at this than others. Once formed, the cells of the brain and nerves are unable to replace themselves, but liver, skin, and blood cells are completely replaced several times a year.

Making cells with half the usual chromosome number, in order to determine inherited characteristics, involves a different type of cell division called meiosis. In this type the chromosomes first become shorter and thicker, as in mitosis, and divide in two; at the moment of fertilization, the chromosomes pair up so that the one from the mother and the other from the father lie side by side.

enzymes, complex proteins that speed up chemical reactions in the cell. They are most numerous in the muscle cells, which need an enormous amount of energy to carry out their work.

Lysosomes—another type of microscopic organ in the cytoplasm—are tiny sacs filled with enzymes that make it possible for the cell to use the nutrients with which it is supplied. The liver cells contain the greatest number of lysosomes.

Substances made by a cell that are needed in other parts of the body, such as hormones, are first packaged and then stored in further minute organs called the Golgi apparatus.

Many cells possess a whole network of tiny tubes that are thought to act as a kind of internal cell skeleton, but all of them contain a system of channels called the endoplasmic reticulum.

Dotted along the reticulum are tiny spherical structures called ribosomes, which are responsible for controlling the construction of essential proteins needed by all cells. The proteins are needed for structural repairs and, in the form of enzymes, for cell chemistry and the manufacture of complex molecular structures such as hormones.

What is a chromosome?

Each nucleus is packed with information, coded in the form of a chemical called deoxyribonucleic acid (DNA), and organized into groups called genes. The genes are arranged on threadlike structures, the chromosomes. Every chromosome contains thousands of genes, each with enough information for the production of one protein. This protein may have a small effect within the cell and on the appearance of the body, but equally it may make all the difference between a person having, for example, brown or blue eyes, straight or curly hair, normal or albino skin. The genes are responsible for every physical characteristic.

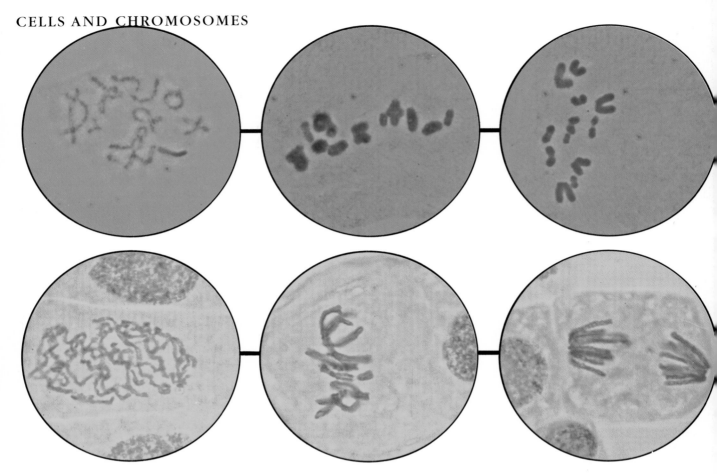

The main difference between the two methods of cell division can be seen above, greatly enlarged. In meiosis (top sequence), the chromosomes are duplicated and then pair up and intertwine, before pulling apart and dividing to produce sex cells containing half the genetic information needed to produce a human being (the remaining half is supplied during fertilization). In mitosis (bottom sequence), pairs of chromosomes separate, and each half divides into two identical parts. These arrange themselves so that when the respective parts move to opposite ends of the cell and the cell divides into two, each new cell will contain the genetic information necessary to replace or duplicate existing body cells. The illustration (right) shows the structure of a chromosome in detail.

Next the chromosomes become very tightly intertwined so that when they eventually pull apart, each new chromosome will contain some of the mother's genes and some of the father's. After this the two new cells divide again so that each egg or sperm contains the 23 chromosomes it needs. The interchange of genetic material during this process of meiosis explains why children do not look exactly like their parents and why

Cell — Chromosomes in nucleus

Structure of a chromosome – made from entwined strands of DNA

Enlarged chromosome structure

Sections of DNA are called genes. Each gene contains the information to make a protein

Single strand of DNA

Hayward Art Group

each person, with the exception of identical twins, has a completely unique genetic makeup.

Problems

Considering the number of cells in the body, and the complexities of their structure and chemistry, it is surprising how little goes wrong with them during the average life, and how few babies are born with deformities. Apart from accidental damage and disease, things only go wrong when there is some abnormality of the chromosomes or of the genes they contain, which then sends out faulty information to the cell. Occasionally the cell may be unable to respond to the messages it receives, although these are correct.

Sometimes whole chromosomes can be responsible for abnormalities. For example, children with Down's syndrome are born with one extra chromosome, while additional sex chromosomes can cause abnormalities in sexual development. Many abnormalities at birth are caused by faulty genes. Other genetic problems, such as muscular dystrophy, do not arise until some time after birth, although these, too, occur from faulty genes. Many aspects of cell life and action have yet to be clarified by science.

Cerebral palsy

Q Is it correct to say that people who have no control over their muscles and their movements are spastic?

A No, although people with other types of disability may have spastic limbs. For example, someone with a severe spinal injury may have spastic legs, though this disability has nothing to do with cerebral palsy. Other disabilities involving paralysis include spina bifida, multiple sclerosis, Parkinson's disease, and the effects of cerebral hemorrhage. People with cerebral palsy have commonly been referred to as *spastics*, though this term is very much disliked by those affected and by their families.

Q Why can't some spastics speak properly, and can anything be done to help them?

A A number of factors can cause speech difficulties in people with cerebral palsy. First, the speech center of the brain may be damaged. Second, a lack of good muscle control makes it hard to regulate breathing and form words. Third, some people who find it very difficult to control their speech production become tense when they try to speak, and this exacerbates the problem. Speech therapy can help enormously, but the best help can come from the listener. Embarrassment on your part won't help; so try to remember that the person speaking is thinking just as quickly as you, but is prevented from speaking normally by physical factors.

Q My sister has a little boy with congenital spasticity. Does this mean that any child of mine will have this condition?

A Don't confuse the term *congenital* with *genetic*. Congenital means that the condition was present at birth or soon afterward; genetic would suggest that some inherited factor caused the baby to be spastic. Only very few cases are caused by an inherited factor, and it is really very rare to find more than one person with cerebral palsy in the same family.

The word spastic *has unfortunately become a slang term for a clumsy, stupid person. In fact, spastic people have cerebral palsy, or spasticity—a disabling disease, but one that may well not affect the individual's intelligence.*

Cerebral palsy, sometimes called Little's disease, is a broad medical term that covers a range of conditions, all resulting in some form of paralysis in early infancy because of imperfect development of, or damage to, the nerve centers in the brain. The damage occurs during pregnancy, at birth, or soon after. The most common form of cerebral palsy is spasticity, or spastic paralysis. There are approximately 300,000 children with cerebral palsy in the United States.

There is a widely held misconception that all spastic people are mentally handicapped, but this is not true. Although some people with this condition may have brain damage that affects their learning abilities, many are of average or above average intelligence.

How the brain is affected

There are three main types of cerebral palsy. In each type a different area of the brain has been affected.

Spasticity accounts for more than 80 percent of all cases of cerebral palsy. In this condition the outer layer of the brain, the cortex, appears to have been

Voice synthesizers can help cerebral palsy children with severe speaking difficulties. The boy below controls his synthesizer using a laser attached to his headband.

damaged. The cortex deals with such functions as thought, movement, and sensation—all vitally important.

In athetosis, damage is centered in the inner part of the brain, on a particular group of nerve cells known as the basal ganglia. These nerve cells are responsible for easy, graceful flowing movement.

The third type, ataxia, results when the cerebellum (situated at the base of the brain) is affected. As the cerebellum is connected to the brain stem, which links the main part of the brain with the spinal cord, it controls balance, posture, and coordination of bodily movements.

Causes

During pregnancy certain illnesses and viruses can affect the fetal brain. Rubella (German measles) in the early weeks of pregnancy is known to cause damage to the fetus. Failure of the placenta (see Placenta) to provide adequate nourishment can also cause difficulties.

Prolonged oxygen starvation at birth is thought to be the largest single cause of cerebral palsy. This may occur during a very difficult or prolonged labor, when the baby's delicate brain tissues, deprived of rich, oxygenated blood, can rapidly deteriorate. Some newborn babies develop jaundice and infections like meningitis and encephalitis, which may cause

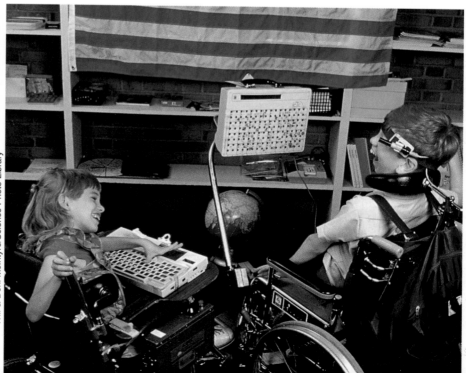

Will & Deni McIntyre/Science Photo Library

CEREBRAL PALSY

brain damage. Injuries to the head can also result in cerebral palsy.

Symptoms

No two people who suffer from cerebral palsy have precisely the same degree of handicap. In some the results of the brain damage are so mild that there is no apparent disability; in others the paralysis can affect all four limbs, speech, hearing, and vision; it may also be accompanied by a mental handicap and epilepsy.

A person with spasticity will have general muscular stiffness, weakness, or paralysis in one or more limbs. It will be difficult to use or control the affected limb or limbs, and deformities can develop if treatment is not available.

This boy has athetosis, which makes it hard for him to control his limbs and head. The facilities and visual aids of a special school will help him fulfill his potential.

How cerebral palsy affects the brain

In spastic paralysis, damage to the cerebral cortex leads to uncontrolled movement, muscular weakness, and varying degrees of paralysis. Ataxia—difficulty in balance, posture, and coordination—results from damage to the cerebellum, and athetosis, characterized by involuntary movement, is caused when the basal ganglia are involved. In all these conditions sight, hearing, and speech may also be affected.

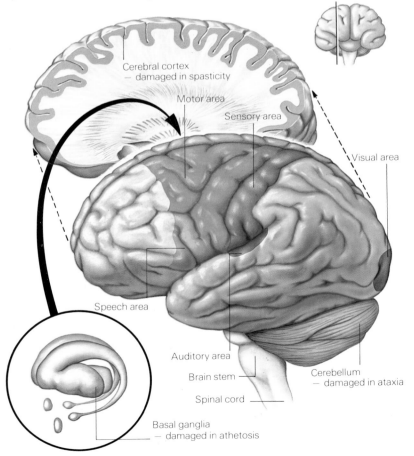

Cerebral cortex
— damaged in spasticity

Motor area

Sensory area

Visual area

Speech area

Auditory area

Brain stem

Cerebellum
— damaged in ataxia

Spinal cord

Basal ganglia
— damaged in athetosis

The paralysis can affect either side of the body (hemiplegia), the legs only (paraplegia), or all the limbs (diplegia, when the legs are mainly affected; and quadriplegia, when the legs and arms are equally involved). The paralysis can either be spastic, that is, stiff and rigid, or flaccid, which is limp and relaxed.

People with ataxia walk in an awkward and uncoordinated manner and usually have very great difficulty in balancing. Those with athetosis are subject to involuntary, awkward movements and have difficulty controlling their limbs and the muscles in their faces and bodies.

Combinations of symptoms can mislead onlookers. For example, the involuntary, writhing movements and awkward walk of some athetoid people, combined with an inability to control facial expression, have earned them the reputation of being mentally handicapped. This is particularly frustrating for those who are intelligent but unable to talk fluently.

Hearing, sight, and speech may also be affected. If speech is badly slurred, the person may have difficulty in communicating and, where the hands are affected, learning can be very difficult and slow. Some people with cerebral palsy also have epilepsy and problems with spatial reasoning are not uncommon.

Treatment and outlook

There is no cure for cerebral palsy, but with therapy much improvement is possible. Physiotherapy can help movement in spastic muscles and speech therapy is essential in assisting communication.

New technological developments have meant that even the most severely handicapped can now hope to live a reasonably fulfilled and satisfying existence.

Frank Kennard

Cervix and cervical smears

Q Are cervical smear tests really necessary? I don't like the idea at all.

A The incidence of cancer of the cervix in American females has been reduced by 70 percent as a result of the widespread use of the Pap smear test. Many thousands of lives have been saved by this test. In spite of this, over 13,000 American females get cervical cancer each year, and over 4000 of these females die each year from the disease. These unfortunate females are mainly those who, for various reasons, did not have a Pap smear test. Many of them avoided the test simply because they didn't like the idea.

Q Isn't a Pap smear painful and embarrassing?

A The doctor or the nurse is not embarrassed, so there is no reason for you to be. It's just routine to them. You will not be able to see what is happening, so it's simply a matter of relaxing. If you can relax and avoid squeezing, the whole procedure is painless.

Q What if my Pap smear test result comes back positive?

A Pap smear tests are reported as normal or abnormal, not as positive or negative. Even if you get an abnormal result, there is no need to panic. It may simply mean that the specimen was questionable and that the pathologist couldn't safely grade it as normal. It may have been taken too near the time of your period, or the smear may have been inadequately preserved. There may be inflammatory changes, not cancer. Just make sure that you have a repeat test.

Q What if the Pap test result really is abnormal?

A Mildly abnormal cells call for a repeat test every three months or so. If there is severe abnormality, you will have to have a biopsy of the cervix, a minor procedure in which a cone of cervix is removed for full microscopic examination. Many females have been saved from real trouble by this procedure.

The cervix is the neck of the uterus, which remains closed until a female gives birth. Cervical smears detect the presence of abnormal cells that can lead to cancer—if discovered early enough, treatment can provide a total cure.

The cervix is the narrowed lower part, or neck, of the uterus. Although the uterus enlarges considerably during pregnancy, the cervix remains closed until the descent of the baby's head during childbirth forces it to open widely. The cervix is the site of various disorders, the most important of which is cancer.

The cervix

Like the rest of the uterus, the cervix is largely muscular and is lined with a mucous membrane. It is almost cylindrical and about one inch (2.5 cm) long, and it is loosely connected to the bladder in front. The lower part of the cervix, which is somewhat conical and rounded, projects into the vagina so that there is a shallow cul-de-sac (or fornix) all around. This part of the cervix is covered with the same mucous membrane that lines the vagina and is readily accessible for examination. In the center of the vaginal part of the cervix is the tiny, circular external os (bone), the mouth of the cervical canal that runs down the cervix from the cavity of the uterus.

Infections of the cervix

Cervical infections are fairly common and can cause inflammation (cervicitis). Infection is usually sexually acquired and may be caused by herpes, chlamydia, gonorrhea, or syphilis. All but the herpes virus respond well to treatment with antibiotics. If persistent (chronic), cervical infections are often associated with pelvic pain and backache; there may be pain on intercourse. Infections with the human papillomavirus and with herpes viruses are believed to be important causal factors in cancer of the cervix. It is probably because of this that sexually promiscuous females are more likely to develop cervical cancer. Such females have a higher probability of acquiring a

Position of the cervix

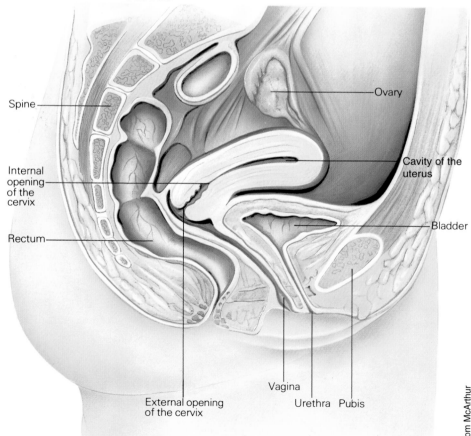

Spine

Internal opening of the cervix

Rectum

External opening of the cervix

Ovary

Cavity of the uterus

Bladder

Vagina

Urethra   Pubis

Tom McArthur

papillomavirus infection or herpes. Some strains of herpes viruses, especially types 16 and 18, have been classified as high-risk strains for cancer.

Cervical erosion

The term *cervical erosion* is a remnant from an earlier misinterpretation of the appearance commonly seen on direct visual examination of the cervix. It is inaccurate, because this appearance is not an erosion or any other form of ulceration, nor is it an inflammation or the result of infection. Earlier gynecologists were convinced that cervical erosion was abnormal, and all kinds of symptoms were attributed to it. Many females underwent unnecessary treatment, especially cauterization with a hot probe.

The term refers to a conspicuous dark, raw-looking appearance of the outer part of the cervix, caused by an extension of the columnar epithelium (inner lining) of the canal of the cervix out onto the usually smooth and lighter-colored covering membrane of the vaginal part. The extension of this velvety red area onto the cervix is especially common during pregnancy, when the high levels of estrogen present cause it to expand and extend. Some contraceptive pills also produced well-marked "erosions."

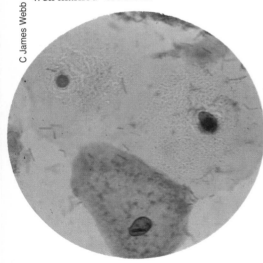

Bleeding and discharge

Occasionally this extension of columnar epithelium, with its more profuse blood supply, leads to a slight, intermittent, bloodstained mucous discharge. It is a rule in gynecology that unexplained vaginal bleeding must never be ignored, so even bleeding from this cause should be investigated. If the cervical smear test gives a normal result in a pregnant female, the condition can safely be ignored.

Cervical erosions are seldom seen after a female goes through menopause. This is a time when estrogen levels are lower,

and any vaginal bleeding at this point must be taken more seriously.

Cervical incompetence

In some females the upper part of the narrow cervical canal is, for various reasons, abnormally open to just under 0.5 in (1 cm) at the point at which it joins the cavity of the uterus. During pregnancy the internal pressure from the increasing volume of fluid surrounding the fetus (the amniotic fluid) tends to force this opening wider, so that the outlet of the uterus progressively expands. As a result, such females may repeatedly suffer the misfortune of painless, spontaneous miscarriages, usually around the fourth or fifth month of pregnancy. Miscarriage may also occur because the abnormal widening promotes premature rupture of the membranes.

This unfortunate condition is known as cervical incompetence, and it is usually, although not always, the result of earlier damage to the cervix during delivery or previous surgery, such as a cone biopsy for suspected cancer, repeated dilatations and curettage, or an amputation of the cervix. When recognized, the condition is easily treated. At some time between the 12th week of pregnancy (when most spontaneous abortions have already

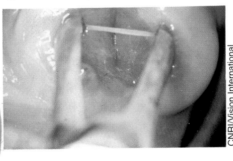

In a cervical smear the cervix is inspected through an instrument called a speculum. A few cells are scraped off, then examined under a microscope, which shows up any abnormalities. Cells to the left are normal.

occurred) and before the 16th week, the cervix is reinforced with a single, strong, purse-string stitch of nonabsorbable material, such as nylon, sewn around it in an in-and-out manner. This procedure, known as the Shirodkar operation, keeps the cervix firmly closed until the baby can safely be delivered. The stitch is then cut and pulled out. This is a simple matter that takes only a few minutes.

Cervical smear

Cancer of the cervix is very common. Fortunately the cancer remains in the surface layer for years before invading the muscle. The smear test can detect it at

this harmless stage. For this reason the cervical smear test should, ideally, be done on all females. The test can detect 90 percent of cell abnormalities, and treatment given during this preinvasive stage is simple, safe, and nearly always completely curative.

The cervical smear test, or Papanicolaou (Pap) smear, was instituted not by a gynecologist, but by an American physiologist and microscopist, George Nicholas Papanicolaou (1883–1962). While investigating the reproductive cycle using vaginal smears, Papanicolaou recognized cancer cells and realized that this was an important method of early diagnosis of cervical cancer. He devoted much of the rest of his life to promoting the test among the medical profession and the general population.

The procedure

The Pap smear test is a simple, virtually painless, and highly reliable method of detecting cancer of the cervix in its earliest stages. The vagina is held open by a small device called a speculum, and a shaped spatula is used in a rotary manner to gently scrape the area around the os for 360°. The most important cells are those at the junction between the lining of the canal and the lining of the vaginal part of the cervix. This is known as the transformation zone, and it is here that cancer is most likely to start.

The almost imperceptible smear of cells obtained in this way is spread on a glass slide, fixed, stained, and then examined microscopically by an expert pathologist who has been trained in the discipline of detecting abnormalities in single cells. The whole technique is known as exfoliative cytology.

Suggested frequency

The test should be done regularly on all females, initially between the ages of 16 and 20 and thereafter every year.

A three-year period between tests is the acceptable minimum requirement, except for those in whom the risk factors apply. These females should have the test at least once a year, or more often if abnormalities are found.

Pap smear tests should ideally be accompanied by microscopic examination of the cervix (colposcopy). This allows accurate localization of the abnormal surface tissue. The instrument used is a long-focus microscope with coaxial illumination that provides the gynecologist with an excellent enlarged view of the vaginal part of the cervix.

Cancer of the cervix

Worldwide, cancer of the cervix is the most common female malignancy.

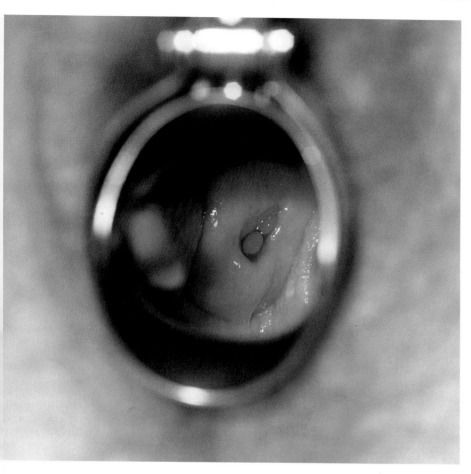

View of a cervical polyp, as seen through a cervical speculum. Polyps are benign growths that may occur on any mucous membrane; cervical polyps are removed if it is suspected they may become malignant.

Because of the Pap smear test, however, in the United States this form of cancer now ranks only number eight in causes of death among females. This is an enormous reduction and highlights the importance of the test.

Even so, the American Cancer Society states that, currently, some 13,500 new cases of invasive cervical cancer occur in the United States each year, with 4400 deaths from the disease. These deaths are particularly tragic when one considers how accessible the site of the cancer is and how easily it can be detected in the early stages if it is looked for.

High-risk factors
Risk factors for cancer of the cervix include starting to have sexual intercourse at an early age, many sexual partners, sexually transmitted diseases, genital warts, repeated pregnancies, and cigarette smoking.

As suggested, the sexual factors probably relate to the increased probability of infection with the human papilloma and herpes viruses (see Herpes).

Research has shown that the DNA of human papillomavirus types 16 and 18 is found in 62 percent of females with cervical cancer, but in only 32 percent of females without cancer. Other studies have shown that cervical cancer is more prevalent in those females who use drugs intravenously and in females who are HIV-positive (see AIDS).

Cervical intraepithelial neoplasia
Cancer of the cervix is preceded, for a number of years, by a recognizable and easily diagnosable preinvasive condition known as cervical intraepithelial neoplasia (CIN), or carcinoma-in-situ.

The epithelium is the mucous membrane lining of the cervix, and neoplasia means a cancerous change in the cells. Intraepithelial means that these changes are still confined to the cells within the lining and thus have not invaded any other tissue.

Cancer that remains at this stage is harmless, although potentially devastating. About 55,000 cases of CIN occur each year in the United States. Half of all cancers of the female reproductive system are in the cervix, and so early detection is essential for a course of treatment, which in many cases will provide a complete cure.

Symptoms
Unfortunately cancer of the cervix often causes no symptoms until it has spread and may cause no symptoms at all before reaching an incurable stage. Sometimes there is bleeding between periods or following sexual intercourse, but there are no dramatic early signs.

Pain and general upset are rare until a late stage is reached and the cancer has spread to other sites. Such pain, which may be felt in the pelvis, buttocks, or lower back, often indicates that the disease is far advanced. It may imply that the cancer has spread widely into the pelvic or abdominal regions.

Involvement of the bladder and the rectum may cause blood in the urine or bleeding from the rectum. The moral is clear. Cancer of the cervix has to be looked for, and the best way to do this is by the Pap smear test.

Complications
Once the cancer has passed from the epithelium into the underlying cervical muscle, the treatment becomes more difficult. If the cancer is confined to the cervix, the choice rests between removing a cone of the cervical muscle or removing the whole uterus (simple hysterectomy). The former has a recurrence rate of about 5 percent; the latter, a zero recurrence rate.

More extensive cervical cancer is difficult to treat successfully, and the choice rests between extensive surgery and radiotherapy (see Radiotherapy). There is no universal agreement on which of these forms of treatment is best. Radiotherapy is widely used—this treatment is usually administered by means of a sealed container of radioactive material being placed in the vault of the vagina and in the cavity of the uterus.

Outlook
The cure rate for cancer of the cervix depends on the extent of its spreading at the time of diagnosis. If there has been spreading to the vagina (see Vagina) and surrounding tissues, the cure rate drops sharply to about 50 percent.

Extensive spreading to the organs of the pelvis and remote spreading to other parts of the body has a very poor outlook. In only about 10 percent of such cases is the patient still alive five years later. But when the condition is detected in its early stages by means of the Pap smear test, there is an excellent chance of cure and recovery for many females who suffer from this type of cancer.

Chest

Q I am an avid gardener, but I find that I get pains in my chest after I have been digging. Could this mean that I have strained my heart?

A Probably not, because most chest pains are related to muscle strains in the chest wall. After all, the chest is not only a cage for the lungs, but also provides the platform from which our arms and shoulders do all their muscular work. It is not surprising that we sometimes get strained or pulled muscles in the chest. The clue is usually the fact that a specific movement or set of movements will bring on the pain. To put your mind at rest, go and see your doctor about this problem.

Q When I broke my ribs playing basketball, I was not bandaged or given any treatment. Why was this?

A Although broken or cracked ribs can be uncomfortable or even painful, the main danger is that the chest movement will be reduced, producing less air flow in and out of the underlying lung. This can cause pneumonia, and it is for this reason that it is unusual to bandage broken ribs.

Q My doctor says I am pigeon-chested. What does it mean? And am I more likely to get ill from chest infections?

A Some people have minor deformities of the chest wall, which are often referred to as a pigeon chest. The most common is a hollowing of the center of the chest at the front, but this does not mean that you are more liable to chest infection than anyone else.

Q Can people still die of pneumonia like they did in the old days?

A Unfortunately, yes. Pneumonia used to be a common cause of death not so many years ago, even in healthy young people, but this is generally no longer the case. However, in people who are seriously ill for some other reason, or are elderly, pneumonia is often the final illness that kills them.

The chest is the protective framework for the lungs and the heart, so it is essential to know when a cough or chest pain needs medical attention.

The chest is a bony cage that contains two of the most important organs in the body: the lungs and the heart. The basic function of these organs is to transfer oxygen from the air to the tissues, where it is essential for the continuation of life.

Structure

The rib cage is located just under the skin of the chest. It totally encloses the lungs and heart on all but their lowest surface, and resembles a bell in shape. It is attached to the spine at the back, and its base is sealed off by the diaphragm, the thick muscular sheet separating the contents of the chest from the abdomen.

In between the ribs there are further muscular sheets called the intercostal ("between the rib") muscles. The chest wall therefore consists of a bell-shaped muscular bag—with the ribs as struts—that, by expanding and contracting, is able to suck air in and out through the windpipe, or trachea, which emerges from the chest into the neck.

The whole of the inside of the chest is lined with a membrane called the pleura. Similar membranes cover the lungs and the heart. When the pleura becomes inflamed, this leads to pleurisy.

The left and right lungs fill the bulk of the chest and are connected by their tubes, the main bronchi, to the trachea. Smaller tubes, or bronchioles, then split off from the main bronchus of each lung in a treelike fashion, carrying air to the air sacs (alveoli) in the lungs, where oxygen is extracted from the air and passed into the blood, and carbon dioxide—which is the body's waste product—moves in the reverse direction.

The heart lies at the front of the chest between the two lungs, inside its own membranous bag. The heart receives blood from the body through its right-sided pumping chambers (the right

Organs of the chest

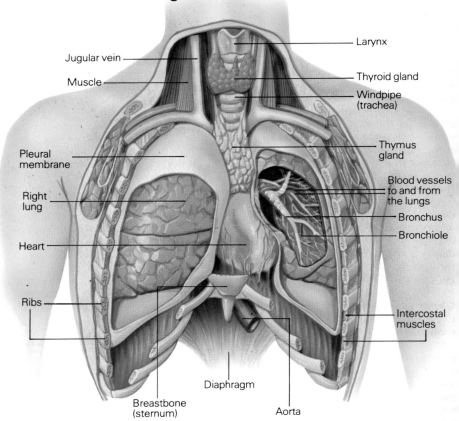

Jugular vein

Muscle

Pleural membrane

Right lung

Heart

Ribs

Breastbone (sternum)

Diaphragm

Aorta

Larynx

Thyroid gland

Windpipe (trachea)

Thymus gland

Blood vessels to and from the lungs

Bronchus

Bronchiole

Intercostal muscles

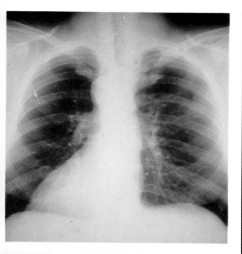

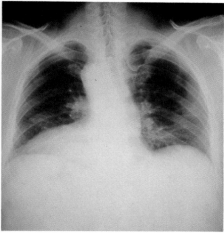

These X rays show how the muscular walls of the chest expand when air is inhaled (top) and contract when it is exhaled (above).

Pain in the chest: when to see your doctor

Type of pain	Other signs	Causes
Central pain, pressing and dull in character	Breathlessness, nausea, or sweating, lasting more than 20 minutes	Angina (heart disease) Heart attack Pericarditis (inflammation of the membrane lining the heart) Indigestion
Central, gripping pain spreading to the neck, shoulders, or arms	Brought on by exercise or emotional excitement	Angina Pericarditis
Anywhere, worse on inspiration (breathing in) or on coughing	May be associated with a cough or an attack of bronchitis	Pleurisy Pericarditis
Central, burning. Worse after food or on bending forward; may be worse at night	Foods may bring it on, and it may be relieved by milk or indigestion tablets	Esophagitis (inflammation of the gullet, a form of indigestion)

When a cough needs medical attention

Type of cough	Cause
Green or yellow sputum coughed up	Bronchitis (inflammation of the lining of the bronchial tubes in the lungs) or pneumonia (inflammation of the lung)
Cough and/or wheezing	This may be true asthma or wheezy bronchitis
Coughing up blood or bloody streaks in sputum	There are many causes of this, but the most serious are tuberculosis or lung cancer

atrium and ventricle) and pumps it into the lungs. Blood returns from the lungs full of oxygen to the atrium and ventricle on the left side of the heart, from where it is pumped out into the main artery of the body—the aorta.

Apart from the heart and lungs, the chest contains the gullet, or esophagus, which carries food from the mouth into the stomach (which lies just below the diaphragm). There is also a gland called the thymus, which lies at the top of the chest in front of the windpipe.

Chest problems
Chest complaints have three main symptoms: pain, coughing, and breathlessness.

Pain in the chest area may arise from the chest wall itself, as a result of pleurisy, or it may arise from the heart. The esophagus, which passes through the diaphragm into the stomach, is also often the source of pain; the acid contents of the stomach may wash back upward, causing inflammation.

In cases of pleurisy (see Pleurisy), the two layers of pleura lining the inside of the chest and outside of the lungs become inflamed and cause pain when they rub together. The pain of pleurisy is worse on breathing or coughing.

Since the lungs themselves do not give direct pain signals, coughing is an important symptom of damage to the lung. Doctors call a cough "productive" when it produces phlegm or sputum from the chest. This may indicate infection, particularly if the sputum is colored green or yellow rather than white. Most coughs, however, do not produce sputum and are simply the result of inflammation of the upper airways, rather than a sign of lung disease. Such coughs usually follow on from a cold.

Breathlessness may be the result of disease of either the lungs or the chest. Asthma is a common cause, particularly in younger people and children, and is accompanied by wheezing. Heart problems lead to breathlessness because the

pumping of the blood has become slightly imperfect; the lungs move stiffly because they are somewhat distended with blood. This situation is referred to as heart failure and is, in fact, quite common in the elderly. In its most serious form, known as pulmonary edema, it can be a life-threatening condition.

Dangers
If a person experiences a new, severe pain in the chest, shoulders, or arms, especially if this is accompanied by breathlessness, nausea, and sweating, medical advice is urgently needed. This also applies if the pain is worse on breathing or coughing.

A doctor should also be consulted promptly if a new cough develops that produces phlegm (see Phlegm) or is accompanied by wheezing, if blood is being coughed up, or if there are bloody streaks in the sputum. Extreme breathlessness with a bubbling cough should also receive immediate attention.

Chicken pox

Q What is the best way to prevent scars from forming from chicken pox? Both my older children scratched their spots, and it would be a shame if my daughter were to scar her face when she gets it.

A Scarring takes place if the spots become infected or if the scabs are pulled off, taking fresh tissue with them, so widening the area of damage.

Preventing itching with an antihistamine drug or calamine lotion is helpful, but it does take some willpower not to scratch scabs. All you can do is explain to her what will happen if she picks the spots on her face and neck, and constantly encourage her to resist the temptation.

Q Could my baby daughter get chicken pox, and if so, is it more serious than in an older child?

A Babies seem to have some natural immunity to chicken pox, and very few cases have ever been recorded. A baby could be seriously, but probably not fatally, ill with chicken pox—but any child under the age of two who develops a rash should be seen by a doctor.

Q My brother appears to have chicken pox for the second time. Is this possible?

A This is unlikely. In general, chicken pox is a one-time-only infection. The first attack might have been scabies (severe itching and spots caused by a mite) or a number of gnat bites occurring together. These can look like chicken pox.

Q My daughter recently spent the day with a child who, I just found out, had chicken pox. How soon will she come down with it?

A Your daughter may show the first symptoms—headache and a vague illness, followed by spots—within ten days, or it could take up to three weeks to develop. Alternatively she may not develop chicken pox at all—there is no certainty that she was infected.

Because it is so easily caught, chicken pox is almost a natural hazard of childhood. But it does not last long and practically never has serious complications, so effective home nursing is a simple matter.

Chicken pox, the medical name of which is *varicella*, is a highly infectious illness, easily recognized by the rash that it causes. It is generally considered a childhood illness. Babies are born with a natural ability to resist the infection (passed on by their mothers), but the resistance wears off by the time the child is three or four years of age, leaving the child likely to catch the infection.

The virus

The virus (germ) that causes chicken pox is the same as that which causes shingles (which has similar symptoms, including a rash) in adults. So an adult with shingles can pass chicken pox on to a child.

Although slightly similar in appearance to smallpox (see Smallpox), chicken pox has nothing else in common with the disease. Smallpox is a much more serious illness, with a 40 percent death rate, and is caused by a completely different virus. The chicken pox and shingles virus is so highly infectious that many outbreaks occur, mainly in children between the ages of two and six. The outbreaks are strongest in the autumn and winter and appear to occur in three- or four-year cycles as new groups of children lose their inborn resistance.

How it is caught

Although the virus is present and alive in the spots that form on a child who catches chicken pox, it is chiefly transferred between people by droplet infection. Someone who already has the virus spreads clusters of the virus in the tiny droplets of water that are exhaled as a matter of course with every breath.

When a child breathes in an infected droplet, the virus starts to multiply and another case of chicken pox begins. Outbreaks cannot begin on their own; there has to be a source, which is almost always another child.

First symptoms

Once the virus enters the body, it needs an incubation, or breeding, period of between ten days and three weeks in order to spread. The first a child will know of his or her illness will be a 24-hour period where there will be symptoms of a vague headache, a sick feeling, occasional slight fever, and sometimes a blotchy, red rash that fades. A parent may note that a child is pale.

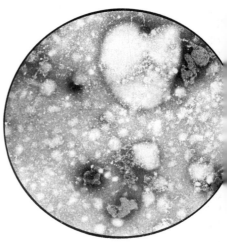

H. A. Davies/Science Photo Library

The chicken pox virus, enlarged about 8000 times, is mainly transmitted through droplets of water in the breath.

The spots

Within 24 hours the first spots will appear. The nature and position of these spots allow a diagnosis to be made. In very mild cases it can be difficult to distinguish chicken pox from gnat bites, but in a full-blown case, with hundreds of spots, the diagnosis is simple.

Spots first appear in the mouth and throat, where they quickly burst, causing pain and soreness. They then appear on the trunk and face, only occasionally affecting the limbs.

Each spot starts as a pink pimple, and within five or six hours, it becomes raised to form a tiny blister, or vesicle, containing clear fluid that is full of viruses. These teardrop spots gradually become milky in color. They form a crust and finally a scab. The time that it takes from the appearance of the teardrop to the formation of the crust is only about 24 hours. During this period the child may be agitated and uncomfortable, and run a temperature of 100° or 101°F (38°C). Some children only have a few spots, while others may have several hundred. Immediately after the crust forms, the spots begin to itch, and this stage may last until the scabs drop off, leaving new, normal skin after one or two weeks.

Course of the infection

Chicken pox spots come out in crops, which means that new ones will appear everyday for three or four days. When examining a child's skin, an adult will notice that the spots will be at different stages even in the same area. This is typical and quite normal. In the majority of cases the condition is very mild. But in some cases the child · is very sick and needs attentive home nursing.

Dangers

In children the dangerous complications of chicken pox are extremely rare. Most children feel well enough to play. Children who are taking steroid drugs or those suffering from leukemia are the only ones likely to be seriously affected, and for them the condition can be fatal. In a small number of cases the virus can lead to a severe form of pneumonia.

Chicken pox can be dangerous in pregnant women, as it can sometimes affect the developing fetus. A woman who has not had chicken pox should be vaccinated against it before becoming pregnant. Chicken pox pneumonia is fatal in adults in more than 20 percent of cases.

Infection

The most common complications arise from infection of the skin at the spot, causing boils or one or two other skin conditions. Similarly spots near the eye may lead to infective conjunctivitis, commonly called pink eye. In such cases treatment with antibiotics is needed.

Cases of arthritis and even inflammation of the heart have been known to follow chicken pox, but they are extremely rare. The only other serious danger is when the virus attacks the nervous system to cause encephalitis (inflammation of the brain), which it may do on the fourth or tenth day of the rash appearing. The patient becomes delirious, and intensive hospital treatment is needed. The chances of complete recovery are high.

Treatment

Children with a high temperature who feel unwell may prefer to stay in bed or lie downstairs to be with the family. Otherwise, there is no medical reason to enforce strict bed rest. The majority of children require no treatment at all.

Any pain from a sore throat or a headache is best relieved with a painkiller such as acetaminophen, or

Chicken pox spots begin to itch as soon as the crusts form, and calamine lotion is a soothing, cooling treatment.

Home care of a child

- Allow the child freedom, and do not insist on bed rest. Give mild painkillers for a sore throat or headache. Reassure the child. The spots may look dramatic, but the patient is rarely very sick
- Consult your doctor if the spots are very large, infected, or extremely painful (for instance, in the ear)
- If the child is not hungry, cut down on food when temperature is high, but offer plenty of fluids
- Explain the need not to scratch, and suggest that the child might like to wear soft cotton gloves as a reminder
- Apply calamine lotion to reduce irritation, or ask the doctor for an antihistamine drug, which will have the same effect
- Make sure strict hygiene is observed— short nails, clean hands, and a daily bath at the scab stage
- Check with the school about isolation of the child. Usually a week is required from the appearance of the spots
- It can be reassuring for your child to ask another child with chicken pox to come to the house to play

---

aspirin, in a child over seven. As there is no medical cure for the virus, the condition is left to take its natural course. Severe itching can be helped with application of calamine lotion, which has a cooling and anti-itching effect.

Alternatively the itching can be reduced with an antihistamine drug. If any of the spots should become infected, they may take longer to heal and antibiotics will be necessary.

Outlook

The majority of children who have had a mild case of chicken pox start losing their scabs after about ten days and will then be completely free of spots within about two weeks.

Where scabs have been scratched, the process will take a little longer. The scabs themselves are not infectious, and those that fall off on their own do not leave a scar. Scabs that have been prematurely picked or have become infected are more likely to scar, and for this reason it is important for children to avoid scratching their scabs.

Chicken pox infection produces lifelong immunity to the disease. But the virus remains in the body and can lead to shingles, which may occur later in a person's life.

A vaccine has recently been developed for chicken pox, and this will probably become one of the standard set of childhood injections.

Child abuse

Q I know my neighbor beats her toddler. I've seen terrible bruises on her face and arms. Whom should I contact?

A A doctor or social worker will give practical help to your neighbor, and no one will know that it was you who contacted them. It would be even better if you could also offer her some help yourself. Ask if you could look after the little girl sometimes; invite the mother in for coffee and encourage her to chat. Your support and friendship could make a lot of difference.

Q Will my child be taken away from me if it's discovered I've beaten her?

A If you cooperate with the people who want to help you to stop beating your child, and you manage to control your urges, then there is no danger of your child being taken away. Everyone would prefer you to keep your child, and it is only as a last resort that children are placed in a foster home.

Q My husband has beaten our baby once or twice. Does he need help?

A Yes, he does. To ignore his beating or to cover up for him can only be bad for the baby. Persuade him to see your local doctor, who will refer him to someone who can help him.

Q I get really mad at my toddler sometimes. Will I end up beating him?

A If you haven't done so before now, the answer is probably no. Most abused babies are beaten in the first year of their life, and if you have managed to control your feelings so far, then you should be safe both now and in the future.

Q Is my mother right when she says that slapping could develop into beating?

A The occasional slap can relieve a parent's bottled-up frustration and is unlikely to escalate into full-scale beating. But if you feel it could become uncontrollable, it is better not to slap a child at all.

Parents who abuse their children are likely to have suffered cruelty in childhood themselves, and so they are emotionally damaged. How can they be helped—and what are the signs that a child is being abused?

Child abuse is a term used to describe the nonaccidental physical (including sexual) abuse of a child by one or both of the parents or another adult, even though the child may in all other respects be well cared for and loved. Injuries can range in severity from the relatively minor to the point where the child actually dies.

Emotional abuse, where the child is taunted or told that he or she is not loved, or made to suffer mentally in other ways, often accompanies the physical abuse, and the scars left from this can linger long after the body has healed.

Causes

Every parent has experienced the helpless frustration that accompanies the nonstop crying of an infant who cannot be calmed. Most parents, however, find that "something" stops them from hitting the child; it is the lack of this internal brake that leads other parents to beat their children—not just once, but a number of times.

It is believed that as many as 20 percent of women experience difficulty in learning to become a mother. A small percentage of these go on to abuse their children, and the cause of this can be found far back in their own childhoods.

Some child abusers of both sexes were beaten or sexually molested themselves as children, and some are aggressive types with a pattern of physical violence

Too many children live in fear of those who should protect them. In 1993 the National Center for the Prevention of Child Abuse reported 786 deaths due to child abuse or neglect (this covered 37 of the 50 states). It is estimated that annually there are about 1300 deaths nationwide, of which about half are due to neglect and half to physical abuse.

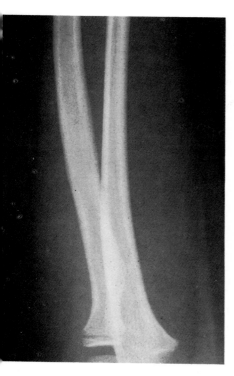

X ray showing child's forearm with a bent bone (left)—the result of a blow. A child's bones are soft and therefore bend rather than break.

in all their relationships—others fall into neither group. Almost all were deprived of good parental care when they were children, which means that they never learned to give and receive love and did not have a successful parent to model themselves on when the time came for them to raise their own children.

Fewer than 10 percent of parents who abuse their children are severely psychologically ill, although half of the mothers who do so are classifiably neurotic, and a third of the fathers are said to have a gross personality defect. Many of them are depressed, passive, reclusive types who demand instant love from their children and fail to understand that for a long time babies are dependent and only aware of their own needs. Crying is interpreted as a sign that the baby does not love them, and the parent's feelings of anger and failure can trigger an attack.

Other potential child abusers are obsessively clean and tidy, and the baby's natural soiling or a toddler's investigative messiness seem like deliberate naughtiness that must be punished. A mother who has had to give up her career or put it on hold to have the child may also feel strong resentment and frustration.

Isolation is another contributing factor to child abuse. A young mother whose own parents live far away, and who does not have friends nearby, may find that her desires and fears center on the baby, and she does not have the natural safety valve of talking with a sympathetic listener. If her marriage is also difficult or unhappy, then the baby will be placed even more at risk. The child abuser may be shocked and horrified at the damage he or she has caused while in a rage. Even though abusers sometimes realize that they are placing unrealistic demands on the children, not even their self-disgust will stop them from doing it again.

Social background

Research reveals that most child abuse happens among the poor and deprived and that the level of intelligence of the abusing parent is low. But statistics are compiled from cases that have come to the attention of the authorities—either from health visitors, social workers, hospitals, or police—and experts are sure that the problem is more widespread.

Child abusers who are well-off are able to seek private treatment for their children. The more intelligent they are, and the higher their social class, the more easily they are able to deceive the authorities as to the true cause of their child's injuries. It is also the case that a doctor is more disposed to believe the explanations of an articulate, middle-class parent.

Some people also believe that there is more chance of a stepchild being abused, or the child of a single parent. But while these cases are represented in the statistics, the fact is that most abuse occurs within a normal family unit.

Another common supposition is that one child is often singled out from a family group for beating. This is sometimes the case, but in most families where one child has been abused, the other children suffer from beatings too. One child may be being picked on at a time, and the house-proud nature of the abusing parent often means that the clean, well-dressed look of the others makes them appear to be unharmed. Closer examination generally proves that the others, at different times, have also suffered unexplained injuries.

Those most at risk

Anything is likely to trigger the violent rage of a harassed potential child abuser. However, some babies are more at risk: premature and underweight babies are in danger, because they need special care and patience and may be sickly and fretful, which is trying to the patience of even the most well-meaning parent.

Emotional abuse

It is impossible to estimate the extent of emotional abuse when it occurs without physical injury. Parents who say, "You're always "clumsy, stupid, lying, unpleasant, ugly" are doing their children great harm. The children begin to believe what is said of them, and it can affect their whole lives. If they are made to feel unloved, they will often unconsciously make themselves unlovable to other people and become antisocial.

It is a vicious circle: the parents feel that they are proved right by the actions of the child, and continue to hurt them with words. No physically abused child escapes emotional battering either. A child who is repeatedly hit for real or imagined naughtiness lives in fear. If physical contact means a blow as often as a hug, he or she may shrink from other people. Since it has been proven that children who are cuddled a lot tend to be mentally brighter, the implication for the abused child is clear. The child who is beaten and then pampered by the guilty parent will end up emotionally muddled and confused.

Preventing child abuse— a self-help guide

The baby has been crying all day and won't be comforted. The toddler has been driving you crazy, and you have a headache. These are moments that any mother or father will recognize, moments when they feel themselves losing control and know they are in danger of lashing out. Punishment given in a blind rage can be dangerous—especially if the child is a small baby.

Here are some suggestions that could help avert a crisis:

- Turn your aggression on an inanimate object: kick the door or punch the wall. The shock of the action may dispel violent feelings
- Telephone someone and tell them how you feel. Talking really helps
- Ask a neighbor or friend to watch your child for a while, and get out of the house. Spend the time walking and thinking until you feel calm
- If you can't get out, remove yourself from the child. Go into the kitchen and make tea. Allow yourself to cry or shout. If you give your angry feelings expression (without violence to the child), they will go away quicker than if you try to "pull yourself together"
- When the feelings have passed, don't just hope that it will never happen again. Seek help from your doctor, nurse, or social worker. They will understand without being shocked and will offer practical aid and advice

CHILD ABUSE

Symptoms

It is harder to spot an abused baby than it would seem. Most parents who abuse their children voluntarily bring them for treatment and are clearly distressed by their children's injuries. Abused children are usually genuinely loved, the beating being performed in a rage by parents with the emotional problems already mentioned. Some parents even have a partial memory blackout about the beating. They do not want to admit to themselves that they inflicted the injuries on their own children, and they are often glib and convincing in their explanation of the "accident" that caused the injury. In other ways, the child may look well cared for, so it is not surprising that the parent's explanation is often accepted.

However, alert doctors and teachers can spot the signs that indicate child abuse. Apart from the physical symptoms, a professional will notice if there is delay in reporting the injury; even parents who bring the child in for treatment may wait a day or two before doing so. Another sign is the child's general attitude: occasionally children may flinch from their parents, but this is not always a reliable sign, as some abused children are extra loving to their parents in an attempt to win their affection.

Injuries

Actual injuries vary, but even when a reasonable excuse is given for the way in which they happened, an examination can prove that the damage is inconsistent with "falling downstairs" or an accidental bang against a door frame.

The most serious injuries are to the face and head: fractured skulls or bruised and cut faces are often seen. *Failure to thrive* may be another sign. This is the term used for children who are underweight and not developing as they should. This could mean that a child is neglected, but in the case of an abused child, unhappiness could be the cause.

Children are abused in different ways, and the list makes unpleasant reading. Some are beaten around the head, punched, kicked, bitten, and thrown across the room or downstairs. Others are burned by cigarettes, thrown against a fire, or even placed in the oven or a boiling bath. Some parents confine themselves to shaking the child, believing that this does less harm—but young babies can suffer brain damage if violently shaken, even though their soft bones may sustain the shock of being thrown to the floor.

Doctors look out for heavy bruising caused by tight gripping around the head or limbs while the child was beaten or thrown. X rays can show up old healed injuries or damage to internal organs.

Treatment

Physically curing the abused child is the easiest part of the treatment, but it does not get to the root of the problem. According to some experts, a severely abused child who is returned ato the parents without their problems being treated stands a 25 to 50 percent chance of being killed or permanently injured.

Sixty percent will be abused again, and an even higher percentage will suffer minor attacks or emotional battering.

So how can the parents be treated to stop them from abusing their children? Certainly an increased knowledge of what to expect from their children at each stage of growth and development is a great help, along with practical aid with child-raising problems.

Doctors and social workers should recognize that sometimes the very obvious nature of the child's injuries is a cry for help from the parent, and it should be answered by offers of support, rather than accusation and disgust.

Above all, however, the best treatment consists of the parent relearning the art of loving and caring for the child, and this is brought about by being loved and "mothered" themselves. The social worker or caring person involved should focus attention on the parent—even in the face of antisocial behavior.

It used to be thought that any kind of parent was better than none at all.

An abused child can be helped to recover physically and emotionally by being fostered in a loving home.

Nowadays, however, if the parent repeatedly abuses the child, it is recognized that it is better for the child's physical and mental well-being if he or she is removed from home and placed in a loving, caring environment with foster parents.

Sexual abuse

Child abuse may also be of a sexual nature, and the damage can be done by family members or close family friends. The number of cases recognized has grown recently because doctors and teachers have learned to recognize the symptoms. However, there is growing awareness that this very serious problem has existed for many years, however hidden inside the family it may have been.

Outlook

The problem of child abuse is becoming more widely acknowledged and understood. Whether a child who has been physically and emotionally abused grows up to be a disturbed adult depends entirely on how the problem is dealt with and at what stage of development. If the abuse stops and professional help is used to treat the physical and emotional scars, there is no reason for the child not to outgrow the terror of the experience.

Child development

Q My one-month-old baby sleeps almost all the time. Is this unusual?

A Sleeping patterns vary. Some babies are naturally sleepier than others. At around 10 or 12 weeks most babies sleep through the night, giving up their midnight feed, and become more wakeful during the day. After three months the baby gradually needs less sleep and will not automatically have a nap after each meal.

Q When can I expect my 11-month-old sister to start talking properly?

A Probably very soon now. Most one-year-old babies have around three clear words and for the rest of the time babble in a way that sounds very like talking. They can understand many words and phrases and will obey simple commands, although they will have also learned to shake their heads when they mean no. But children do vary very much as to the age at which they start to talk.

Q When should a baby start on solid food?

A A baby has no need of solid food until the age of about three months. When a baby is drinking two pints of milk a day and is still hungry (but not overweight), it is a good time to start solid food. More than two pints of milk is too bulky for a baby's little stomach and the concentrated calories of solid food are needed.

Q My toddler screams and refuses to go to nursery school. How do I make him more independent?

A A child has a natural drive toward independence that can't be forced. It could be that your child is too young and has been made to feel insecure by your attempts to leave him with strangers. Once he is secure in the knowledge that a separation from you doesn't mean losing you forever, he might be happier about going to nursery. Perhaps you could wait a little while until he becomes less dependent on you.

A child's life from birth to age five is a fascinating series of changes. A helpless infant gradually turns into a sociable human being who is ready to enter school. So what progress can parents expect—and how can they help their child to develop healthily and happily?

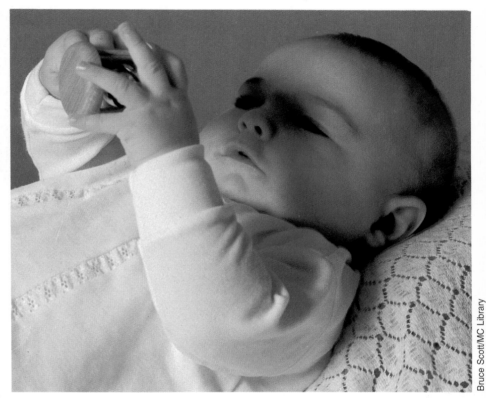

In the first six months a baby will learn to grasp objects with both hands.

Children develop at different rates according to their inborn potential, and their progress is also influenced by factors such as their surroundings and how much attention they receive. However, the sequence of physical development and the acquisition of new skills does not change. A child may be more advanced in some areas and slower in others—but the order in which he or she develops and learns will be the same.

Birth to six months

Feeding: During the first three months of life a baby gets all the nutrients necessary from milk, ideally breast milk.

If bottle-feeding is decided on, milk that has been specially prepared for infants should be bought and the formula carefully made up so that the feeding is not too concentrated. Formula milk should be used until the baby is a year old (using cow's milk before this age can lead to milk allergy).

Solid food should be introduced from about the age of three or four months in tiny amounts. By the age of six months, the baby will be eating three meals a day with a bottle or breast-feed at night. The solids should be finely mashed and the baby given rusks and cut-up vegetables and fruit to handle.

Crying: Crying is a baby's only method of communication. A parent finds out by trial and error why a baby is crying and soon learns to interpret the cries. Small babies usually cry while being undressed or if roughly handled.

From six weeks onward almost all babies will stop crying if they are cuddled. By six months babies also cry because they are bored or lonely but will usually stop when picked up by their mother or father.

Physical development: During the first six months, the baby learns to support his head and to roll over by himself.

Sally and Richard Greenhill

A baby has a strong will to do things without help—in time this infant will learn to feed himself without too much mess.

Eventually he will sit up with a little support, and if his hands are held, he will jump up and down on someone's lap. He will learn to coordinate hand and eye and will be able to reach out and grasp objects with both hands. He will likely cut his first tooth by six months.

Social development and play: From the start, a baby likes to look at a human face above all things and enjoys the sound of a human voice best. By four weeks she will be making cooing and gurgling noises, and at around six weeks the sounds will be phonetic and the infant will "talk back" when spoken to.

The first smiles will come at about six weeks, too, and the baby will smile in response to a smiling face and a human voice. As physical skills develop, the baby will want interesting toys to look at and grasp, and she will enjoy being talked to, held, and gently played with.

Relationship with mother: By four months a baby is usually more relaxed and happy with his mother than with anyone else. A small baby will treat his mother's body as an extension of his own and react with pleasure to the sound of her voice and to her face. He relies on her for play and entertainment.

Six months to one year
During this period a baby starts to crawl. She is interested in everything but does not have the coordination to be gentle with objects. Everything is put in the mouth—this is a small baby's way of learning about the world.

Feeding: During this time the baby can eat three meals a day at ordinary family mealtimes, supplemented by snacks in the morning and afternoon. His digestive system will be able to cope with the food that the family eats as long as it is minced or cut up. However, some mothers prefer to give their babies commercial foods.

The baby will start to be able to drink from a cup and will want to feed himself. Some babies are still having supplementary bottles, which should be of formula milk until the age of one year.

Crying: At this age a baby mainly cries out of frustration and anger at not being able to do the things she wants to do, and also from pain if she hurts herself crawling or attempting to walk. She also cries when left alone—each time a parent leaves her for any length of time, it is like a major separation.

Social development and play: The baby is far less sociable with strangers

A young child's first attempts at learning a new skill are always thrilling for a parent. Here a mother teaches her small daughter to ride a bicycle.

than before and may be suspicious and really frightened of them at times. He needs more things to play with now.

Physical development: Over these few months the baby learns to sit up without support, and then to crawl. She will start to pull herself up to stand—some babies leave out the crawling stage altogether. Once standing, she may move around the room by holding on to furniture. She also becomes much more practiced at using her hands.

By the end of their first year, most babies will have cut their two upper front teeth, as well as the two lower ones and one molar.

296

Relationship with mother: The baby becomes increasingly attached to his mother in a highly emotional way. He also becomes fond of other members of the family and pets. But he needs his mother's presence constantly, although he will play happily by himself as long as she is around. He is highly disturbed when separated from her. The baby is unhappy when his mother shows disapproval, but his memory is so short that he is likely to repeat the thing that he was told not to do a minute beforehand—so punishment does no good at this stage.

One to two years

This is the stage between babyhood and childhood and can be frustrating for the toddler who wishes to do more than he is physically capable of, and quite tiring for the mother since the toddler increasingly demands his own way.

Feeding: Most mothers understand the need for their child to have a good, mixed diet, but sometimes their preoccupation with this leads to feeding problems. The child herself is a guide to whether she is eating enough of the right things. An infant that is healthy, growing, and energetic is getting all her food needs met.

Sleeping: Most toddlers of this age have trouble settling down for the night. All will cry when their mother leaves the room. The best solution may be to pop in every five minutes till the child settles. Tuck him in with loving words, and say goodnight again. A child treated like this will not feel lonely and abandoned. He should not be allowed out of his crib or it will become a difficult pattern to break.

Walking: Once a toddler has taken his first few steps, his walking ability will increase rapidly. By 16 months most can toddle well.

By 20 months most will be able to run and jump with both feet, but at this age he may prefer to be taken from place to place in a stroller or in his mother's arms.

Talking: A baby's first words will usually be the names of loved ones and pets. Then she learns the words for favorite foods and drinks, followed by parts of the body, clothes, and everyday articles.

Social development and play: The toddler's increased mobility means that he is into everything. He is extremely curious and experimental and wants to copy what adults or other children do.

His imagination and imaginative play increase. He is still shy with strangers but may be pushy with other children.

Toilet training: Toilet training can only begin when the toddler is aware that he has wet or soiled himself. This can occur any time between one year and 15 months, and this is when the toddler begins to indicate to his mother that he has a full diaper.

Bladder control follows later—it is far harder for a toddler to "hold on" when he wants to urinate. It is no use trying to train him to urinate in the potty if he is still wearing diapers. He must be allowed the occasional accident.

If the mother can remain calm and unemotional, toilet training is likely to be easier. Dirty diapers or pants are not naughty—they are unfortunate.

Relationship with mother: The toddler is still very reliant on his mother. He seeks more protection and support than ever before, still feels great anxiety over any separation, and resents people who take

By copying his father, this young child is learning to feed himself confidently using chopsticks.

Q My one-year-old sister is very shy, even with close family friends. How can I help her to become more sociable?

A It is natural for a baby of her age to be shy and dependent on family members. It is a stage that will pass in time, when she is ready to be more sociable. If you try to force her, then her fear of others will increase.

Q I babysit for a two-year-old boy. How do I deal with his temper tantrums?

A Tantrums are very common in a toddler, and some children continue to have them until they are four years old. It would be far more worrying if the child never expressed frustration or bad temper in this way. Try to avoid frustration: suggest acceptable things to do rather than just saying "don't" when the child does something of which you disapprove. Allow him to express his aggressive feelings in play. Don't lose your temper as well; a calm, reassuring attitude will soothe him. Hold him so that he cannot hurt himself, and never give in afterward—or he will believe that a tantrum is the way to get what he wants.

Q How can I help my baby niece who has colic?

A Unfortunately there is no absolute cure for colic. It is also called evening colic, because it tends to strike after the late afternoon or early evening feed. It usually starts during the first two weeks of life and rarely lasts longer than nine weeks. It is distressing, for a colicky baby is not even comforted by being cuddled. You may just have to wait until the attacks pass, since they usually will.

Q My three-year-old son knows lots of words, but he can't make sentences yet. Is this normal?

A Most children know about 800 words by age three, and it is about this time that they start putting together sentences of four or five words.

up his mother's time. But he is seeking independence and resents his smallness and dependence on adults and the power they can wield; so he will become increasingly negative and assertive, testing his own power against that of the adult world.

Tantrums are common at this age—and for the next year or so. The child is not being willful or naughty, but just reacting to a buildup of frustration that he is too young to control.

Two to five years
This preschool age sees the child transformed from the baby dependent on his mother to a social human being.

Toilet training: Some children will be able to use the potty efficiently by the second year. Other children can be as old as three or well into their fourth year before they are completely potty trained.

Physical development and play: Play is the child's equivalent of work. Young children must have space to play and equipment to play with if they are to develop their physical skills.

The development of physical skill also fosters self-confidence, independence, and self-reliance and assists emotional development. Social and emotional development are helped by fantasy games.

Social development: Social behavior with other children goes through three recognizable stages, though the transition is gradual and the stages do overlap. During the first stage a child is indifferent

At nursery school children become used to playing with other children, cooperating and sharing their toys happily.

or aloof with other children, preferring to play alone. In the next stage hostility is shown—others are seen as rivals and there may be jealousy. The third stage sees a child become friendly and cooperative, playing happily with other children and sharing toys.

Most children of three and over benefit from time spent at a nursery or child center. The range of equipment available is likely to be far greater than at home, and a nursery will also encourage a child to learn to do things for himself that his mother might automatically do for him at home. As he gets to the stage of friendly cooperation with other children, he learns to give and take.

Relationship with mother: By the end of the first few years the child has gone through the stage of being dependent on his or her mother and has entered the stage of resistance. This will go on into the third year, but as he or she becomes more mobile, physically capable, and self-reliant, the relationship should start to settle down.

When the child comes to realize that mother always returns after an absence, his separation anxiety will automatically decrease, and if he is otherwise confident, he will enjoy the occasional time away from home, perhaps with grandparents. The calmer and happier his first two tempestuous years are, the more likely he is to become a happy and sociable child.

Chinese medicine

Q How can I check if a practitioner is qualified?

A Make sure that he or she is registered with a recognized professional body. Members have to be qualified to belong to the body and will be bound by their Code of Ethics and Code of Practice. Qualified practitioners of acupuncture, herbal medicine, and tui na should have trained for at least three or four years.

Q How do I know which treatment to choose?

A Although acupuncture, herbal medicines, and tui na massage can all be used to treat a wide number of illnesses, it is usually best to choose the treatment that most appeals to you. Acupuncture is more widely available than other Chinese therapies, and some acupuncturists are also herbalists. Tui na practitioners and qigong teachers are harder to find, although the number of people practicing these is on the increase. You should be able to obtain any relevant dietary advice you need from any Chinese practitioner.

Q Is it possible to teach myself how to do qigong exercises?

A It is important to learn qigong exercises from a qualified teacher. In some instances qigong has proven to be quite dangerous when not done correctly, and people have made themselves very ill by doing the exercises without the proper training.

Q Is the Chinese diet based on vegetarianism?

A Although much of the recommended diet is based on grains, pulses, and vegetables, the Chinese believe that a healthy diet is one that contains about 2 to 3 oz (60 to 90 g) of meat, three or four times a week. This is because the proteins, vitamins, and minerals found in meat products help to form the blood and prevent blood deficiencies. If you decide not to include meat in your diet, it is important to eat plenty of pulses and grains for protein, along with rice, lentils, and fresh vegetables.

For centuries Chinese medicine was considered unscientific and was treated with skepticism and suspicion in the West. But in recent years it has become more widely accepted, and today many people use it as an alternative to, or to complement, traditional medicine.

Chinese medicine is based on a philosophy that has evolved over thousands of years. It involves five different therapies: acupuncture, herbs, tui na massage, qigong exercises, and diet. Although each of these therapies can be practiced individually, they all complement each other, and they all have the same underlying principles.

The theory

Three main components in Chinese medicine are used in a diagnosis. These are Yin and Yang, the Vital Substances, and the Five Elements.

Yin and Yang represent the two opposing, but complementary, sides of nature. Everyone has their own unique balance of Yin and Yang, and when Yin and Yang are in harmony, the body is healthy. When they are out of balance, however, the body becomes ill.

The body also contains the Vital Substances Qi (pronounced chi), blood, and body fluids. Qi is an abstract concept that is usually translated as energy or the life force, which the Chinese believe to be the root of all human beings.

Although it cannot be seen under a microscope, Qi circulates through the body in invisible channels called meridians. If the Qi becomes deficient or the flow is blocked, this causes a lack of resistance to diseases and depleted energy. The restoration of its flow is vital to regain health.

A pharmacist in a Chinese hospital dispenses herbal medicines from his stock of powdered herbs.

Q Should I tell my doctor I am using Chinese medicine?

A You should always tell your doctor if you intend to use any form of Chinese medicine. This is especially important if you are having regular treatment or medication. Most doctors do not mind their patients trying these alternatives, especially if traditional medicine has failed to cure the problem. Even if your doctor does not approve, it is still better that he or she should be aware of any treatment you are having.

Q Is oil used during tui na massage?

A Chinese massage does not always require the use of a medium such as oil on the skin. When one is used, it is chosen to suit the particular illness that is being treated. Pure talcum powder and balms like tiger balm may be used, as well as woodlock oil and Dong Qin Gao, which is made from wintergreen mixed with menthol in a petroleum jelly base.

Q What are Chinese acupuncture needles like?

A In the past these were made from bamboo or even stone. Today the needles are usually made from stainless steel, although some practitioners use gold or silver needles. The needles are solid, with a very fine shaft and a sharp point. They come in different lengths, depending on which part of the body they are used. Many acupuncturists use single-use disposable needles; others may use an autoclave to sterilize their needles with steam pressure.

Q Where do Chinese herbs come from?

A Most of the herbs used in Chinese medicine do actually come from China or Hong Kong. Each herb has to be harvested at just the right time, often when it is fully matured. Once they are collected, the herbs are separated, because different parts of the plant may be used in a variety of prescriptions. They are then dried before being cut into smaller pieces and exported to the West.

A stall selling medicinal herbs in an Oriental market. In front are sacks of loose plant and animal extracts; small plastic bags of dried herbs can be seen on shelves.

Blood is seen as a fluid that nourishes and moisturizes the body, while housing the Shen or Mind-Spirit. Shen gives us the ability to think, analyze, and discriminate.

The state of a person's Qi (life force) and blood are dependent on the state of his or her constitution, which is dictated by the strength of the Jing Essence. Jing is stored in the kidneys and helps us to move through the different stages and cycles of our lives. Jing is inherited, and the amount a person has at birth has to last throughout his or her life.

Body fluids

Body fluids called Jin Ye are the most substantial of all the substances in the body. The Jin fluids are the light and watery liquids, such as sweat or saliva, that are found near the surface of the body. The Ye fluids are heavier and are found deeper inside the body. If the body fluids do not flow freely, they can obstruct the movement of Qi and blood.

The Five Elements

The Five Elements correspond with everything that makes up the universe—wood, fire, earth, metal, and water. Each is associated with two different internal organs, a Yin organ and a Yang organ. Water, for example, is associated with the bladder, which is a Yang organ, and the kidney, which is a Yin organ. The Five Elements are interconnected; so when one of the organs and its associated element are out of balance, the other elements are also affected.

Making a diagnosis

Chinese medicine is holistic (taking into account both the mind and the body of the patient). This means that both the patient's physiological and psychological state will be considered when making a diagnosis. The practitioner will therefore gather as much information as possible about the patient's symptoms before making a physical examination, including looking at the tongue and facial color and taking the pulse. A full diagnosis may take anything up to two hours.

Acupuncture

This is the best-known treatment, and it is endorsed by the World Health Organization for a wide range of conditions. Acupuncture involves the incision of needles into acupoints on the skin. These acupoints lie along the meridians—the channels along which Qi (the life force) flows. The aim of the needles is to disperse any blockages and bring the Qi back into balance. Acupressure is very similar, except that massage techniques are used to stimulate the acupoints rather than needles.

Most acupuncturists use the Five Elements to discover which organ is the root cause of the condition. The Vital Substances will also be taken into account, since they may be deficient or obstructing a particular organ.

Moxibustion can be used with acupuncture to speed up the healing process. Heat from herbal charcoal, or from rolled-up cones of the herb moxa, is applied to the end of the acupuncture needle to promote the flow of Qi and to restore the body's balance.

Herbal medicine

Chinese herbal medicine can be used for many of the problems that can be treated by acupuncture, although it is best known for its success in treating skin conditions such as eczema and psoriasis. The practitioner examines the patient first to determine which organs are out of balance and whether the Yin and Yang energies are in harmony.

Herbal medicines are made from the roots, stems, bark, leaves, seeds, or flowers of many plants, as well as from some mineral and animal products. About 6000 medicinal items are recorded in the Chinese pharmacopeia (the official list of medicinal substances), and around 400 of these are in common use today.

The herbs are prepared in a variety of ways and then made into pills, powders, or tinctures. Some external preparations are also used on the skin as ointments, creams, or herbal plasters.

Herbal medicines are usually combinations of herbs known as a prescription. To make the prescription the herbalist carefully blends together a number of herbs, each of which has a specific application. Many of these prescriptions have been created by eminent Chinese herbalists over the last 2000 years. They differ from Western herbal medicine in that each prescription is a mixture of herbs specially tailored to the patient's needs.

The most common way that these herbs are used is in the form of an herbal decoction boiled up from dried herbs—a fresh bag of herbs is boiled up each day. Sometimes an herbalist will use patent herbal pills that have been made by grinding up the herbs and mixing them with honey or with a paste. These pills are often slightly cheaper than dried herbs and are commonly used for treating deficiencies or acute problems. Powders made of ground-up herbs can be taken directly or mixed with water as a drink. Tinctures are made by extracting the constituents of herbs in a mixture of alcohol and water.

Different tastes

The herbal decoctions or powders vary in taste, and the Chinese have created five main categories of taste: pungent, sour, sweet, bitter, and salty. There is also a neutral, bland taste that has no flavor. The tastes have different effects on the body. The sour, bitter, and salty herbs are more Yin and have a downward-moving and internal effect. The sweet, pungent, and neutral herbs are more Yang, with an outward-moving and exterior effect.

Along with the five tastes, the four energies—hot, warm, cool, and cold temperatures—are also important when deciding which herbs to use. Temperature refers to the effect the herbs have on the body rather than whether they themselves are physically hot or cold.

Once a prescription has been given, the patient needs to see the practitioner once a month if suffering from a long-term, chronic problem. Acute illnesses such as a cold, cough, or stomach upset require more frequent visits, as herbs may only be prescribed for a few days.

Qigong exercises

The word qigong (pronounced chee-gong) was first used in China in the 1950s to describe a large number of different Chinese exercises. Qigong became very popular in China in the mid-1980s because increased freedom meant that the exercises, which had been closely guarded secrets within families for generations, were able to be taught in the open. These exercises are used to strengthen and transform Qi energy, and such is their success in China that many myths and legends have grown up around them.

Qigong aims to improve spiritual development in addition to keeping the body healthy. Many practitioners of acupuncture or massage practice qigong to help their healing ability. Those who practice regularly over a long period are thought to develop special gifts such as seeing into the future. Although a lot of the exercises are based on Taoism and Buddhism, qigong does not entail any religious commitment.

Chinese doctors recognized that gentle exercise can stimulate the flow of Qi so

An elderly patient receives acupuncture treatment for facial palsy, which usually affects one side of the face, making the eyelid and the corner of the mouth droop.

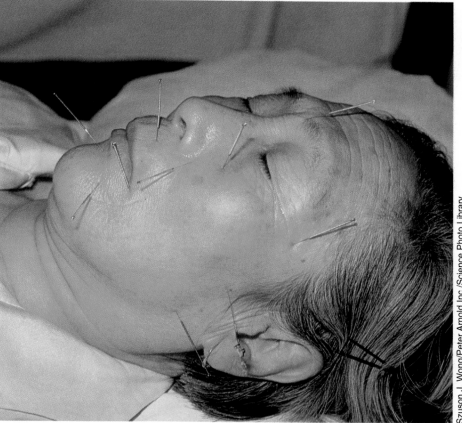

Szuson J. Wong/Peter Arnold Inc./Science Photo Library

that it flows smoothly around the body, thus stimulating the circulation of energy. Some of the exercises are designed to improve the functioning of different organs in the body, while others help to overcome specific problems. Many exercises have more than one beneficial effect: for example, the dragon-swimming exercise" has been used extensively by the Chinese to help them lose weight, and it is also thought to strengthen the kidneys, spine, and the lower abdomen.

Qigong exercises are all based on three key elements—posture, relaxation, and a focused mind. They can be grouped into four main categories: sitting, standing, moving, and spontaneous moving.

Sitting qigong is a form of meditation involving breathing exercises and internal movements such as contracting the anus. Standing qigong involves standing perfectly still in a posture that will help to develop the Qi. Moving qigong is performed in a gentle, relaxed way and requires deep concentration and good posture. Spontaneous moving qigong is the most unusual form of this exercise, and it involves standing very still until small spontaneous movements occur, such as shaking.

It is important to learn qigong from a qualified teacher. Many teachers will teach different types of qigong for different uses, such as for martial art or for healing. Once the student has learned

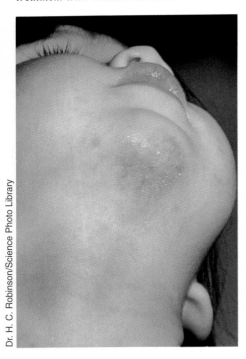

Eczema—a red, oozing rash that itches—is a condition that often responds well to treatment with Chinese herbal medicine.

Dr. H. C. Robinson/Science Photo Library

the exercises, he or she can continue to do them on a daily basis at home.

Tui na

Tui na is a type of therapeutic massage and is one of the oldest forms of Chinese medicine. However, it is still in its infancy in the West, where there are only a relatively small number of qualified practitioners. *Tui na* literally means "push grab," because the massage is usually quite vigorous and fast. It can involve massage techniques such as rolling, pushing, kneading, rubbing, pinching, and pressing.

Tui na is beneficial in relieving both acute and chronic joint problems, such as a bad back or a painful knee. It can also help the patient to relax, although it is seldom used just for relaxation. It can be helpful for many of the problems that are treated by acupuncture or herbal medicine. The massage is often carried out at specific acupuncture points on the body or along a meridian line.

Once the masseur or masseuse has made a diagnosis, a treatment will be chosen to suit the patient's energy balance. The massage can be given without removing any clothes, although the area to be treated may be covered with a towel or cotton cloth. Treatment usually takes around one hour and will probably need to be frequent at first, being reduced gradually as the condition improves.

There are various techniques that can be used for self-massage, but these are best taught by a qualified practitioner.

Chinese dietary therapy

Chinese dietary therapy is based on eating the correct proportion of different types of food, also taking into account the temperature, taste, and quantity of the food, and how and when it is eaten. The Chinese believe that a good diet is important not just for physical well-being, but also for mental health, because everything we eat ultimately becomes one of the Vital Substances, such as Qi, blood, or body fluids. If one of the digestive organs is not functioning properly, this can lead to fatigue, poor skin, and poor hair condition, as well as many digestive disorders. It can also affect concentration and memory.

A healthy Chinese diet will contain more grains, fruit, and vegetables, and less meat, sugar, and fat than most Western diets. The diet should be made up of 40 to 60 percent grains and pulses, 20 to 30 percent fruit and vegetables, and about 10 to 15 percent meat, fat, dairy products, and seafood.

The Chinese class all food as either hot, warm, neutral, cool, or cold. The term *temperature* means the warming or cooling effect the food has on the body, rather than whether the food itself is physically hot or cold. It is generally considered best to eat foods that are neither too hot nor too cold, such as rice, which is considered to be the most nourishing grain for this reason. Food should also be cooked, as raw food is "cold" and therefore harder to digest.

How and where food is eaten is important too, since people should be in a relaxed state when eating so that the digestion can work properly. Food needs to be eaten at regular intervals and should be well chewed to aid the digestive process.

It is thought that drinking liquids should be avoided at mealtimes, as this interferes with digestion. It is also advisable to stop eating when three-quarters full so that the stomach has time to empty before the next meal.

The Chinese believe that the correct diet will help to maintain good health in a patient after he or she has undergone treatment through acupuncture, herbal medicine, or massage. Correct diet is also thought to help if used alongside any of the other Chinese therapies.

As with all Chinese medicine, it is very important to go to a fully trained practitioner for treatment and advice. One of the best ways of finding a practitioner is through personal recommendation or alternatively through one of the various professional bodies.

Common illnesses that can be helped by Chinese medicine

Acupuncture, herbal medicine, and tui na can be used alongside qigong and Chinese dietary therapy to treat a wide variety of illnesses, including the following:

Breathing problems: asthma, coughs, bronchitis, hay fever
Circulatory problems: angina, high and low blood pressure, palpitations, poor circulation, varicose veins
Digestive complaints: gallstones, gastritis, indigestion, nausea, stomach ulcers, constipation, diarrhea
Emotional conditions: anxiety, depression, eating disorders, panic attacks
Gynecological problems: heavy periods, menopausal problems, premenstrual syndrome, postnatal depression, vaginal discharge

Chiropody

Q What exactly are ingrowing toenails, and how should they be treated?

A The nail of the big toe sometimes curves under at the sides and grows into the tissue around it, causing inflammation and an infection. It is a very painful condition, usually caused by cutting the toenails in a curve and down at the sides (rather than straight across at the end) or by wearing tight shoes.

Your chiropodist will be able to treat an ingrowing toenail by removing the ingrowing edge of the nail, along with any nail splinters, under a local anesthetic. He or she will then clean and dry the area, apply an antiseptic, then sterile cotton or gauze, a sterile dressing, and finally, tubular gauze.

Q I was sick recently and had to spend a lot of time in bed. Now that I'm able to get up, I notice that my feet are flat and painful to walk on. Will they stay like this?

A No. This is a temporary condition. Because you have not been using the muscles in your feet, they have become flabby and weak and cannot support the arches. Your chiropodist can give you some special foot exercises to do every day that will strengthen the muscles and help you to gradually regain the arches.

Q I do a lot of running, but recently I have had a pain in the ball of my foot that gets worse whenever I run. What could be causing this?

A You may have a fracture in one or more of your foot bones (metatarsals). Running subjects your feet to repeated stress, and this can cause fractures called March fractures. These fractures produce pain in the ball of the foot, which gets worse following any prolonged exertion. The same thing can happen after taking a long walk. The diagnosis can be confirmed by X ray, and if you do have a fracture, your foot will need to be strapped in, and you will need to rest it for at least a few weeks until the fracture has repaired itself.

Foot disorders cause a great deal of pain and sometimes disability. Qualified chiropodists can diagnose and treat a wide range of problems and give advice on how to keep the feet healthy and painfree.

Chiropody, or podiatry, is the diagnosis and treatment of feet and their ailments. It is unusual for everyday foot problems to be treated by physicians or surgeons. Instead they are dealt with by chiropodists or podiatrists who have had specialized training. In addition to examining the feet and applying dressings, chiropodists perform minor surgical procedures under local anesthesia and identify those patients who do need to be treated by a physician or surgeon.

The most common foot disorders that chiropodists deal with can be put into three basic categories: those that arise from biomechanical factors; those caused by infection; and those that are caused by general disease. As a person gets older, existing problems may get worse and new ones can develop.

Biomechanical disorders

The feet have two main functions: to support the weight of the body and to act as a lever to move the body forward when a person walks or runs. Many demands are placed on the feet, from the fine balance required by a ballet dancer to the propulsion required by an athlete. These extremes of activity, in addition to the everyday activities of standing and walking, place mechanical stresses on the feet. Abnormal or excessive stress, for example, as a result of bearing heavy weight or wearing inappropriate footwear, can cause foot disorders. Bearing heavy weight does not just mean carrying heavy loads—it is also a problem for obese people.

One of the best ways of avoiding stress-related foot problems is to make sure that comfortable shoes are worn and that they fit properly. Narrow or pointed shoes, high heels, platform soles, and shoes that do not hold the feet in place can cause all kinds of problems.

Flat feet

When babies are first born, they appear to have flat feet, but the arches develop as the tendons, muscles, and ligaments get stronger with use. If the arch of the foot does not develop or if it disappears, then the condition known as flat feet occurs. The feet can become flat if the whole structure of the arch collapses. This type of flat foot does not usually cause any pain or discomfort and is nothing to worry about, though an individual may find that his or her shoes wear unevenly. The most common cause of flat feet is rotation of the joints in the feet so that the arches seem to disappear. This

This patient's left big toenail is ingrowing toward the second toe. The surrounding skin is swollen and bleeding, with an infection at the skin fold called paronchyia.

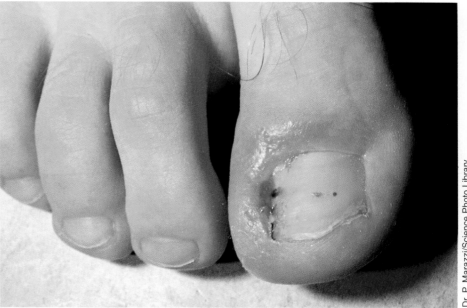

Q I work in a store on Saturdays, and my feet are often aching by the end of the day. Why is this?

A Aching feet are a very common problem. Standing for a long time, doing a lot of walking, and being overweight can all help to make your feet ache. The pain happens because the supporting muscles get tired, and the ligaments become stretched through supporting the load on the arches. A podiatrist will apply a figure-eight strapping to your foot and ankle to relieve the symptoms, and he or she will advise you on the type of shoes you should wear to give your feet the firm support that they need.

Q My second toe is bent into an inverted "V" shape and rubs on my shoes. Is there anything I can do about it?

A This is a common complaint called hammertoe. You should wear shoes deep enough to remove the pressure on the joint, and padding will help to relieve the pain. Your podiatrist can give you a splint to straighten the toes.

Q Why does my podiatrist look at my shoes whenever I visit him?

A Your podiatrist will check your shoes for size, shape, style, suitability, and also any signs of abnormal wear on the heels, soles, and tops. Abnormal wear on the soles or heels, or distortion of the tops, may indicate certain foot disorders, and this inspection will help to diagnose the problem.

Q I am training to be a ballet dancer. I have constant problems with my feet, especially bunions. Is there anything I can do to prevent or reduce the effects of strain on my toes?

A It is important for you to see a podiatrist regularly, especially if you are planning to have a career in ballet. The podiatrist will check to see that your ballet slippers fit correctly and will advise you on general foot care.

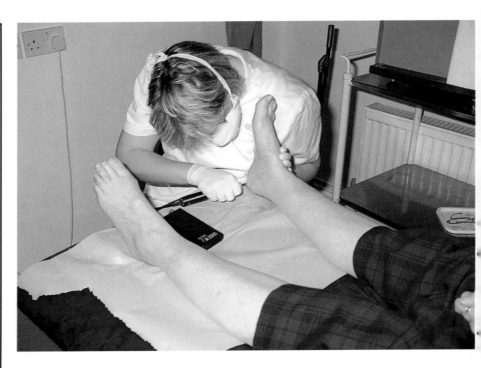

Sometimes the chiropodist uses a machine to file down calluses—areas of thickened skin caused by prolonged pressure or friction—on a patient's feet.

can cause pain and discomfort in the feet and also in the ankles, knees, and lower back, because the rotation in the feet affects the way that a person stands and walks. Chiropodists treat patients with this type of flat feet by using special inserts for the shoes, called orthoses; the type of orthosis will depend on where in the foot the rotation has occurred. Some times the shoes may need to be modified.

Bunions

A bunion (see *Bunions*) is an abnormal enlargement at the outside edge of the joint between the foot and the base of the big toe and is a very common disorder. The joint, which is often swollen and tender, points outward at a sharp angle, while the big toe points inward. The other toes become affected and corns can develop, because the deformity causes increased stress on other parts of the feet.

Bunions tend to develop in people with an inherited weakness in the toe joints. They are made worse by wearing badly fitting shoes, especially those with high heels and pointed toes; so it is not surprising that more women than men are affected. Once the deformity has started, it tends to get worse and will not correct itself, even if shoes are not worn.

If a bunion is painful, a person should see the chiropodist, who will remove any corns that have developed and give treatment to relieve the pain. This may include protective padding to ease the pressure on the joint; shoe alterations, such as a balloon patch on the side of the shoe; or an appliance, such as a shield, that fits over the tender joint and protects it.

Corns and calluses

Corns and calluses are areas of skin that become thickened by constant pressure, often caused by wearing new shoes or shoes that do not fit properly, and once they have developed, pressure on the corns and calluses causes tenderness in the tissues underneath. Corns (see *Corns*) are small and develop on the toes, while calluses are larger and develop on the soles of the feet. Wearing high heels can also cause calluses, since this type of shoe puts more pressure on the ball of the foot. Some people have a natural tendency to develop calluses because of their more delicate skin type.

The chiropodist will remove the thickened skin of a callus with a scalpel, then apply an antiseptic and a padded dressing. If the skin is dry, the chiropodist will probably recommend that an emollient be applied twice a day to soften the skin and prevent further calluses. With corns, the chiropodist will remove the nucleus with a scalpel, and as with calluses, an emollient should be applied.

Infections

Foot infections may be caused by bacteria, viruses, or fungi. Bacterial infections are not very common, but if a person does get one, the chiropodist will prescribe either an antiseptic, if the infection is mild, or an antibiotic, if it is more severe or persistent. Some groups of people are more prone to bacterial infections: these include older people, particularly those with poor circulation; people with certain medical conditions, including diabetes mellitus; those with poor nutrition or anemia; or those who are taking certain medicines such as corticosteroids and immunosuppressive or cytotoxic drugs.

Verrucae (warts)

The most common viral infection is a verruca (see Verruca, p. 2106) , which is a wart on the sole of the foot. The virus enters a skin cell, where it multiplies and spreads to adjacent cells. The hard, horny swelling this produces usually gets pushed under the skin by standing and walking, which may irritate the sensitive nerve endings and cause pain. Most people catch verrucae at the swimming pool,

A chiropodist presses and manipulates the foot of a patient during an examination. Problems treated may include bunions, hammertoes, and foot ulcers.

Damien Lovegrove/Science Photo Library

since the virus finds it easier to get into the skin cells when they are wet.

If a verruca develops, it is advisable to wear rubber shoes when going swimming; at home, use a personal bath mat and towel so that the virus does not spread to other family members. A verruca does not always cause pain, and if it is left alone, it will usually disappear within six to eight months. If it lasts much longer than this or is painful, a chiropodist should be consulted.

There are no effective drugs that can kill the verruca virus. Therefore treatment involves killing the skin cells that contain the virus. Most chiropodists do this by using either chemical cautery, cryotherapy, or electrosurgery.

Methods of removal

Chemical cautery is effective, produces rapid results, and is not usually painful. The chiropodist will apply a caustic chemical, taking care not to spread it onto the surrounding healthy tissue. A circular

pad with a hole in the middle is placed over the verruca and covered with a zinc oxide plaster. After about seven days, the chiropodist will remove the dead tissue from the foot, and if the verruca has not been completely destroyed, he or she will apply more of the caustic chemical and a fresh dressing.

In cryotherapy the infected tissue is cooled to very low temperatures. This causes ice crystals to form in the fluid inside and around the cells, and the cells then rupture. The temperature in the tissues must be reduced to at least $-4°F$ ($-20°C$) for the treatment to be effective. It is a technique that requires only a single treatment, but it can be painful.

Electrosurgery is also a single treatment technique that destroys the tissue by heat. If the chiropodist is using this method, the patient will be given a local anesthetic, as there may be a little pain.

Fungal infections

Other problems that are associated with wearing shoes are fungal infections. These are quite common, because shoes help to create the warm, moist conditions between the toes, in which fungi thrive. The fungi digest the dead skin that the body sheds each day and can also cause inflammation and damage to living skin cells—in severe cases, they can infect the toenails.

Fungal infections can be treated with an antifungal paint or ointment, which should be applied twice daily until two or three weeks after the symptoms disappear. If the toenails are infected, they may take up to 18 months to clear. The best way to prevent fungal infections from recurring is to wash the feet at least once a day and dry them thoroughly, especially between the toes. Antifungal powders can also be used inside the shoes.

General diseases

Older people and those who have diseases that cause reduced sensation in the feet or diseases that affect the circulation, such as diabetes mellitus and peripheral artery disease, should take special care of their feet and should never neglect any cuts or sores that do develop. Poor circulation means they take longer to heal than in healthy people, and they can become seriously infected without attention from a chiropodist.

Diseases such as arthritis, in addition to affecting the joints in the feet, can make it difficult for a person to reach their feet, and this can also be a problem as people get older. If this is the case, a chiropodist should be visited on a regular basis so that he or she can cut the toenails and treat any minor problems before they develop into more serious ones.

Chiropractic

Q What is the difference between the methods used by an osteopath and a chiropractor?

A Although they offer similar treatments, compared with an osteopath (and physiotherapist), a chiropractor is seen to use manipulation as the main form of treatment, as opposed to soft tissue or massage techniques. Some will also offer dietary advice. In the US osteopaths are medically qualified and they are usually consulted primarily for their medical expertise.

Q Are chiropractors medically qualified?

A No, but the standards of chiropractic preclinical education are now recognized to be equal to those of medicine. US students must have credits from at least two years of a bachelor's degree course before they can start their chiropractic training. They train for four to five years full-time and study medical sciences in addition to the required chiropractic techniques.

Q Is chiropractic treatment painful or uncomfortable?

A This depends largely on the type of problem, your sensitivity, and the way in which individual chiropractors make adjustments. As a general rule, the more painful the condition, the more likely it is that brief discomfort may be experienced. Many patients feel tired after treatment, and stiffness or soreness may occur for a day or two afterward. Pain could increase as tight muscles readjust, but this is unlikely. If you are concerned, contact your chiropractor.

Q How can I find a good chiropractor?

A Your doctor can refer you to a fully qualified, registered chiropractor; otherwise the chiropractic associations will usually supply a list of registered chiropractors. The initials DC after a qualified chiropractor's name stand for doctor of chiropractic.

Chiropractors diagnose joint conditions and use manipulative techniques to improve the function of joints and to relieve pain and muscle spasm. Chiropractic is primarily used in the treatment of back pain.

Manipulating the spine is one of the oldest healing therapies in the world. A 5th-century votive relief excavated from the Aesculapian hospital in Piraeus, Greece, shows the healer Aesculapius manipulating the upper thoracic spine. But by the 19th century, medicine was increasingly starting to involve only scientifically proven treatments.

In America most medical progress was being made on the East Coast, but elsewhere, in rural areas in particular, where there were fewer trained doctors, there was a dissatisfaction with medical methods. This encouraged a general interest in natural healing, including bonesetting. It was not until September 1885, however, that chiropractic was "discovered," when the healer Daniel David Palmer treated caretaker Harvey Lillard for a 17-year-old injury. Lillard had been bent over his work when he felt something give in his back. At almost the same time he lost his hearing. Palmer repositioned the vertebra that had moved, Lillard's hearing allegedly improved, and chiropractic began.

Early theories

Two decades earlier the founder of osteopathy, Andrew Taylor Still, had developed the theory that many ailments stem from distortions or malfunctions in the structure of the body. Although the theories are similar, Palmer's first spinal adjustment convinced him that the basis of all disease lay in the spine, because the human nervous system was affected if the vertebrae of the spine were misaligned. Palmer talked to doctors and taught himself anatomy and physiology, and then developed his own system of treatment.

Palmer came up against much opposition from the established medical profession and in 1906 was jailed for three months for practicing without a medical license. Meanwhile his son, Bartlett Joshua, took over the Palmer Infirmary and Chiropractic Institute—it was not long before he had turned it into a profitable concern.

Shortly after Daniel's release, father and son parted company. Daniel Palmer spent the next seven years attempting to establish schools as he traveled through the Indian Territory, California, Oregon, and Canada. He died in 1913—the year that Kansas became the first state to license chiropractors. Bartlett Joshua continued to work at the school, influencing the chiropractic profession until his death in 1961. He introduced X-ray analysis, and

A patient consults a chiropractor. Chiropractic is based on the theory that almost all physical complaints can be traced to an incorrect alignment of the bones.

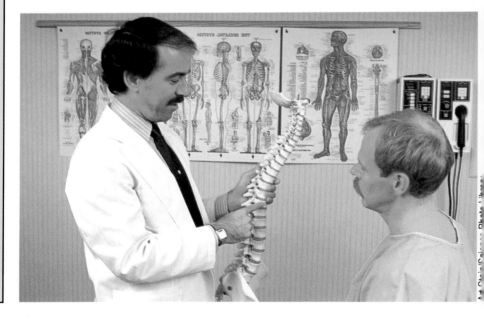

A chiropractor attempts to correct the nerve function in this man by manipulating the spinal column. Many disorders may be caused by poor alignment of the bones.

practor seeking relief from back pain. The most common problem area is the lower back. Mild backaches usually disappear within a few weeks, in which case they do not require treatment. But when the pain becomes prolonged or recurrent, or after a sudden sprain or strain or heavy fall, it is advisable to seek expert advice.

The next most common problem area is the neck. Incorrect posture and tension can cause the neck muscles to tighten, and this may refer pain to other areas of the body, particularly the shoulders and arms. Whiplash can also be helped by chiropractic treatment, as can many sports injuries, such as joint or ligament sprains, muscle strain, or intervertebral disk damage. Chiropractic may also reduce pain caused by the aftereffects of injury or surgery where traditional methods of treatment have failed.

What happens in a consultation

On a first visit, the chiropractor will ask about the patient's medical history and whether prescribed drugs are being taken. He or she will also want details of any injuries. Questions may sometimes be asked about lifestyle, such as working and

together with other early chiropractors, used this to pioneer new techniques and methods of study. Bartlett Joshua insisted on a purist approach and opposed those who incorporated other methods of natural healing.

In the 1930s Bartlett Joshua developed the hole-in-one technique, believing that if the top two vertebrae were aligned, the full health of the patient could be achieved. This policy was revised in 1958 in line with other major chiropractic colleges in the country.

In 1974, two years after Congress had voted to make chiropractic available under Medicare, chiropractic became legal throughout the US. In the same year, the Wisconsin Workers Compensation Board identified chiropractic as the most economic form of treatment for back pain, and studies repeated in other states drew the same conclusion.

Today chiropractic has emerged as a major form of treatment for back pain, with an estimated one in fifteen Americans consulting a chiropractor at least once a year.

How it works

The basic principle of chiropractic is that the architecture of a healthy spine is designed to assist normal body functioning. Chiropractors manipulate joints which have been subjected to abnormal pressures that have damaged their function. The chiropractor's aim is to restore normal joint functioning and thereby improve overall health.

All of the body's joints contain cells called mechanoceptors, which register movement. Stimulating these mechanoceptors produces pain-relieving hormones, or endorphins, which is one of the reasons why soft tissue massage around the joints may also be effective.

When to see a chiropractor

Treatment is suitable for people of all ages, although only a specialist should manipulate babies, and it is essential that women who are pregnant inform the chiropractor of their condition before the consultation. A few chiropractors specialize in the treatment of animals.

Since chiropractors aim to restore the correct functioning of the joints, any person with an appropriate joint problem is likely to benefit. Occasionally organic illnesses have been successfully treated, but the majority of patients go to a chiro-

---

Conditions the chiropractor can treat

The following common conditions may be helped or relieved by chiropractic treatment:
- Neck pain caused by posterior joint and ligament strain
- Tension headaches due to problems in the upper cervical spine and muscle spasm
- All back pain, except when there is a serious underlying pathological cause or where nerve roots are so trapped that surgical decompression is necessary
- Thoracic spine pain involving the costovertebral joints
- Lower back pain due to facet joint, sacroiliac, and ligament strains, causing associated muscle spasm and referred pain
- Occasionally disk herniation or an abnormally protruding disk
- Nerve root irritation—including cramplike leg pain—caused by lateral spinal canal stenosis, the narrowing of the canal carrying the spinal cord
- Peripheral joint problems, such as rotator cuff tendinitis and shoulder capsulitis—types of shoulder inflammation—tennis elbow, and carpal tunnel syndrome—numbness, tingling, and pain in the thumb, index, and middle fingers
- Problems in hand and foot joints
- Knee ligament sprains and minor meniscal tears
- Ankle injuries

Q How long does a course of treatment last?

A The number and frequency of treatments depend on your needs and the chiropractor's approach. Chronic conditions generally take longer to treat than recent, acute problems. Each time you visit, the chiropractor will reassess your condition. Most patients receive between four and twelve treatments. Patients with conditions that are not completely curable may need to return at regular, longer intervals for improvements to be maintained.

Q What causes the popping when the chiropractor adjusts my spine?

A Often a slight click is heard as an adjustment is made. Patients usually assume that this is the noise made by a vertebra going back into place. But the only joints that can move at all during spinal adjustment are the facet joints that link the vertebrae. The noise is caused by the joint surfaces being forced apart during manipulation. This alters the balance of pressure from the synovial fluid surrounding each joint. The "pop" is similar in principle to cracking the knuckles.

Q Is chiropractic treatment completely safe?

A No medical treatment is completely safe, but the risk of complications arising from chiropractic treatment is minimal, especially on referral and with the use of X rays to safeguard against misdiagnosis. In the 1970s an investigation of chiropractic by the New Zealand Commission led to a report that concluded that "there can be no doubt that chiropractic treatment is effective for musculoskeletal disorders" and that it is "remarkably safe." Subsequent research has supported this. In the unlikely event of an accident, most chiropractic associations have complaints procedures. In cases of malignant tumors, tuberculosis, acute arthritis, fractures, and some bone diseases, manipulation should never be carried out, and it should rarely be done in cases of prolapsed disks. All chiropractors should adhere to safety guidelines.

eating habits. Information is treated as confidential.

A thorough physical examination will follow, when the patient is asked to take off outer garments and go through a series of maneuvers. During the exercises, the chiropractor assesses posture, leg length, and mobility. The chiropractor also uses palpation, or analysis by touch, at various times to enable himself or herself to judge skin and muscle tone, ligament and bone condition. A light rubber hammer is used to test leg and arm reflexes.

Healthy reflexes mean that clear messages are being sent from these areas to the spinal cord via the nervous system, and that the area is free from disturbance. Other tests may be chosen also, depending on the type of problem presented. If necessary, X rays may be taken.

Treatment is sometimes given at the end of the first consultation, but not if X-ray results are required. Occasionally the chiropractor decides that a condition is unsuitable for treatment, and he or she refers the patient back to the doctor. Although chiropractors are trained to make a diagnosis, if a condition is particularly painful or chronic, it is advisable to see a doctor before visiting a chiropractor.

Treatment

Many patients who seek treatment for back pain have developed postural problems. In order to maintain balance, the body compensates for any postural distortion, and it does this by causing one or more counter distortions elsewhere in the spine or pelvis. This is the main reason why treatment may involve areas other than the site of pain and why a number of visits may be necessary.

Treatment includes soft tissue work along with manipulation. Patients are usually asked to lie on a special couch, but could be asked to sit, kneel, or stand. The two main types of manipulation are direct adjustment and toggle recoil. Direct adjustment involves a rapid, shallow movement that is sometimes accompanied by a "pop." Any pain is usually from inflamed tissues rather than caused by the adjustment. Toggle recoil involves carefully positioning the patient before performing a split-second thrusting movement. This is said to induce relaxation around the joint tissues and to allow the joint to return to normal mobility and function. Back, leg, or arm joints may be manipulated, and sometimes the skull and face are manipulated.

Some chiropractors offer mechanical means of pain relief, such as ultrasound, but they are used for short periods only. Most chiropractors prefer to restrict their services to manual techniques. In the US members of the American Chiropractors Association incorporate other therapies into their treatment, placing particular emphasis on the importance of nutrition and vitamin and mineral supplements.

An osteopath pulls back the legs of a small boy, lying on his front. Manual techniques and therapeutic procedures may be used to diagnose and treat dysfunction.

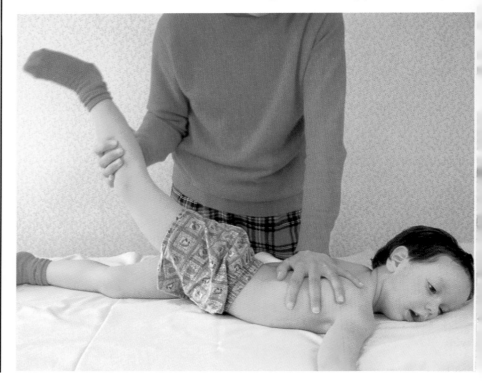

Cholera

Q Will I need to have a cholera vaccination if I go on vacation to India, and will I need a certificate to prove I have had the vaccination?

A Cholera vaccinations are voluntary in many countries, but countries like India strongly recommend that you are vaccinated. However, those traveling from India to certain other countries will need an International Certificate of Vaccination. The best thing to do is to get details of all vaccinations needed from your travel agent, or direct from the embassy of the country you intend to visit, and then get a set of vaccinations from your doctor.

Q Can poor housing and overcrowded conditions cause cholera?

A Cholera remains a threat to all communities where sanitation and hygiene standards are poor. However, the disease is not regularly found in the United States these days, because we do not have a population of carriers (people who carry the bacteria but show no symptoms). But with foreign travel becoming more widespread, it is easier for an unidentified carrier to come into a city and start an outbreak. It is only because water supplies are so carefully controlled, and because of the high standard of personal hygiene in homes, that cholera does not affect the United States.

Q Why does cholera appear after some form of natural disaster, such as an earthquake?

A Cholera breaks out whenever drinking and cooking water have been contaminated by infected excreta. In earthquake areas drainage pipes for sewage water may crack and leak into wells or rivers providing clean water. Where large numbers of people are living and cooking together in temporary camps, the disposal of excreta may be poor and hygiene virtually impossible, due to lack of water. A cholera epidemic can also occur as a result of food contamination, when flies feed off sewage and then settle on food.

Cholera is an acute infection that is spread in water contaminated by human feces. Today it usually occurs only in areas where hygiene and sanitation are poor.

Cholera is an extremely serious, highly infectious, and often fatal bacterial infection of the intestine. The bacterium causes profuse watery diarrhea and vomiting, which leads to death through a massive dehydration of the body tissues.

Causes
The bacterium causing cholera is known as the *Comma bacillus*—a reference to its short, commalike shape. It can be transmitted either by those infected with cholera or by those who have survived it. The fouling of a fresh water supply by the excreta and vomit of an infected person is the most common cause.

Symptoms
There is an incubation period of between 12 hours and six days. About 90 percent of people infected show symptoms; the remainder suffer few or no ill-effects.

The disease starts with uncontrollable diarrhea, nausea, and massive dehydration, followed by raging thirst. The kidneys or heart might fail, and the patient may die at this stage, but in many cases the condition improves. However, if the damage to the heart or kidneys has been too severe, the disease is fatal.

Treatment
Prompt medical treatment can reduce the mortality rate from 50 to one percent. Rehydration is the most important element. Although this is usually done using intravenous fluids, rehydration can be done orally. Where treatment is delayed, the death rate rises. Mild cases recover spontaneously, but in serious cases of cholera, the outlook depends on the severity of the fluid loss and the medical treatment received.

TAKE CARE
Preventive measures
Before entry into a cholera area
- Be vaccinated: this lasts for six months to a year
- Take tetracycline antibiotics for further protection if infection is likely

In a cholera area
- All suspected victims should be isolated
- Burn all soiled linen and contaminated items
- Identify and treat those who carry the disease but are unaffected by it
- Boil all water
- Avoid uncooked food that may have been sprayed or watered with contaminated water
- Protect food from flies and other insects
- Maintain scrupulous personal hygiene. Wash hands after going to the lavatory and again before handling food
- Carefully dispose of all sewage

Where vaccination against cholera is necessary

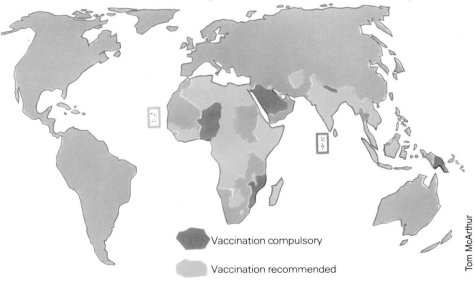

■ Vaccination compulsory

░ Vaccination recommended

Tom McArthur

Cholesterol

Q Will eating a low-cholesterol diet help me avoid getting heart disease?

A It might help, but only if it is combined with other measures. First, if you smoke, it is pointless doing anything until you have stopped, because smoking causes the arteries to contract and so makes them more likely to clog. Other precautionary measures are taking regular exercise, weight control, and generally avoiding stress wherever possible.

Q Does a high blood cholesterol level run in families? Several of my relations have had heart attacks. Is there any connection?

A Yes, there are a number of well-known medical conditions where abnormalities of the fats and cholesterol in the blood are inherited. People who are thus affected may need intensive treatment with both diet and drugs.

Q My son has always been teased about being fat. Does this mean that he has a high blood cholesterol level?

A Not necessarily. People who are very overweight consume more food than they need, storing the excess food energy in the form of fat. Their blood cholesterol largely depends on the makeup of their diet, in the same way as it does with thin people. But the chances are that your son is also eating the wrong kinds of foods. You could help him most by trying to improve his eating habits and encouraging him to cut his consumption of fast food, ice cream, cakes, and candy. Be sure not to nag him too much—losing weight too rapidly or eating less food than he needs would be equally damaging to his health.

Q Are there any danger signs of a high cholesterol level?

A Yes, there are. Deposits of cholesterol can be seen in the skin. These look like little yellow, spots and can be found over the elbows or ankles, or at the inside corners of the eyes on the lids.

A certain amount of cholesterol is essential to health, but too much can contribute to artery disease and heart attacks. Careful attention to diet and lifestyle will help to avoid potential problems.

Alan Duns/MC Library

These foods contain large amounts of dietary fat and should be consumed in moderation.

Cholesterol is a fatty or oily substance that normally forms part of the wall around each cell in the body. It is also a basic building block of the steroid hormones, a major group of the body's chemical messengers. Unfortunately cholesterol can become lodged in the walls of the arteries, where it contributes to the condition called arteriosclerosis, or hardening of the arteries, which causes heart attacks and strokes—a major cause of death in the Western world. The body usually makes sufficient cholesterol, but levels may be increased by extra amounts in the diet from animal fats and eggs.

People at risk
A number of factors contribute to the risk of an individual having arterial or heart disease. Smoking and a family history of these conditions are as important as the level of cholesterol in the blood.

Cholesterol levels vary for a number of reasons, including the total amount of fat in the diet and whether that fat is of animal or vegetable origin. People in the US derive about 40 percent of their food energy from fats. Surveys of other groups of people who traditionally eat a less fatty diet suggest that if this figure were reduced to below 30 percent, cholesterol levels would probably be lowered. Such a reduction could be accomplished by replacing fats with carbohydrates (starchy foods such as bread, potatoes, and rice). In addition to this, fats of animal origin—the so-called saturated fats—seem to increase cholesterol levels, whereas the

unsaturated fats, such as sunflower, safflower, and corn oil, do not appear to increase the overall cholesterol intake.

What happens in the body
Only a quarter of the cholesterol that circulates in the blood comes directly from the digestive tract, where it has been absorbed from food. Some of the cholesterol in the blood returns to the liver, where it is broken down and secreted as bile by the gallbladder. Any excess may enter the walls of the arteries.

It has been discovered that the body binds cholesterol with protein to form lipoproteins. There are two forms of lipoprotein: a low-density (or lightweight) form called LDL and a heavy-density form called HDL. LDL contains more fat than HDL and therefore floats, which is why it is the more lightweight substance. The LDL can thus be regarded as the bad lipoprotein, which deposits cholesterol in the walls of arteries.

The HDL, on the other hand, seems to operate in reverse by mopping up loose cholesterol from the arteries and elsewhere in the body and carrying it back to the liver, where it is broken down in the bile and excreted.

It has also been discovered that if people have a greater proportion of HDL in the blood, the effect is beneficial. The only known way to increase HDL is through exercise. Although a great deal of research is being carried out into these two different substances, not enough is yet known about exactly how they work. However, it is clear that lowering the level of cholesterol has produced good results in preventing heart attacks.

Altering the diet
Many people ask what food they should eat to lessen their chances of suffering a heart attack. There is no definitive answer, but most experts agree that a sensible mixed diet can only help.

First, the consumption of sugar (found in many commercially made foods) should be reduced to a minimum. Carbohydrates are best eaten as bread, potatoes, rice, and beans. Meat should be eaten only once every two or three days, and more vegetable protein, fish, and poultry should be eaten. Fats should be half of vegetable (polyunsaturated fats) and half of animal origin. No more than four eggs per week should be consumed.

Chorionic villus sampling

This modern, painless diagnostic technique can be used in the very earliest stages of pregnancy to detect a variety of possible disorders in a developing fetus.

Q My doctor has suggested that I should have a chorionic villus sample taken. If it shows that there is something wrong with my baby, will the doctors be able to cure it?

A Unfortunately not. Like all screening procedures, chorionic villus sampling can only point out a possible problem with an unborn baby. If the test does show that the baby has a problem, you will have a choice between continuing with the pregnancy, knowing what the outcome will be, or having an abortion. Medical treatment can only begin after the birth. It is important to remember also that a negative result does not guarantee a perfect baby, because there are defects, such as heart conditions, that the test cannot pick up.

Q Can I refuse to have a chorionic villus sample done if the hospital offers me one, or will my doctor insist I have it?

A You cannot be forced to have any test in pregnancy. Your doctor or the hospital may offer you a variety of tests that they feel would provide useful information, but you do not have to have them. It may, however, help you to be clearer in your mind if you discuss the matter with a counselor before making your final decision.

Q I have three daughters and have just discovered that I am pregnant again. My husband desperately wants me to have a son this time. Would chorionic villus sampling be a good way to find out the sex of the baby? My husband would be so disappointed if it is a girl that I would consider an abortion.

A Chorionic villus sampling is a serious medical procedure that is intended to discover fetal abnormalities at an early stage. If you are not considered to be at risk, no doctor would agree to perform the procedure simply to learn the sex of your unborn child. From what you say, there seems to be severe stress in your marriage. Perhaps you and your husband should consider undergoing couples counseling or marriage guidance.

Chorionic villus sampling (CVS)—also known as chorionic villus biopsy (CVB)—is a technique for obtaining information about an unborn baby that can be performed as early as eight weeks after fertilization. Results can be obtained within a few days. This gives it an advantage over the similar technique of amniocentesis (when a sample of the amniotic fluid surrounding the fetus is removed by means of a syringe for testing [see p. 64]), which can only be performed from the 16th week after fertilization and takes several weeks to give results.

Why it is done
Chorionic villus sampling is used to test for a variety of chromosomal, metabolic, and genetic abnormalities, including Down's syndrome, cystic fibrosis, spina bifida, thalassemia and Tay-Sach's disease, and sex-linked abnormalities such as Duchenne muscular dystrophy and some forms of hemophilia. Unlike amniocentesis, it cannot detect neural tube defects.

Like amniocentesis, the test is generally offered to older pregnant women, because the procedure does carry some risks, and the likelihood of chromosomal abnormalities is higher in older mothers.

When taking a villi sample through the abdominal wall, the doctor holds a white ultrasound scanner on the mother's abdomen, which gives a picture of the inside of the uterus on the screen.

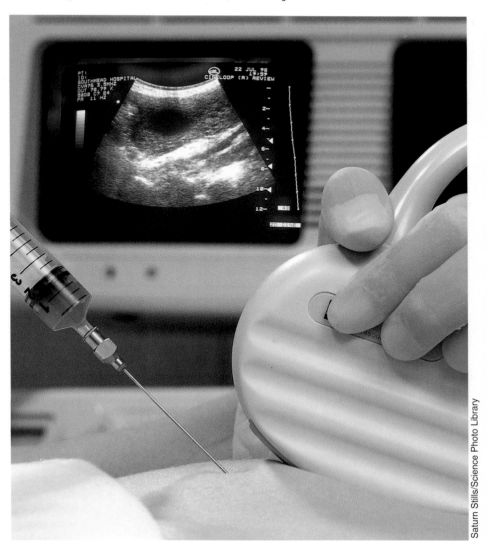

CHORIONIC VILLUS SAMPLING

It may also be offered to younger women at risk, either because of their family history or because of a previous pregnancy with chromosomal abnormalities.

How it works

Early in pregnancy the embryo forms two parts—one becomes the fetus and the other the placenta, which carries nourishment to the growing fetus. The part that forms the placenta starts out as fingerlike chorionic villi (literally, shaggy hairs). These villi burrow into the wall of the uterus, where they come into close contact with the mother's blood vessels. The placenta does not start to form before 12 weeks, and the villi are removed for testing before then. The tests can be carried out between eight and 11 weeks.

Because the villi are formed by division of the original fertilized egg, they have the same chromosomes, including any genetic abnormality, as the embryo. So it follows that if the villi test positive for any chromosomal abnormalities, then the embryo itself will.

How the test is done

The test is carried out in the hospital under local anesthetic. If the women is particularly anxious about the procedure she may be given a sedative before the test begins. A small sample of the chorionic villi are obtained by one of two methods. In one method a fine, flexible tube is passed through the vagina and the cervix (the neck of the uterus) and guided to the villi by means of an ultrasound scanner; then a sample of the villi is sucked out by a syringe. In the other method a needle is passed through the abdominal wall, as in amniocentesis, again using ultrasound to locate the villi. The procedure is slightly uncomfortable, but not painful, and takes about one hour.

The cells are then cultured and chromosome analysis is performed. The main

In the pairing of chromosomes in a girl with Down's syndrome, the 21st set has an extra chromosome, which produces the disability. This is one of the defects that can be detected by a chorionic villus sample.

advantage of the procedure over amniocentesis is that if any abnormalities are found, the mother will be aware of them much earlier. For many women it is easier to decide to have a termination early in the pregnancy rather than around 20 weeks, as happens with amniocentesis.

Possible complications

One of the reasons why chorionic villus sampling has not completely replaced amniocentesis as a means of diagnosing abnormalities is that the risk of miscarriage is slightly higher, at 0.5 to 1 percent (the rate for amniocentesis is 0.25 to 0.5 percent). In some cases, even when miscarriage does not occur, the wall of the uterus can be damaged, which may cause complications at birth. There is also the possibility that chorionic villus sampling may cause limb deformities in 0.03 to 0.1 percent of cases. Other rare problems include nutritional and growth problems later on in the pregnancy.

Who is offered the test

If a doctor feels that an expectant mother is at significant risk of carrying a fetus with one of the conditions that can be detected by chorionic villus sampling—perhaps an earlier blood test has given cause for concern—he or she may offer a chorionic villus sampling. The risks and benefits will be explained, and the woman will be made aware of the possibility of terminating the pregnancy if the fetus is found to be affected. Most hospitals offer counseling, which should be given before the decision to have the test and again afterward if the sample shows some abnormality. If termination is legal where she lives, the expectant mother will be offered this option. And even though for some women termination is out of the question, for religious or other reasons, knowing in advance that their baby is going to be handicapped helps them to prepare before the birth so that they are ready to cope both mentally and practically when the baby is born.

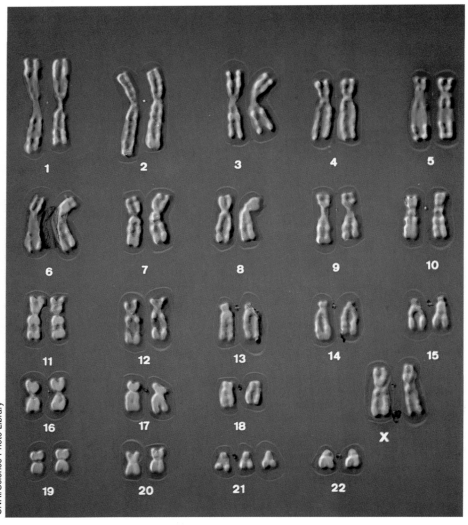

Before having the test:

- Consider seriously whether this form of testing is for you. Some women prefer not to know the possible outcome of their pregnancy before the birth itself

- If counseling is not offered to you, ask for it

- Consider whether the increased risk of a miscarriage is acceptable to you

Chronic fatigue syndrome

Q I first read about chronic fatigue syndrome only a few years ago. Is it a completely new disease?

A It has been known for a long time that viral infections are often followed by a period of depression and tiredness. This is particularly noticeable in conditions such as mononucleosis. Doctors have known about chronic fatigue syndrome for some time, but there was a lot of publicity about it in the early 1980s, and the diagnosis has been more common since then.

Q I have heard people refer to the "yuppie syndrome." Is this the same thing as chronic fatigue syndrome?

A Yes, it is. The term *yuppie syndrome* came into existence for three main reasons: it mostly affects people below the age of 40, it has a tendency to affect those who are exhausted by a stressful lifestyle, and it received public attention around the same time as so-called yuppies (young urban professionals) did.

Q My brother has been diagnosed as suffering from chronic fatigue syndrome. My father thinks that he's just lazy. Could my brother's condition be all psychological?

A Certain psychological states can have outwardly the same effect as chronic fatigue syndrome. However, if a doctor has diagnosed the syndrome in your brother, his condition will be mainly a physical illness. Nevertheless, the condition does cause some psychological depression, and support from those near him—including you and your parents, and close friends— will be a great help.

Q A friend tells me that there was an epidemic of CFS at her husband's office. Do such epidemics actually happen?

A Most of the time it is a single individual who is affected by CFS, but epidemics sometimes do occur in hospitals, schools, offices, and factories, where people spend a lot of time together.

Chronic fatigue syndrome has only come to be commonly recognized in recent years. However, sufferers have been only too aware of the condition for some time.

The main characteristic of chronic fatigue syndrome (CFS) is continual physical tiredness, which may be as severe a state as incapacitating exhaustion. There is usually also mental tiredness. It is closely related to myalgic encephalomyelitis, more commonly known as ME. CFS, which is also known as postviral fatigue syndrome, and ME both occur following viral infections.

Symptoms

The feeling of physical tiredness that accompanies CFS varies in its degree and may be accompanied by aching muscles. Physical exercise often makes the symptoms worse. The mental tiredness may be associated with emotional disturbances, which arise either from the condition itself or from the frustration sufferers can feel because of the exhaustion.

The general tiredness can have drastic effects on sufferers' lifestyles. They are often unable to work or take part in social activities for some considerable time. Some people are completely incapacitated for all practical purposes.

Causes

Beyond the fact that both CFS and ME follow viral infections, little is known about the real causes of either of these conditions. CFS generally follows a series of infections, whereas ME tends to follow a single infection. There is some evidence that infections of the digestive system, which later move into the rest of the body, may be involved. But other viruses—such as those that cause influenza, mononucleosis, and rubella (German measles)—may also cause the conditions. Recent research shows that some continuous viral infection is involved in both the conditions, with improvement occurring when antibodies to the virus disappear from the bloodstream.

Recovery

There are no specific treatments for CFS or ME other than time and plenty of rest. Because of the depression that is caused by the conditions, which can in itself hinder recovery, it is particularly important that the mind, as well as the body, is cared for and nurtured. A generally healthy diet (see Diet) and lifestyle can only help to speed recovery, as can a positive mental attitude.

People with CFS and ME recover, and neither condition is ever fatal. However, recovery may take some months, especially with ME, and this can be very dispiriting for the sufferer, especially if seeming recovery then falters for a while.

An inability to concentrate and excessive tiredness after only a short time at work are symptoms of chronic fatigue syndrome.

Circulatory system

Blood pumped by the heart is constantly circulating around the body. This journey has several essential purposes—among them, to supply the body's cells with food and oxygen and to clear them of waste products.

Q My daughter sometimes complains of pins and needles. Does this mean there is something wrong with her circulation?

A The pricking sensation of pins and needles is actually the irritation of a nerve, caused when blood supply is restricted for some reason. Most often this comes about through lying in an awkward position, but it can also be a sign of circulatory disease that has damaged the blood vessels. If the problem persists, take your daughter to the doctor.

Q I am considerably overweight, and my doctor has warned me that it is harmful to my circulation. Why is this?

A When you are overweight, you carry too much fat. This has to be stored somewhere, and a fatty buildup often occurs in, among other places, the heart and arteries. As a result, the arteries cannot carry as large a blood supply as they previously could. This causes further problems: to keep the blood flowing around the system, the heart has to work extra hard, which may strain it. A heavy body also requires extra effort when simply moving around, and this, too, could strain the heart. So it is worth trying to shed your extra pounds.

Q My teenage daughter keeps on fainting, but she looks completely healthy. Do you think she might have problems with her circulation?

A The most usual cause of fainting is a temporary fall in the amount of oxygen reaching the brain, and this is a common problem in adolescents, particularly girls. It often has a mental cause, for emotional disturbance can make the arteries widen, lowering the blood pressure and preventing blood from being pumped up to the brain. This sort of fainting has been known to occur frequently in groups of girls, but it is something they usually grow out of. If the fainting spells increase or cause your daughter to become worried that she may be ill, make sure that she sees her doctor promptly.

The circulatory system is a closed network of blood vessels—the tubes that carry blood around the body. At its center is the heart, a muscular pump that has the task of keeping the blood in constant motion as it progresses on its journey.

The circulatory system

Jugular vein
Carotid artery
Innominate artery
Subclavian artery
Pulmonary vein
Hepatic veins — cut
Inferior vena cava
Brachial artery
Kidney
Spermatic artery
Radial and ulnar arteries
Femoral artery
Superficial veins
Tibial artery

Innominate vein
Superior vena cava
Aorta
Heart
Cephalic vein
Renal artery
Basilic vein
Renal vein
Inferior mesenteric artery
Abdominal aorta
Spermatic vein
Great saphenous vein

Arteries and arterioles

Blood begins its journey around the circulatory system by leaving the left side of the heart through the large artery known as the aorta. At this stage blood is rich in oxygen, food broken down into the microscopically small components known as molecules, and other important substances, such as hormones (the body's chemical messengers).

On the early part of its journey, blood flows through relatively large tubes called arteries. It then passes into smaller vessels known as arterioles. These lead to every organ and tissue in the body, including the heart itself.

Artery

Fibrous outer layer
Muscular layer
Elastic white fibrous tissue
Inner lining of endothelial cells
Valve

Vein

From the arterioles, the blood enters a vast network of minute vessels called the capillaries. It is here that oxygen and life-maintaining molecules are given up in return for waste products.

The veins

Blood then leaves the capillaries and flows into the small veins, or venules, where it starts the journey back to the heart. All the veins from the various parts of the body eventually merge into two large blood vessels, the superior vena cava and the inferior vena cava. The first collects blood from the head, arms, and neck, and the second receives blood from the lower part of the body.

Both veins deliver blood to the right side of the heart, and from here it is pumped into the pulmonary artery (the only artery to carry blood with no oxygen). This artery takes the blood to the lungs, where oxygen from air breathed in is absorbed into it, and the waste product, carbon dioxide, is given up and breathed out.

The final stage of the journey is for the now oxygen-rich blood to flow through the pulmonary vein (the only vein that carries oxygenated blood) into the left side of the heart, from where it starts its circuit once again.

Distribution

The blood is not evenly spread throughout the system. At any given moment about 12 percent is in the arteries and veins that carry it to and from the lungs. About 59 percent is in other veins, 15 percent is in other arteries, 5 percent in the capillaries, and the remaining 9 percent in the heart. Nor does the blood flow at the same rate in all parts of the system. It spurts from the heart (see Heart) and through the aorta at a brisk 13 in (33 cm) per second, but by the time it reaches the capillaries it has slowed down to a gentle 0.1 in (0.25 cm) per second. The flow back through the veins gradually increases in speed so that blood is delivered back to the heart at about 8 in (20 cm) per second.

Pulse and blood pressure

One of the main guides a doctor has to the condition of a patient's circulation is the pulse (see Pulse), for it is a mirror of the heartbeat. Arteries have elastic walls that expand every time the heart pumps a wave of blood through them, and it is possible to feel this happening if an artery near the surface of the body is found and pressed against a bone. One such place is at the wrist.

The normal pulse rate is between 60 and 80 beats a minute, but varies widely. Thus, a doctor taking a pulse is not only counting the beats, but feeling for changes in their strength and regularity.

Blood pressure (see Blood pressure) is different from the pulse rate—it is a measurement of the force with which the heart pumps blood out into the arteries.

The circulation of blood throughout the body is automatically regulated according to certain activities, so that it is always in the places where it is most needed.

A blood pressure measurement is often taken on the upper arm, because this is where the opening through which the blood passes is narrow enough to resist the flow. The instrument used to measure blood pressure consequently works on the principle that if the flow of blood through the artery is temporarily closed (by inflating a special bandage around the arm), the time taken for the flow to be reestablished at full strength is a measurement of the force of the heartbeat.

If the blood pressure is higher than normal, the heart is probably having to work harder to push the blood through the circulatory system, and this may indicate that there is some disease in the system. For example, there might be arteriosclerosis, or a narrowing of the arteries. Clearly the smaller the opening in a blood vessel, the harder the heart has to work to pump the blood through it. If the heart works too hard over a long period of time, its life may be shortened, and this is why doctors are constantly on the lookout for high blood pressure.

Further controls

In fact, the width of the blood vessels also controls the circulation. Changes in the width of the blood vessels can be brought about by two means: the nerves and the hormones (see Hormones).

If for some reason the blood pressure drops, the kidneys respond by producing a hormone called angiotensin. This substance makes the arteries grow narrow, allowing the the blood pressure to rise back to its normal rate.

Distribution of blood in the body

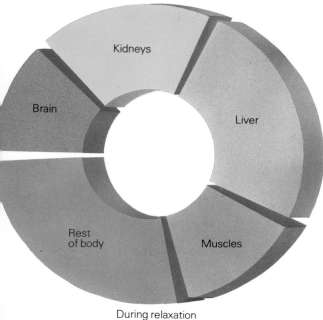

During relaxation

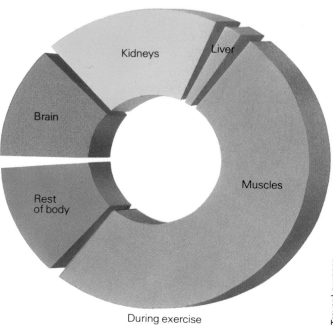

During exercise

Trevor Lawrence

Circumcision

Q If our baby is a boy, my husband wants him to be circumcised. Will it be painful?

A On a young baby there is so minute an area of foreskin to be snipped away that the infant will hardly notice. A soothing dressing is put on immediately, and so there should be no infection.

Q My boyfriend is circumcised and insists it makes him a better lover. Is this true?

A There is no scientific evidence to show that the circumcised man has a firmer erection or a better technique than the uncircumcised man. I suspect your boyfriend's self-confidence, or lack of it, could be at the root of his views.

Q I heard that a woman married to a circumcised man is less likely to get cancer of the cervix. Is this true?

A This belief has been held for a long time, many people arguing that Jewish women have a much lower risk of this kind of cancer because their husbands are circumcised. But two studies, one American and one British, failed to show any difference in the incidence of cancer of the cervix between wives of circumcised and uncircumcised men.

Q My daughter wants to know if girls can be circumcised, but I said it would only be done to males. Was I right?

A In girls, the clitoris—a small organ situated in front of the urethra—also has a hood like the male penis, but this is not normally removed for either religious or hygienic reasons in the West. Female circumcision, which sometimes involves the sewing together of the vaginal lips, is still common in some parts of the world, although it is considered barbaric in Western countries. It makes intercourse very painful for women (insuring that wives remain faithful), and a woman has to be "opened up" for childbirth and resewn afterward, causing terrible pain and a high risk of infection.

Circumcision has been practiced the world over, mainly for religious reasons. In the West the operation is becoming rarer, but it is still performed for medical and religious reasons. It is an easy and safe procedure.

Baby boys are born with a sheath or hood covering the glans, or tip, of the penis. This hood is the foreskin, or prepuce, which extends from the skin of the penis; it reaches forward over the glans, then turns back onto the penis itself. In the nonerect penis, the foreskin has to be pulled back to expose the glans, but in the fully erect penis, much of the glans is exposed automatically.

Circumcision refers to a cutting away of the foreskin so that the glans is permanently exposed. In a baby it is a quick and almost painless procedure. In older children and adults an anesthetic is needed during the operation.

Religious reasons

Circumcision may be carried out for religious reasons or because of health or medical problems. Worldwide, the largest religious group practicing circumcision of infants are the followers of the Moslem faith. Circumcision is also practiced on a large scale by members of the Jewish faith, preferably when the children are between two and ten days old. Orthodox Jews have their sons circumcised during religious ceremonies, when the boys are eight days old.

Circumcision and health

In the United States circumcision is performed principally as a measure to aid hygiene, because washing beneath the foreskin can be easily overlooked. However, the American Academy of Pediatrics has stated that routine circumcision is unnecessary. In the United Kingdom and certain other countries, circumcisions are nowadays usually performed only for medical reasons.

The most common medical reason is the condition of phimosis, or the inability to pull back the foreskin. Phimosis is more likely to occur after inflammation of the glans and foreskin, a condition called balanitis. The preferred age range for circumcision in cases of phimosis is three to five years old. However, the problem may arise later in childhood or in adulthood, and circumcision may become necessary.

Paraphimosis is a condition in which a pulled back foreskin cannot be brought forward over the glans. This may cause painful swelling of the penis tip. The patient may need to go to the hospital for a slit of the upper part of the foreskin, carried out under an anesthetic.

Aftercare

Removal of the foreskin leaves a raw area on the penis that requires daily attention and care. In a newborn or young infant, irritation from the urine in a wet diaper, or the presence of infection in the urine, means there is a risk of a small ulcer forming at the tip of the penis. Therefore the baby requires frequent diaper changes and more frequent bathing during the healing period. Petroleum jelly can also be applied to the sore area to help speed the healing process.

Local dressing of the sore area of the penis is usually advised by the doctor, and this might be, for example, gauze covered with soft yellow paraffin or an antiseptic water-repellent cream. But generally speaking, the risks of infection are very slight.

In an uncircumcised male, the foreskin of the nonerect penis covers the glans, or tip. Circumcision exposes the glans.

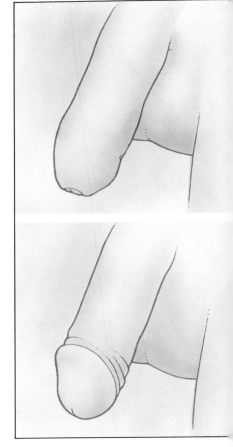

Cirrhosis

Q How much alcohol can I drink before I develop cirrhosis of the liver?

A French experts estimate that the consumption of 40 grams of pure alcohol a day for up to ten years will cause cirrhosis in most people. This is the equivalent of drinking ten glasses of beer or ten whiskies every day for that period of time. What matters is the total quantity of alcohol consumed: the choice of drink makes no difference.

Q I have been a heavy drinker for some time. How do I know whether I have damaged my liver?

A There are usually no symptoms in mild cirrhosis, and simple blood tests will not indicate how much permanent damage has been done to the liver cells. The only sure way of making a diagnosis is to have a small piece of the liver examined under the microscope, and in your case this may not be necessary. Talk to your doctor about your drinking problem—and cut down. Better yet, stop altogether.

Q My father has been told that his heavy drinking has affected his liver. Is there any chance that it may recover?

A This depends very much on the severity of the damage. Liver cells do possess a tremendous capacity to repair damage, but it is unlikely that a cirrhotic liver will be able to replace all the lost tissue. Once the cirrhotic process takes hold, the disease is irreversible, regardless of whether the original cause is removed.

Q I had cirrhosis over a year ago, and I am now better. Can I start to drink again?

A Certainly not, if you truly have cirrhosis of the liver, whatever the cause. The disease is not reversible, and you should seek advice from your doctor if you feel you cannot control your drinking. However, if you had a bout of jaundice, due to hepatitis, without permanent damage, you may resume drinking if your doctor says there is no serious risk involved.

Although cirrhosis of the liver can develop after a bout of infectious hepatitis, it mostly affects heavy drinkers. If it is detected early enough, treatment can be effective.

Cirrhosis is a liver disease characterized by a progressive destruction of liver cells (hepatocytes); these are then replaced with fibrous tissue, which gradually leads to hardening and reduced effectiveness of the organ. Clumps of small nodules give the cirrhotic liver its characteristic knobbly appearance.

Causes

The most common cause of cirrhosis is alcoholism. The quantity of alcohol needed to damage the liver varies with each individual, but it is generally accepted that drinking for 10 years at the rate of 10 cans of beer a day, or 10 single shots of whiskey, can cause cirrhosis. Viral hepatitis (there are two types: A and B; see Hepatitis) can

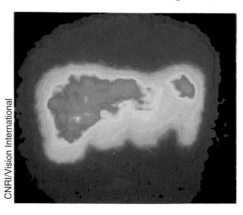

also lead to cirrhosis. The virus responsible may be transmitted in blood from hypodermic needles or blood transfusions, and in contaminated drinking water. Type A hepatitis very rarely causes cirrhosis.

Symptoms

In mild cirrhosis there are usually no symptoms. The onset of the disease is gradual, and many of the symptoms are the result of toxic chemicals accumulating in the body, and of internal bleeding, due to lack of the necessary clotting factors in the blood.

Brain function is impaired, bile accumulates in the skin causing severe itching, followed by jaundice and the contraction of the liver. The abdomen swells, and fine red lines, caused by small veins, appear on the skin.

In men, the testicles may shrink and the breasts may begin to grow, because the liver is no longer able to cope with the small amounts of female hormone that are normally present in the body.

Dangers

In the most severe cases of cirrhosis, death can result in one of two ways: either from an irreversible coma or from bleeding, which is caused by the rupturing of the enlarged veins around the esophagus (gullet). When bleeding is very extreme, the patient will die, usually within only a few minutes of the rupture

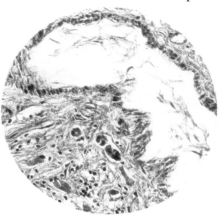

The microscope picture (above) is of a section of tissue taken from a liver affected by cirrhosis. The picture (left) is taken with radioactive isotopes.

occurring. Cirrhosis is also a major cause of cancer of the liver.

Treatment

When the cause of the disease is alcohol abuse, the treatment is abstinence. Protection against type B viral hepatitis can be given by vaccination or, on an emergency basis, by an injection of gamma globulin, which is rich in antibodies against the virus. Sufferers from viral hepatitis should be isolated until they are no longer infectious, which can be determined by blood tests, and should abstain from alcohol for six to twelve months. Once the cirrhotic process is fully established, there is no effective treatment.

Outlook

The liver cells possess a remarkable capacity to repair damage, but ultimately a point of no return is reached, beyond which cell destruction outstrips cell replacement. Once the cirrhotic process is past this point, the disease progresses relentlessly, even if the original cause has been removed, and death usually follows within ten years.

Cleft palate

Q Does my daughter's cleft palate mean that she will be unable to speak normally?

A Not if surgery is performed early enough to repair the damage and therefore prevent speech problems. Your daughter's progress will be checked regularly after her operation, and if she is not developing normal speech, she will receive speech therapy when she is about four years old. The chances of her having normal or near normal speech by the time she reaches school age are very good.

Q My baby has been born with a cleft palate. Does this mean I can't breast-feed him?

A Your baby may find it difficult at first to breast-feed, but he should be able to manage with some practice. If problems persist, try spoon-feeding; this is usually successful. It may help to lay your baby on his stomach while feeding, because this reduces the chances of milk going down the air passage.

Q My first child had a cleft lip. Does this mean my next child will have the same defect? And does the fact that I am 38 make it more likely?

A If neither you nor your partner had a cleft lip, then the chances of your next child having one are slim. If, however, either of you had a cleft and your child had the same type of cleft, there is a 15 percent risk of any further children you have inheriting it. There is no evidence to suggest that having children later in life causes the appearance of any type of cleft.

Q What kind of problems should I expect my baby, who has a cleft palate, to have?

A Your baby may experience some feeding difficulties, but the most pressing problem is with speech. Cleft palate is sometimes accompanied by mental retardation and/or deafness, in addition to poorer health in general. But provided that everything else is normal, once surgery on the palate has been performed, your child should be completely normal.

One in every 2,500 babies is born with a cleft palate, a cleft lip, or both these conditions. Fortunately surgery can improve appearance, and speech therapy helps to overcome problems in communication.

The palate is the roof of the mouth: the front part is hard and is called the hard palate; the back part is soft and is called the soft palate. Most of the hard palate is formed as part of the upper jaw bone, whereas the soft palate is made of muscle. The soft palate is lifted up to close the back of the nose in swallowing and is lowered to let air escape through the nose to produce the sounds "n," "m," and "ng."

Causes

No one knows exactly what causes cleft palate or cleft (hare) lip. One of the most likely possibilities is that the condition is inherited. Clefts run in families, with relatives frequently showing the same type of cleft, but cleft lip is more common in boys and cleft palate in girls. In a pair of identical twins, if one twin has a cleft, the chances are three to one that the other will have a normal palate and lip.

Other possible causes are deficient tissue development or poor circulation in the face during the growth of the fetus.

Symptoms

Clefts are divided into types, depending on where they occur: in the lip only, in the ridge behind the teeth (alveolar), or in the palate. All three types can occur together, but because the palate joins in the front part, and then closes forward toward the lip and back to the soft palate and uvula (the flap of tissue that helps to prevent food entering the air passages when swallowing), clefts are more common in the lip and uvula than in the front part of the palate.

The types of cleft can vary greatly: they range from a groove in the lip or uvula to a complete separation of the two halves of the palate and lip. Clefts may be one sided; if they are two sided, they occur in alveolar clefts and lip clefts, with a cleft on either side of the two front teeth.

At birth these clefts are clearly visible, but there is a condition called submucous cleft in which the muscles of the two halves of the palate have not joined, although the skin covering the palate has. A submucous cleft may cause speech problems, because the soft palate does not move normally and cannot close off the passage of air through the nose.

Outlook

Because nearly all clefts are repaired early in infancy, it is extremely rare for an adult to be left with an obvious deformity or poor speech. After surgery and dental work speech will usually develop normally, though where there are special difficulties and the child has not achieved normal or near normal speech by the age of four or five, therapy may be required. Generally by school age most children born with a hare lip or cleft palate are speaking well.

Normal palate

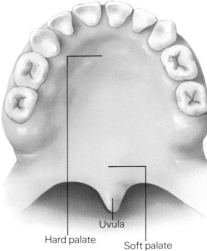

Uvula

Hard palate　　Soft palate

Cleft palate

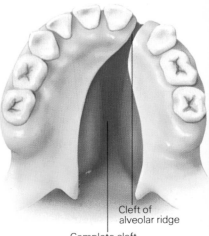

Cleft of alveolar ridge

Complete cleft of the palate

Unlike a normal palate, the two sides of a cleft palate remain separate. This occurs during a baby's development in the uterus.

Club foot

Q My baby was born with a club foot, which has now been corrected. If I have more babies, are they likely to have the same condition?

A Club foot is not directly inherited, but there is some genetic connection, which means that having one child with the condition gives a relatively greater chance that other children will have the deformity. Ask your doctor about genetic counseling, which is provided for parents who want to discuss these risks.

Q I had a bad fright while I was pregnant. Could this be the reason why my baby son has a club foot—or was it something to do with my diet?

A It is extremely unlikely that a bad fright caused the problem, and there is certainly no evidence to support this idea. There is also nothing to suggest that nutritional deficiencies during pregnancy play a part. It is thought by doctors that the deformity is due to a halt in the development of the foot.

Q I have heard that a child's foot can be put in plaster casts to set it into the correct position. Is this true?

A This measure is sometimes used, but it is only part of the treatment—repeated manipulation is more important in coaxing the foot into the correct position. Casts and splints are then sometimes used to maintain the position, if this is necessary.

Q If a child has club foot, is he or she likely to have other physical or mental disabilities?

A It depends on whether this is an isolated deformity, as is the case in most cases of club foot. A few cases are linked with other disorders, such as congenital dislocation of the hip, or may arise through conditions such as cerebral palsy (when the child is spastic) or spina bifida (a defect in the spinal wall). Where club foot occurs by itself, there is no reason to fear that the child will be mentally retarded or affected in any other way.

A small number of babies are born with a club foot, but it is a condition that can be corrected—sometimes very easily—if treated early enough.

The term *club foot* (medically known as congenital talipes) is usually applied to a deformity, present at birth, in which the bones in the ankle are incorrectly placed. When this happens, the sole of the foot faces inward and the toes point down.

Causes

The cause of this condition is far from certain, and it is likely that several factors play a part. Some hereditary influence may be responsible.

An early theory suggested that an abnormal position of the fetus in the uterus, or pressure on the fetus because of lack of uterine fluid, might play a part. This is uncertain, however, because a

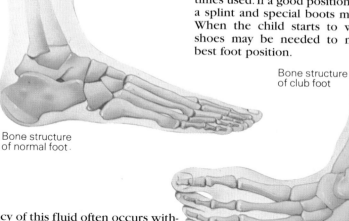

Bone structure of normal foot.

deficiency of this fluid often occurs without any resulting deformity, and it is known that the fetus constantly moves its limbs while still in the womb.

A halt in the development of the feet may be part of the explanation—there is a stage in the normal growth of the feet when they do appear to be clubbed, but usually this is just an earlier stage of development. There is no known reason why an arrest occurs in some cases.

Symptoms

In the typical club foot, the foot is bent downward and the ankle twisted, so that the sole faces inward. In a few instances the foot can be readily manipulated into the normal position, and such cases usually recover in a few weeks with the minimum of help. Most, however, cannot be

fully corrected so easily and will need more prolonged treatment.

Occasionally the foot is deformed in the other direction—it is bent upward and the sole faces outward; another type of deformity affects the front part of the foot only. It is important that these problems should be distinguished as soon after birth as possible, because without attention, the deformity may progress, and the child will develop an abnormal gait. Early treatment is therefore vital.

Treatment

The earlier the treatment starts the better, for in the first few weeks of life the deformity may respond to fairly simple measures. Repeated gentle stretching of the foot will encourage it into the correct position. Bandaging between stretches will help keep it there.

Splints and plaster of paris are sometimes used. If a good position is achieved, a splint and special boots may be worn. When the child starts to walk, special shoes may be needed to maintain the best foot position.

Bone structure of club foot

Advertising Arts

In a club foot, the bones in the ankle are in the wrong position, causing the ankle to twist. Usually the foot is bent downward, and the sole faces inward.

When simple measures fail to correct the condition within a few weeks, surgery may be needed to prevent the deformity from becoming permanent. This is required in around 50 percent of cases of true club foot, but an operation is almost always successful. Thus, on the whole, the outlook is favorable, as most cases of club foot respond well to either a simple form of treatment or surgery.

Cocaine and crack

Cocaine and crack are dangerous drugs that are in general use among drug abusers. Crack, in particular, has become increasingly common in recent years, and it is causing great social and criminal problems.

Q Can cocaine and crack affect the ability to drive safely?

A Yes. Research in Memphis, Tennessee, has shown that a high percentage of males arrested for reckless driving had substantial levels of cocaine in their bloodstreams. Nearly all of these males were found to be intoxicated, too, although, for the purposes of the study, all cases of alcoholic intoxication had been excluded. Incidentally the figures indicated an alarmingly high level of usage of cocaine.

Q Do the normal police tests for alcoholic intoxication reveal cocaine intoxication?

A No, but this is a growing danger to the public and a concern to both medical and legal authorities.

Q Why does the media always connect cocaine with crime?

A For starters, cocaine and crack are illegal drugs, vended by criminals. The trade is so lucrative at all levels that those engaged in it will go to any lengths, including murder, to promote it. Cocaine and crack are expensive, and many of those using these drugs cannot legally find the money needed to support their habit. As a result, they may resort to burglary, mugging, prostitution, or extortion to get it.

Q Why do some of my cocaine-using friends laugh when I suggest that it is dangerous?

A It is uncommon for recreational users of moderate doses of cocaine to suffer more than minor side effects, and these may seem unimportant to them. A proportion of users, however, find that they cannot continue on small doses, may resort to crack, and continue to increase the amount taken. These users are likely to damage themselves in one way or another.

Q Where did crack get its name from?

A When crack is heated for smoking, it makes a cracking sound, giving it its name.

Cocaine, once exclusive to the working people of the Andes of South America, has become the most widely abused dangerous drug in the Western world. The use of its purified form—crack—is now very commonplace.

Cocaine is a natural alkaloid derived from the leaves of the *Erythroxylon coca* and *E. truxiuense*, small shrublike trees indigenous to Columbia, Peru, and Bolivia. For centuries the hard-working natives of these countries have chewed the leaves of the coca plant to increase their endurance, relieve their hunger, improve their strength, and promote a sense of well-being.

Cocaine was rarely used as a recreational drug until the late 1960s, when the cost of amphetamines became prohibitive as a result of federal restrictions on its illegal distribution. By the late 1980s, almost 20 percent of young adults had used cocaine at least once, and 5 percent were using it regularly. Today usage is far more widespread.

The effects of the drug

Cocaine acts upon the neurotransmitter dopamine, which stimulates the brain. Cocaine blocks the re-uptake of dopamine into the nerve endings in the brain. This uptake normally reduces the ability of dopamine to stimulate the brain, so cocaine, by blocking its re-uptake, increases stimulation. The effects are similar to those of amphetamines (see Amphetamines), but less persistent.

Cocaine and Freud

Cocaine was largely unknown to Western medicine until the Austrian psychiatrist Sigmund Freud became interested in it. In 1883 he tried the drug to see if he could relieve his habitual tiredness, depression, and stomach cramps. To his delight, all his symptoms disappeared. The results impressed him so much that he began to prescribe cocaine to friends, colleagues, patients with heart disease, and those with "nervous exhaustion" following morphine withdrawal. Predictably the only effect was to substitute cocaine addiction in place of morphine addiction.

Undaunted, Freud continued his research. He concluded that the greatest value of the drug was in temporarily strengthening the body. He also recommended it to relieve indigestion and in the treatment of anemia, asthma, and alcohol and morphine addiction. He was

Powdered cocaine is usually taken by being sniffed into the nose, whereas crack can be smoked in a pipe or injected.

James Prince/Science Photo Library

Alexander Tsiaras/Science Photo Library

convinced that the drug was an aphrodisiac. Having noticed the numbing effect of the drug on the mouth, Freud recognized its possible value as a local anesthetic, but because he left the promotion of this application to a colleague, he was denied credit for the only valid medical use of the drug. Ironically the other uses he suggested came to be seen by himself and others as undesirable and misguided.

After about 1886 Freud no longer took cocaine or recommended its use as a general stimulant. The drug, however, soon became widely popular as a mental stimulant and promoter of a "high." It is prepared by mashing coca leaves, dissolving out the drug, and preparing the hydrochloride salt. Illegally imported in that form, it is then cut with inert materials to increase its bulk and street value.

Crack and addiction

Crack is a highly purified and powerful form of cocaine extracted from the cruder product with alkaline water or ether. It is volatile on heating and is readily absorbed through the lungs—a high results, with a short period of intense pleasure. This feeling is strongest on the first use and is not experienced to the same intensity again. The intensity of the sensation is matched by the danger, and the incidence of toxic effects is much higher than with the weaker preparation. Crack quickly leads to dependence in some users, and there is no way of knowing in advance who will become addicted and who will not.

Some people seem to have little difficulty in keeping usage under control, but around 15 percent of users take larger and larger doses until they are as dependent on the drug as heroin addicts. Laboratory animals, given the choice of injecting themselves with cocaine or taking food, prefer the cocaine and continue to inject until they are exhausted or dead.

The likelihood of severe addiction depends on how the drug is taken. People who are smoking crack (freebasing) or injecting it (shooting) are much more likely to become addicted than those who are only snorting the drug. In freebasing, up to 80 percent of the dose can get to the brain in about ten seconds. As with any other major drug, addiction may lead to serious medical, social, financial, and legal consequences.

Medical effects

Cocaine increases the heart rate and narrows the blood vessels, raising the blood pressure. It initially widens the air passages in the lungs and shrinks the lining of the nose, making breathing easier. After use, however, there is a rebound stuffiness of the nose and a tendency to resort to the drug to relieve it. The effects of the high dopamine levels on the brain are identical to those of amphetamine. Euphoria, increased awareness, and mental stimulation are strong, and there is a decreased sense of fatigue. Motor activity is increased but coordination reduced.

Many people imagine that cocaine and crack are harmless. Medical evidence shows, however, that they are often extremely dangerous, especially crack. The most common physical effects include epileptic-type fits, loss of consciousness, running and bleeding nose, sore throat, sinusitis, pain in the chest, coughing blood, pneumonia, severe itching ("cocaine bug"), irregularity of the heart, loss of appetite, and stomach upset.

Some of the chest and throat problems are probably caused by the high temperature of the inhaled cocaine fumes. The nose and sinus disorders are due to the constricting effect of cocaine on the blood vessels in the nose lining. This is sometimes severe enough to destroy part of the partition between the two halves of the nose, leaving a perforation. With increasing doses, coordination becomes ever more affected, and tremors and then seizures occur. Eventually the respiratory centers in the brain stem are blocked and death follows from respiratory failure.

Crack can lead to a short-lived, acute form of mental illness called cocaine psychosis. The symptoms include severe depression, agitation, delusions, persecution fantasies, hallucinations, violent behavior, and suicidal intent. People with cocaine psychosis often have lucid intervals in which they seem normal and will often deny using the drug. This mental illness usually follows long binges or high doses of the drug.

The consequences of crack usage are serious: it is an illegal drug with a high rate of medical problems, including addiction.

Cold sores

Q Whenever I get anxious, I feel a prickling sensation in my lower lip—and a cold sore comes up. Is there any connection between cold sores and stress and anxiety?

A Possibly, but stress itself will not necessarily produce a cold sore unless your body has somehow learned to use such situations as a trigger. Such a response is more likely to occur when a person is run down, which could account for the feeling of not being able to cope that accompanies anxiety in many people.

Q I always seem to get a cold sore just before a special occasion, when I want to look my best. Is there any way I can stop this from happening?

A Unfortunately not. Once the blisters have appeared, they have to run their course. The only thing you can try to do is to avoid catching a cold at such a time, which could either act as the initial trigger or simply aggravate the existing condition.

Q Do cold sores have a tendency to run in families?

A This has not been proven, but the inability to develop sufficient immunity to the virus that causes cold sores may be hereditary.

Q My mother suffers from cold sores. She insists on kissing my baby whenever she visits, whether she has them or not. Can cold sores be passed on in this way?

A The cold sore virus can probably be passed on to very young children this way. So when your mother has a cold sore, you should very tactfully persuade her not to kiss your baby until the sore is better. However, most children have come into contact with the virus by the time they are five and have developed their own immunity to it. Therefore, people over this age are unlikely to catch a cold sore from anyone else through kissing. Neither will kissing trigger a cold sore in anyone who periodically suffers from them.

A cold sore is an unsightly nuisance but not a serious health hazard. Many people develop a natural immunity to cold sores, and symptoms can be alleviated in those who are affected.

Cold sore is the term used to describe blisters (see Blisters) that form around the mouth and inside the nose. These blisters most often appear toward the end of a cold—hence their name.

The sores can be irritating and unsightly, and cause a lot of local discomfort, but they are not dangerous. They are produced by a virus called herpes simplex. Most people have been exposed to the virus by the time they are five years old and build up a natural immunity that is so effective that they never produce cold sores. Unfortunately, for the minority who suffer from them, they are a real nuisance.

The herpes simplex virus is related to the herpes virus that attacks the genital area. The latter is a sexually transmitted disease, and an immunity to the cold sore virus does not mean that one is immune to genital herpes.

Causes

Once the herpes virus has infected the skin, it remains hidden there, lying dormant between attacks. The body produces a partial immunity that controls the virus for most of the time, until a trigger causes it to flare up. This trigger can be a cold, a bout of flu, a chest infection, or a sore throat.

Exposure to sunlight or harsh winds can also act as triggers. Some women have a tendency to develop cold sores a few days before or during their menstrual period.

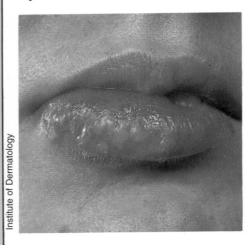

Institute of Dermatology

The typical cluster of tiny blisters forming a cold sore: these feel itchy and hot, then become painful. The healing process starts when they begin to dry up.

Symptoms

People who suffer recurring attacks of cold sores soon learn to tell when one is about to begin: there is a sudden, itchy tingling in the skin of the affected area, which can start up to two days before the cold sore erupts.

An inflamed cluster of tiny blisters then develops. These blisters fill up with a yellowish-white fluid and feel itchy and hot, a sensation that is followed by tenderness and some pain.

Occasionally the inflamed blisters may burst within two to four days of appearing, but in all cases they start to heal by drying up. The sore should be left alone while a crust forms; this will eventually fall off.

Dangers

There is very little danger of the skin tissue scarring (see Scars), except in the most severe cases. However, it is important to touch the sores as little as possible, as this may cause them to spread.

The protective crust should never be scratched or picked before the cold sore is fully healed and dried out. If it comes off, the sore could become reinfected, and the whole healing process would then be prolonged unnecessarily.

Treatment

Once the virus has infected the skin, there is no cure for it but patience. Some doctors have used smallpox vaccinations in an attempt to immunize sufferers against severe attacks, but the effectiveness of these is doubtful.

In the early stages before the sore has erupted, while the skin is itching and tingling, an antiviral solution may be applied to the affected area. This can stop the sore from developing further. Some people have found that applying ice cubes to the tingling area at this stage is also of some use.

Once the cold sore blisters have appeared, there is no treatment that will stop them from running their course. There are preparations on the market, however, that will relieve the itchiness and pain, even though they will not shorten the healing period.

Outlook

Most cold sores heal naturally within two weeks or so—the process will take no more than three weeks at the most.

Colon and colitis

Q I have chronic colitis. Is there any chance that my children will catch it?

A No. Although the cause of chronic colitis is uncertain—it may be a bacterial infection or a result of psychological disturbance—it is not at all contagious.

Q If I have chronic colitis, am I likely to get cancer of the bowel in later life?

A It is highly unlikely. Modern drug treatment with salazopyrin is very effective and will usually control the symptoms. If the disease is severe, the colon, or a portion of it, can be removed. Only 5 to 10 percent of those patients who have chronic colitis for ten years or more develop colonic cancer.

Q I sometimes have severe diarrhea after I eat certain foods. How can I tell if this is colitis or not?

A If you are certain that you are not merely suffering from a stomach upset, and that specific foods trigger diarrhea, you may be having an allergic reaction and be suffering from acute colitis. See your doctor. If the diarrhea is constant, possibly containing mucus, pus, and blood, and you are anemic and dehydrated, you should be examined by your doctor for chronic colitis. The lining of the colon is examined by a colonoscope: if you have chronic colitis, the appearance will resemble red velvet and bleed readily on contact.

Q My father gets attacks of acute colitis. How should they be treated?

A He should go to bed, have plenty of fruit juice to drink, and take kaolin and morphine mixture or codeine to reduce the severity of the diarrhea and pain. If his colitis is the result of an allergic reaction to foods, he should simply avoid them.

Q Nothing helps my colitis. Do I need an operation?

A When normal treatment proves insufficient, your doctor may consider surgery as an alternative.

Colitis is unpleasant and debilitating. But while chronic colitis can become serious, and a long-term problem, acute colitis is usually easy to treat.

The function of the colon is to move solid material from the small intestine to the anus and to absorb salt and water delivered to it from the small intestine. Colitis is an inflammation of the colon's mucous membrane.

There are two kinds of colitis. Acute colitis is often a result of an infection or an allergy, and lasts only a short while; chronic, or ulcerative, colitis is much more serious, can have serious complications, and requires prolonged treatment. Chronic colitis is most common in the 20 to 40 age group, but can occur at any age.

Causes

Acute colitis is caused by infections such as amebic and bacillary dysentery; typhoid; enteroviruses; and, most commonly, allergies to certain foods. The cause of chronic colitis is unknown, but there are a few possible theories. Bacterial infection and allergies to milk and milk products have been cited. It may also be the result of emotional stress.

Symptoms

In both acute and chronic colitis, the symptoms are abdominal pain, followed by an explosion of watery diarrhea. In chronic colitis, there may be as many as 15 to 20 bowel movements each day. Large quantities of mucus, pus, and sometimes blood are passed with the movements. On occasion there is rectal tenesmus (an urgent need to defecate without results). In more severe cases dehydration, anemia, loss of appetite and weight, vomiting, and high fever may be present.

Treatment and outlook

For acute colitis, rest in bed is advisable. Doses of kaolin (see Kaolin) and morphine mixture will stop the diarrhea.

The mainstay of treatment for chronic colitis is salazopyrin (a combination of antibiotic and aspirin-like drugs), taken three times a day. A liquid preparation of hydrocortisone can be given as a suppository, and this has a marked soothing effect. Diet should consist of bland, high-protein food, with only a small amount of fruit and roughage. Psychotherapy, when the cause is psychological, may help.

With acute colitis, the outlook is excellent so long as the cause of the illness is removed. Some patients recover after a single attack of chronic colitis, but for a greater proportion it may become a fact of life, but one that can be controlled.

How colitis affects the body

Colitis is inflammation of the colon. Here (inset) it is chronic and has caused ulcers in the mucous membrane.

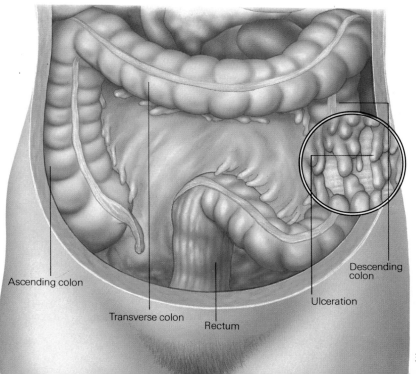

Ascending colon

Transverse colon

Rectum

Descending colon

Ulceration

Frank Kennard

Colonic irrigation

This controversial treatment is used by some holistic practitioners for a variety of bowel and other problems. It has recently gained popularity.

Q What is the difference between colonic irrigation and an enema?

A Colonic irrigation is more thorough than an enema. It penetrates further into your bowels, and the treatment lasts longer. In an enema the water is left in your intestine, but in colonic irrigation there is a constant flow in and out. Enemas tend to be performed by doctors or nurses, whereas colonic irrigation is more likely to be part of holistic medical treatment.

Q Is the treatment very embarrassing or painful?

A The patient wears a special gown designed to preserve as much modesty as possible. There may be slight discomfort when the speculum is inserted, but that is all. Your colon will start to feel full before the water flowing into it is released, but this is an unfamiliar, rather than an unpleasant, sensation. The water temperature is adjusted by the therapist to a comfortable level.

Q Is the treatment completely hygienic?

A Yes, if it is properly performed. Equipment is either disposable or disinfected using hospital-approved techniques. The piping system is completely closed so that there is no smell or external contact with the water. The water used is purified or filtered.

Q Do I need to prepare for the treatment in any way?

A Not really. The more relaxed you are, the better the treatment will work, but most people are nervous before their first treatment; this will be taken into account. You are allowed to eat beforehand, but it is not advisable to have a large meal. There is no need to rest after the treatment—practitioners say that many people feel immediate benefits in terms of more energy and a greater sense of well-being—but you are quite likely to need to visit the bathroom as soon as the treatment is finished, and you will feel very empty afterward.

The colon is the major part of the large intestine, and it is the last part of the digestive tract, in which the final processes of the digestive system take place. In it, water and water-soluble nutrients are absorbed, and some vitamins are synthesized. The remaining matter, which consists of toxins, mucus, dead cells from the rest of the digestive system, and indigestible food (roughage), is moved along the colon by the expanding and contracting of its walls (an action called peristalsis) and is gradually dehydrated until it forms a fecal mass. This waste material is then stored in the rectum before being eliminated as feces.

Inner wall

The colon has an inner wall that consists of a mucous membrane designed to absorb the liquids. It also produces mucus that lubricates the waste matter and makes it easier for it to pass along the colon. If waste matter accumulates on the walls of the colon, this system stops functioning properly. The waste matter builds up in the colon and causes a variety of problems throughout the body.

Colonic irrigation, also known as colonic hydrotherapy or colonic lavage, is a method of cleaning out this accumulated waste matter and helping the colon to return to full working order.

Historical techniques

Colonic irrigation is not new. Similar practices were mentioned in 1500 BC in the ancient Egyptian document *Ebers Papyrus*, and again by the 16th-century French surgeon Ambroise Paré.

In the present day, with bowel disorders said to affect one in three people in the West and cancer of the colon second only to heart disease as a cause of death, colonic irrigation has become popular once again.

Colonic health

Much of the work done in the colon is carried out with the help of billions of microbes—bacteria, viruses, and fungi. These produce vitamins, break down toxins, and protect us from infection. However, the delicate balance of this internal ecosystem can very easily be disturbed by a number of factors, including stress, pollution, drugs, lack of exercise, and the wrong diet.

When this happens, waste matter builds up, restricting the normal activity of the colon, and the problem may get worse over the years. Not only can this cause minor health problems, such as intestinal discomfort, gas, and constipation, but it can also cause more serious ones, like colitis (chronic inflammation of the bowel), or diverticulitis (where infected sacs appear in the colon), and even cancer.

Toxins

According to holistic therapists, if toxins are not properly broken down and eliminated, they can be reabsorbed by the body. They can then cause all sorts of problems ranging from headaches and fatigue to frequent bouts of infection, candida, and acne, in addition to less specific problems such as lack of sex drive and premature aging.

The unhealthy gut

Colonic irrigation practitioners believe that few people leading a modern Western lifestyle have a really healthy gut. Ideally humans should eliminate the contents of the bowels two to three times a day, but many people do not even manage to do so once each day.

Diarrhea (see Diarrhea) is another unpleasant problem. It is caused by food passing too quickly through the body so that much of it is left in the colon.
- Sometimes the wrong diet can cause the body to make too much mucus. This

---

Problems for which colonic irrigation may be prescribed:

acne
allergies
arthritis
bloating
candida (thrush)
chronic fatigue
colitis (colonitis)
constipation
Crohn's disease
diarrhea
diverticulitis (diverticulosis)
flatulence (gas)
frequent infection
headaches
hemorrhoids
irritable bowel syndrome (IBS)
itching anus
migraine
stomach pains

can leave behind a gluelike coating on the bowel wall that may then build up and solidify over the years, causing problems in the gut.

The treatment

Most people are referred to a colonic irrigation practitioner by another holistic therapist, such as a naturopath, a homeopath, or a herbalist, in connection with some specific problem. However, even when a specific problem does not exist, colonic irrigation practitioners suggest that their treatment is also a useful therapeutic measure that can be undergone at the change of the seasons, for instance, or during a period of prolonged stress, such as after a death in the family or the breakup of a marriage.

An important part of the first consultation is the advice on the correct diet and lifestyle to complement the treatment.

The procedure

The actual irrigation itself takes from half to three-quarters of an hour. Having changed into a special gown and having had the process explained in detail, the individual will be asked to lie flat on the treatment table and relax.

A sterile speculum (a kind of surgical instrument that is used for holding open a cavity in the body) is inserted into the rectum, and then water at low pressure is introduced through an inlet tube and fed progressively in waves into the colon while the water, waste, and gas is piped away through another tube—the evacuation tube.

While this is going on, the therapist will be gently massaging the abdomen to stimulate peristalsis and to promote the evacuation of waste. Afterward the patient may be given a suppository-type implant made either of herbs, to help loosen the accumulated waste, or of microbes, to help reestablish the gut's healthy ecosystem.

Frequency of treatments

The number of treatments a patient will need depends on how long the problem or problems have existed, how severe they are, and how relaxed an individual is during the treatment. The efforts that the patient makes regarding diet and exercise to back up the treatment are also taken into account.

Some people may only need one session, but others may require several, with follow-up sessions at widely spaced intervals over the course of, say, a year. Initially the usual recommended number is four to six, at weekly intervals.

The conventional view

Some doctors believe that colonic irrigation can bring temporary relief for a range of ailments, but that it is not a long-term cure. Others believe that it is simply a useless form of quackery or that prolonged use of colonic irrigation can weaken the body's natural ability to expel feces, and that, at worst, the practice is dangerous.

Certified practitioners

Because colonic irrigation is a fairly controversial treatment, it is important to always make sure that the therapist is reputable, and preferably is someone who is fully trained and experienced in a body-based holistic therapy.

The therapist could even be a conventional practitioner, such as a nurse or doctor. At the very least it is important to insure that the colonic irrigation practitioner has a thorough knowledge of anatomy and physiology.

In a healthy colon feces are produced as water, and nutrients are absorbed through the walls of the colon from the digested food passing through it. Problems can arise when an accumulation of waste matter builds up on the walls of the colon, interfering with the absorption process.

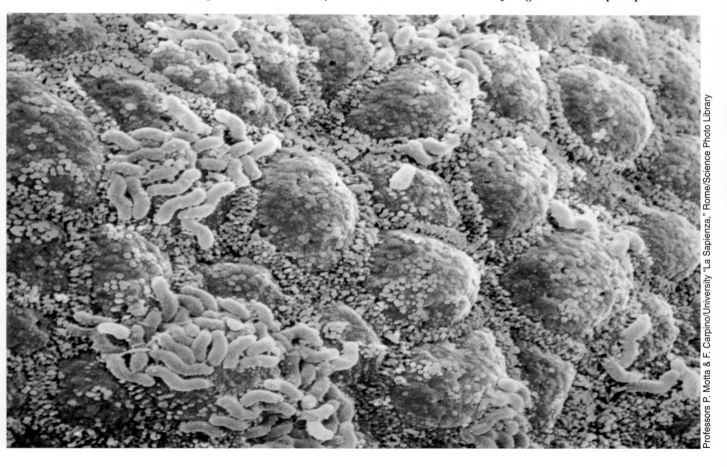

Professors P. Motta & F. Carpino/University "La Sapienza," Rome/Science Photo Library

Color blindness

Q If my son is color blind, will it affect his schoolwork?

A Color blindness does not affect the ability to see color, only the ability to distinguish between certain colors. It should not affect your child's learning to read, though in schools where arithmetic is taught by using colored bricks, it may cause confusion. If you are worried that your son may be color blind, take him to an optometrist and have his eyes tested.

Q I am a painter and decorator, and I sometimes find it hard to distinguish colors. How can I tell if I am really color blind?

A If you are a man and color blindness runs in the family, then there is a good chance that you might be. Perhaps some of the colors on paint charts all look the same to you, or a chance remark from someone has alerted you to the fact that they can distinguish between shades that you can't.

A test by a set of Ishihara cards will determine whether you are color blind. These cards have bold numerals printed on them in dots of various tints, set against a background of dots of a different hue. If you can't read the numerals, then you will be interpreting the color of the numeral and background dots as the same. Therefore, you are color blind. Unfortunately these tests are not infallible, because some color-blind observers can differentiate between the different colored surfaces.

Q Is it true that color blindness can be caused by tobacco or alcohol poisoning?

A Tobacco and alcohol will not cause color blindness alone, but they can lead to a gradual deterioration in all aspects of vision. Alcoholism can cause blindness in severe cases. Methyl alcohol, the type found in methylated spirits, can lead to rapid, permanent blindness. Smokers and chewers of very strong tobacco mixtures may have foggy vision, especially if they also drink heavily. However, this is very rare among today's cigarette smokers, because the tobaccos used are not rough enough.

Color blindness is a fairly common condition that occurs more in men than women, but it is rarely a serious disadvantage to those affected.

Color blindness is the inability to distinguish between different colors. The most common form involves the confusion of red and green; in the other, rarer forms, all colors are seen as black and white.

Color blindness is very common: about one in 20 men and one in 200 women are affected. Many people are unaware that they are color blind until they have their eyes tested by an optometrist.

Most cases of color blindness are hereditary. Women can transmit red-green color blindness without themselves being affected. They can only have red-green color blindness if their father had it and their mother was a carrier. The rare forms affect both sexes equally. Color blindness can also skip a generation and show up in grandchildren.

Causes
The causes of color blindness are unknown. Color is perceived by certain cells, called cones, in the retina of the eye. These contain pigments (coloring matter), which determine the color certain cones will respond to. In the inherited form, color blindness may be due to a lack of one of these pigments.

Sometimes color blindness can occur because of a disease of the retina or optic nerve (the nerve connecting the retina to the brain). This rarer form of color blindness is progressive and associated with a general deterioration of vision, unlike the inherited variety where the ability to see detail is unaffected and the condition never worsens.

Symptoms
In the common, inherited form, the red-green color blind person will see the colors red and green as the same hue, the

A person with normal vision would see these fruits and vegetables as below. Someone with red-green color blindness would perceive them as they appear opposite.

Paul Brierley

326

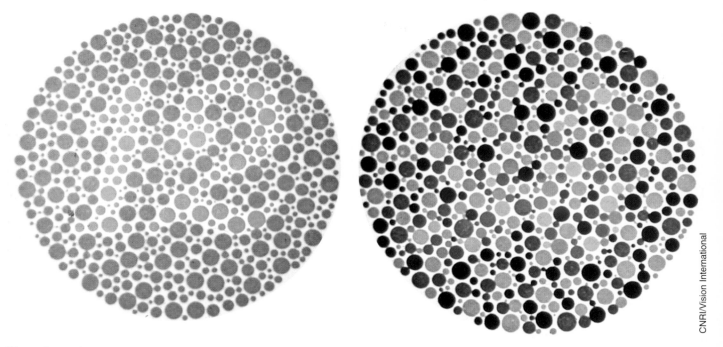

CNRI/Vision International

All people can distinguish the figures against the background in the card on the left—the first of a series used in testing for color blindness. If someone cannot see the dark red "9" in the second card (shown above) they are green-blind; if, on the other hand, they cannot see the lighter red "6," they are red-blind.

two colors being distinguished only by their intensity. Because the disability is present from birth, people suffering from this form of color blindness will have to gradually learn to associate certain tones, textures, and intensities with what people of normal vision see as red and green. In the rarer form, only black and white are seen, and the vision worsens progressively.

Employment problems

Color blindness is not a handicap to everyday life, but when someone's job depends on information conveyed by color, then it could become a barrier to employment. Careers in areas such as graphic design and color photography would obviously be unsuitable.

Red and green are the universal stop/go, port/starboard colors, so engine drivers and sailors should not be color blind. But traffic lights can be distinguished by the position of the lights, so color blindness is not a bar to driving.

Treatment

There is no cure for the inherited type of color blindness. The weakening of vision associated with a diseased retina or optic nerve may be improved or arrested.

Outlook

Color blindness from birth is a harmless condition of which many people are unaware, though unfortunately it may prohibit a person from entering certain occupations. If a person does notice that his or her ability to discriminate between colors is deteriorating, then it may be due to an eye condition that can be treated.

Color therapy

Q Is color therapy a belief system, and can it work even if you do not believe in the existence of the aura?

A Exposure to different colors causes very subtle molecular changes to the cells, so it is not necessary to believe in the aura to reap the benefits. However, it will help considerably if you have an open mind. Color therapy is very gradual. You may be instructed to do certain things, such as visualize a color; wear, or surround yourself with particular colors; or make your own solarized water.

Q Is color therapy the same as art therapy?

A There are a number of similarities. Meditation and contemplation of a work of art is used in color therapy. However, whereas color therapy treats the body and mind through the aura, art therapy focuses on the painting or sculpture that the client creates and on the relationship that develops between the client and the therapist. Color therapy is used to heal physical illness, whereas art therapy only treats the unconscious aspects. Both therapies, in their own ways, aim to bring unconscious feelings to a conscious level, where they can be explored with the therapist. In art therapy the technical ability to draw is of much less importance than the expression and exploration of unconscious feelings.

Q Is it possible for a person to use color therapy techniques on him- or herself?

A There is certainly much to be gained from attempting self-therapy if you have an adequate understanding of the powers of color. However, in the initial stages, it is usually better to seek guidance from a qualified therapist. Because the aura is a very delicate and complex entity, it can easily be adversely affected by over- or understimulation with color. A color therapist may also suggest beneficial color choices for clothes and the colors used for paint and soft furnishings in rooms in which you live and work.

Color therapy is one of the most ancient healing therapies in the world. Its roots can be traced back to the mythical lost land of Atlantis, and it is still important today in the healing techniques used in Ayurvedic medicine in India.

Color therapy encompasses many different practices. Stained glass, solarized water, oils enriched with color, gemstones, and crystals are all used to harness the subtle energies and vibrations of light and color. Color therapy may benefit a variety of health problems and promote harmony in a person's natural rhythms and energies.

Electromagnetic spectrum

Visible color is just one part of the electromagnetic spectrum. At one end of this spectrum are radio waves, which cannot be seen. Traveling up the spectrum, through infrared, visible light, ultraviolet light, X rays, gamma rays, and cosmic rays, the frequencies become higher and the waves shorter. Most of the spectrum is invisible to the human eye, but it is used in many scientific and medical applications.

Visible light, which is made up of eight colors, is in the middle of the spectrum. Each color is a form of radiation with its own vibrational frequency. Color therapy uses all the colors of this spectrum, their vibrational forces being manipulated to cause molecular changes at a cellular level. Each cell in the body can be affected by color, so that even blind people may benefit from this type of therapy.

The whole person

Each human being is said to be made up of a body, mind, and spirit. These different components must work together in harmony for the complete well-being of the whole person. The cells and organs of the body are in a state of constant movement, causing vibrational frequencies that are akin to those of color and sound. Practitioners of color therapy believe that colors can be seen in the aura, and that if they become fuzzy and

---

Color therapy and other disciplines

- Reflexology, followed by applications of color to problem sites, can be a very powerful and therapeutic technique
- Yoga, used in conjunction with a knowledge of color, is effective for harmonizing the physical body. Techniques include color breathing, visualization, and meditation
- Gemstones resonate sounds and colors, and their healing properties can be harnessed by positioning the stones in precise patterns on the physical body

---

Color therapy is shown on a chart bathed in a color complementary to the healing color. The patient will then be exposed to therapeutic colors in a treatment room.

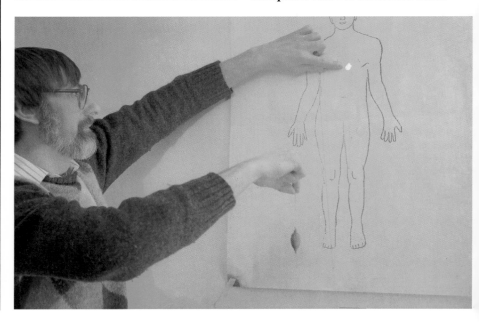

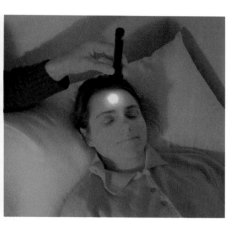

The patient lies on a flat surface while the color therapist projects a light onto her frontal chakra in a room that has been lit with a complementary color.

unclear to any great extent, this may indicate that a problem is present in the mind, body, or spirit, or all three.

The aura

Said to be an invisible cloak of electromagnetic energy around the body, the aura is a multicolored light energy with several layers, each one radiating its own color. The aura absorbs white light and then directs its different vitalizing rays around the body. Color therapy is used to identify areas of disharmony, and to find the colors that are required to retune a person's aura.

The aura has seven energy centers called chakras. Each chakra has its own dominant color, and each is linked to a gland in the endocrine system and certain physical organs.

Types of color therapy

Aura-soma is a nonintrusive color therapy that draws on certain aspects of herbal medicine, aromatherapy, and mineral supplementation. A patient undergoing this therapy is asked to select four bottles of dual-colored healing oils. A range of 95 different color combinations are used, such as gold over yellow, turquoise over pink, and blue over green, which together make up a glimmering rainbow of color. The aura-soma system hinges on the belief that a person is naturally drawn to the colors that reflect his or her own individual healing needs.

The therapist interprets an individual's color selection, identifying the characteristics of the soul and spirit in the first bottle; childhood and the recent past are represented in the second; and the current state is indicated in the third. The energies that are drawing toward the person are represented in the last bottle. Even the colors missing from the

---

The nine major colors of visible light: their meaning and therapeutic uses

Red—strength, energy, sexuality, power, alertness; used for low blood pressure, lethargy, impotence

Orange—joy, independence; used as an antidepressant and for low blood pressure, muscle cramps, spasms

Yellow—intellect, objectivity, critical thinking, reason; used for rheumatism, arthritis, digestion

Green—harmony, balance; used for cleansing purposes, cancer

Turquoise—purity, calmness; used as an anti-inflammatory and for AIDS/HIV, tension

Blue—relaxation, peace, expansion, growth; used for high blood pressure, stress, asthma, migraine, burns

Violet—dignity, honor, hope; used for lack of self-respect, infection

Magenta—release, meditation; used for change, freedom

White light—(all of the above colors) innocence, isolation, wisdom; used for clarity, neutrality, as a diuretic, and emotional stabilizer

Pigment colors

Black—depth; used to attract humility
Gray—dedication; used for pride (rarely used)
Brown—dedication, commitment; used for selfishness (very rarely used)

---

selection have a significance. The therapist may recommend the use of a special preparation, such as a color-enriched healing oil, for application to the body and relevant chakra area.

Hygeia color therapy is a system that uses colored (qualified) light transmitted through stained glass. The consultation begins with a counseling session. The patient will then be asked to sign along the back of a special chart on which a representation of the human spine is drawn. (The spinal cord is the body's central column of energy that links the brain with the organs of the body.) Using the energies transmitted through the signature, the therapist will then dowse each individual vertebra with a pendulum to locate hidden problems.

When the therapist has discerned which colors are needed, the patient may be treated in a variety of different ways. He or she may be asked to put on a white gown and enter a treatment room, where he or she will be subjected to a sequence of carefully timed exposures to colored lights. Sometimes small stained glass filters are used to concentrate color on a particular area of the body. For example, a turquoise filter may be used in the treatment of an infected finger, and a green filter may be used to treat a cyst.

The patient may also be given solarized water. This consists of simple spring

---

water that has been encased in a filter of colored glass and exposed to sunlight in order to change its chemical makeup. Red glass will make the water taste sour and is used to provide energy; under blue glass, water will taste sweet and promote relaxation. Water solarized with yellow is good for arthritic conditions; green is used for cleansing; and turquoise strengthens the immune system. The healing power of these waters is very gentle, and therefore the results will not be felt immediately. Solarized creams can be used in a similar way.

Color in the home

Color therapists believe that the careful use of color in the home can enhance a person's comfort and sense of well-being. Before choosing colors, it is important to consider the room's function and size. A room will seem smaller if it contains a lot of red, orange, or yellow. It will seem larger with blue, white, and indigo. Green maintains proportions and is considered good for cardiac circulation, but a predominantly green room can be tiring. Blue is a calming, restful color that helps to expand the mind, so it is a good choice for a bedroom. Red is powerful and may overstimulate the nerves and ego.

Color and balance

Clothes can act as color transmitters, and therapists recommend that a color should be worn either next to the skin with nothing over it, or with white underneath it. Those who are sensitive to cold weather should try wearing red, especially on the hands and feet. Even looking at the color red can raise a person's temperature.

Balance is one of the secrets of good health, and a color worn or otherwise used therapeutically is best balanced with its complementary color, to provide the greatest benefit for the individual.

Complementary colors—those opposite each other on the chart—are used together.

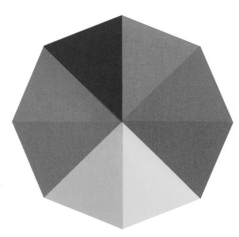

Colostomy

Q Will a colostomy bag show under my normal clothing?

A No. In fact, there are a few very well-known television personalities who have had colostomies.

Q I have just had a colostomy. Do I have to eat more to maintain my correct weight?

A Remember that the colon, or large intestine, absorbs nothing but water and salt from the material that we have eaten. Extra food will just mean extra weight gain in the usual way. A well-balanced diet and sensible eating avoids diarrhea and offensive gas. There is no need to eat extra food.

Q Will a colostomy stop me from exercising, and if so, how can I keep fit?

A This operation should not interfere with sports in any way, with the possible exception of swimming. It is best not to overdo things, but do continue with your sporting activities. It will keep you fit and give you increased confidence. The more normal a life you can lead, the better.

Q My father has just had a colostomy, and he is very depressed. How can I help him?

A Try and put him in touch with someone who is recovering well from the same operation. He might get great help from talking over the matter with someone in the same situation and seeing how they cope. Do not make a fuss over him, and treat him as you normally would. Get him to keep up all his interests and to find new ones if he can. If the depression persists, he should discuss it with his doctor.

Q Will my colostomy affect my sex life? I'm so afraid that this will turn my husband off.

A A colostomy will not affect your ability to make love, but a lot will depend on your attitude and that of your partner. If you have any difficulties, you may both need counseling.

A colostomy is performed when there is a blockage in the colon. Despite having to wear a colostomy bag, an individual can live a full life.

A colostomy is a surgical opening made in the front of the abdominal wall. Feces (waste material from the colon, which is the major part of the large intestine) can be passed out from this opening instead of taking the usual route via the rectum. The operation is performed when there is a persistent obstruction in the passage of feces along the colon to the rectum.

The location of the obstruction in the colon determines the type of surgical procedure that is performed and the position of the colostomy. Colostomies performed on the right side of the colon open on the right side of the abdomen and discharge liquid feces. Those performed on the left side open on the left side of the pelvis, and they pass much

more solid material; this is because more liquid has been absorbed from the food during digestion by the time it has reached this part of the colon.

Why is it done?

A colostomy is undertaken only when there is no alternative method of dealing with the obstruction in the colon.

Most often the obstruction to the passage of feces is due to a tumor, but the operation is also performed to treat certain other bowel diseases, for example, ulcerative colitis. Tumors that develop high up in the colon may be dealt with simply by removing the affected part of the colon and joining the two ends together. But when the tumor grows

Left-side colostomy

Waste is collected in a colostomy bag, which can be on either side. In a left-sided colostomy, feces are solid and the bag does not have to be worn constantly. The belt is for extra security at night.

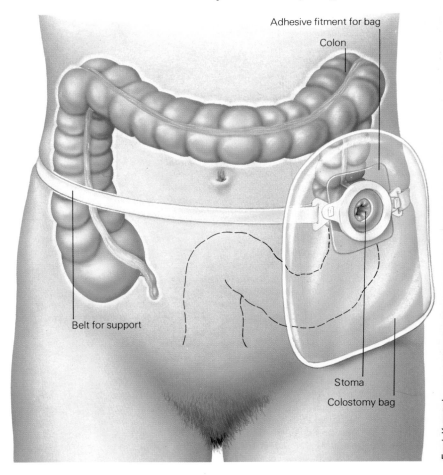

Adhesive fitment for bag

Colon

Belt for support

Stoma

Colostomy bag

close to the rectum, this cannot be done, and a colostomy is performed in the left side of the abdomen. When the whole length of the colon is diseased, an opening is made on the right side.

Coping with a colostomy

The method of dealing with a colostomy depends on the site where the opening was made. Right-sided colostomies discharge liquid matter continually. A drainage bag must be worn at all times, and unfortunately there is no control over when the opening will discharge.

Left-sided colostomies, on the other hand, produce solid material, because there is more colon available to absorb water from the feces. After things have settled down following surgery, most people discharge their feces once or twice every 24 hours, often just before or after breakfast. Others have their major movement after the evening meal, but in any one individual the colostomy functions at approximately the same time each day.

Most physicians and surgeons suggest using a colostomy bag for solid material, and, with practice, this need only be worn in the morning or in the evening. The colostomy wound tends to close up, and people are taught to prevent this by gently inserting a finger into the opening at least once a week.

This stoma (opening) care travel kit contains all that is needed for changing a colostomy bag discreetly when away from home.

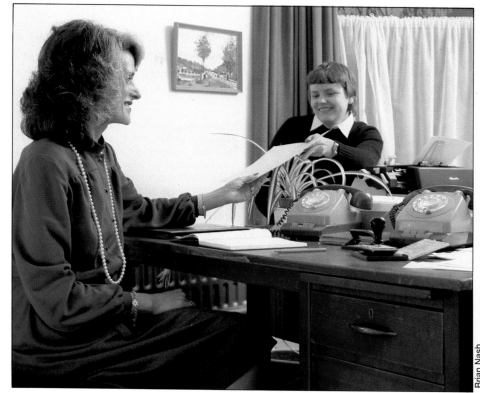

Brian Nash

The importance of diet

The greatest enemy of someone with a colostomy is diarrhea. Loose stools cause the colostomy to function irregularly, and this can be embarrassing. Certain foods are known to cause this sort of trouble, particularly uncooked vegetables, fruit,

The most important thing after having a colostomy is to come to terms with it and to continue living as before.

whole wheat bread, cereal, beer, and certain types of wine. Most people are able to identify the particular type of food that causes them trouble and can avoid it.

Medication may be given to slow down the action of the colon, thus allowing more water to be absorbed. Commonly used products that increase the bulk of the feces are methylcellulose or kaolin. Drugs derived from opium, such as codeine, are extremely efficient at slowing down the action of the colon.

Offensive-smelling gas can sometimes be a problem, but this can also be avoided by not eating certain foods—and most people know the things that disagree with them—or by taking a supplement that sweetens the odor, such as chlorophyll pills.

Outlook

A colostomy operation does not shorten an individual's life, and an opening on the abdominal wall does not make him or her more prone to infection.

The greatest difficulty is in coming to terms with the disability, and it is not unusual for a period of depression to follow surgery of this type. It may be helpful to talk to someone who has had a colostomy for some time.

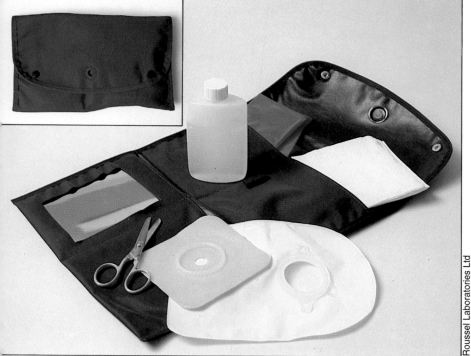

Roussel Laboratories Ltd

Coma

Q In medical shows on TV, unconscious patients are often sent for a CT scan. What is this for?

A Computerized tomographic scanning, also called computerized axial tomography (CAT) scanning, is a technique for producing two-dimensional images of the brain (or other parts of the body). For a CT scan of the brain, you lie on a table with your head inside the scanner. The scanner rotates around your head, taking X rays from many angles. A computer reconstructs the images as slices through the brain. The slices show internal structures more clearly than a normal X ray and can be used to tell if there is brain damage or a tumor present.

Q Is persistent vegetative state the same as a coma?

A Patients with severe brain damage often make slow, but steady, recoveries. In some cases, although there may be some initial improvement, this stops after a while. If the patient remains unconscious without further improvement, but is able to breathe without a mechanical ventilator, the condition is known as a persistent vegetative state. The patient will be fed, usually by a stomach tube, and given treatment to prevent the formation of pressure sores. Patients may stay alive in this comatose state for many years.

Q Why do some patients have their life support machines turned off?

A If there has been permanent damage to the vital centers in the brain stem that control functions such as breathing, heart rate, and temperature, the patient is said to be brain dead. There is no possibility that they will recover, and even if treatment is continued, their heart will stop within a few days. Waiting for death under these circumstances is distressing for relatives and medical staff, while equipment that may be needed to save another patient's life is used. So it is common for life support to be withdrawn once the patient has been certified as being brain dead.

The deep, sleeplike state of unconsciousness is triggered by certain changes taking place in the brain. The causes and severity vary, but in its most extreme form—the coma—it may be very long lasting.

The brain is far more complex and sophisticated than even the most advanced computer. Linked with the nervous system, it controls all of an individual's movements and bodily processes, such as breathing, heartbeat, and bowel function, in addition to controlling the senses and functions, such as speech, memory, and intelligence.

Different areas of the brain control different functions, and there are a number of critical areas, including the cerebral cortex, the thalamus, the brain stem, and a group of cells within the brain stem called the reticular formation, that play an important part in maintaining consciousness itself. If anything causes changes in these key areas, for example, if a person receives a severe blow to the head that results in bleeding in the brain, or if there is an illness or some form of poisoning that alters the chemical balance of the brain, then the individual may become unconscious.

Losing consciousness

If a person becomes unconscious, the electrical activity of his or her brain changes. This activity can be measured using a machine called an electroencephalograph or EEG. Special silver

Coma patients experience varying degrees of unconsciousness. This patient is able to breath by himself, and his eyes are partially open. Some sufferers live for many years.

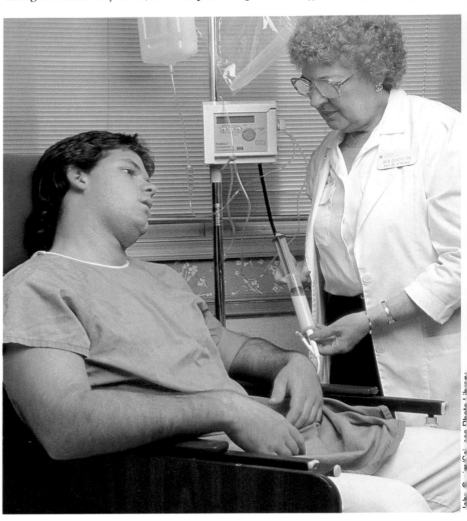

electrodes are attached to the skin on the scalp and connected by wires to the machine. The brain's electrical impulses are shown as a pattern of waves. The pattern varies according to the degree of alertness or unconsciousness. During unconsciousness the pattern is very slow, with about three waves per second. When someone is coming around from unconsciousness—or awakening from sleep—the waves start to increase in frequency until the pattern of waves is rapid and jagged at full consciousness.

Unconsciousness is a sleeplike state, but it is much deeper than sleep, and if a person is unconscious, he or she will be completely unaware of his or her surroundings and will not respond to external stimuli, such as noise. In some cases unconsciousness lasts for just a few seconds (for example, a concussion that may be suffered following a blow to the head), but in its most extreme form it may last for many weeks, and the sufferer is said to be in a coma.

A coma is a very serious condition. It affects the activity of the whole brain, and even reflex actions, such as coughing and tendon reflexes (the type of reflex experienced when the physician hits the knee with a tendon hammer), are absent. A person in the very deepest coma may not respond even to the most painful stimuli.

Major causes of comas

The most common causes of comas are bleeding (hemorrhage) in the brain, a brain tumor, shock, and blood poisoning.

A severe blow to the head may rupture one or more blood vessels, causing a hemorrhage. Another common cause of hemorrhage is a stroke. Most people who suffer strokes are over 65, but they can happen at any age, especially in people with high blood pressure. Whatever the cause, a brain hemorrhage can rapidly lead to unconsciousness and, if the bleeding is severe, to a coma.

Brain tumors, both benign and malignant, can eventually lead to a state of coma. Because the bones of the skull make it impossible for any type of tumor to expand outward, the soft brain tissue becomes dangerously compressed as the tumor gets bigger. Unless it is treated, there will be permanent brain damage, and if the affected area is one of those that controls consciousness, the sufferer will go into a coma and eventually die.

In the condition known as shock, the circulatory system collapses; once this happens the blood supply to all the vital

The electroencephalogram (EEG) records the electrical activity of the brain through electrodes attached to the scalp.

organs, including the brain, is reduced. When the brain is no longer receiving enough blood, the collection of symptoms, called shock syndrome, become apparent. These include sweating, blurred vision, rapid breathing, and faintness that can lead to unconsciousness and coma. This type of shock can be brought on by massive internal or external bleeding, heart attacks, and loss of body fluid caused by various illnesses, for example, cholera.

Someone who has been poisoned by fumes, chemicals, or drugs may become comatose. Some drugs, for example, barbiturates (see Barbiturates), depress the activity of the brain stem, one of the parts of the brain controlling consciousness. An overdose of this type of drug will therefore cause unconsciousness and, unless it is quickly treated, a coma.

Carbon monoxide poisoning (which can be caused by inhaling an excessive amount of fumes from an automobile or other vehicle) can result in a coma because it reduces the amount of oxygen in the blood, leading to an oxygen deficiency in the tissues of the brain.

Other causes

Two other causes of comas are diabetes (a disease caused by a deficiency or lack of insulin produced in the pancreas) and hypothyroidism (a disease caused by underactivity of the thyroid gland, which causes all chemical processes in the body to slow down).

A diabetic coma (see Diabetes) is the result of the body using fat instead of glucose to provide energy, and poisonous acids called ketones forming as a by-prod-

uct. This can happen to a person before his or her diabetes has been diagnosed or treated, or if his or her treatment is neglected. An overdose of insulin, leading to very low blood sugar, can also cause a coma. People who suffer from hypothyroidism may go into a coma brought on by cold weather or certain drugs, especially some types of sedative.

Some infections can also cause a coma. Most of these are viral. The virus can spread to the nervous system and brain from an infection such as mumps, measles, glandular fever, herpes simplex, or HIV, causing inflammation of the brain cells, or encephalitis. In most cases the infection only causes encephalitis and not, subsequently, coma.

Treatment

The treatment of a coma depends upon the initial cause. If it has been caused by bleeding, surgery may be needed to release trapped blood or clots, relieve the pressure on the brain, and repair the damaged blood vessels. It may also be possible to remove part or all of a brain tumor with surgery, and this may be followed by radiotherapy to kill remaining tumor cells.

Until recently, any kind of coma that lasted for more than 24 hours usually resulted in some form of permanent brain damage, but advances in treatment have impoved. A life support system now takes over vital brain functions, including breathing and maintenance of blood pressure, allowing time for treatment to be effective and natural healing to occur. However, the longer a coma lasts, the less chance there is of a complete recovery.

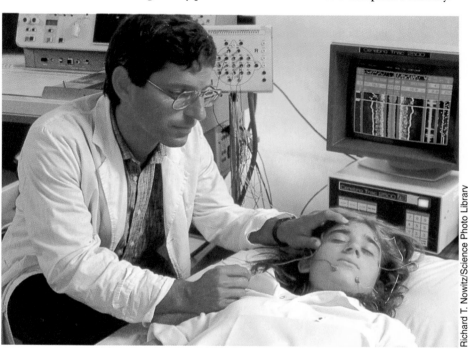

Common cold

Q I've often been tempted to try cold cures that I see in advertisements. Do these work?

A There is no such thing as a cold cure, but some commercial products can relieve the symptoms of colds. These contain substances called antihistamines, which have the effect of helping you to sleep. But, unfortunately, once you get a cold, it must run its course.

Q My father always seems to have more colds in the summer than in the winter. Why is this?

A He may be suffering from hay fever, which has symptoms that can often mimic those caused by cold viruses. Such allergic reactions are usually seasonal, and this is an important clue. However, if someone becomes allergic to material that is present in the air all year long, such as house dust, it can be quite difficult, without tests, to distinguish between an allergy and the common cold.

Q Are there any special foods I can eat that can protect me from colds?

A Some people feel that taking large quantities of vitamin C, contained in citrus fruits or in the form of ascorbic acid preparations, provides some protection. Hence the old belief in honey and lemon mixture. However, experiments have not yet proven whether this helps.

Q I've heard that standing in a draft can cause you to catch a cold. Is there truth to this?

A No. But it is possible that a period of exposure to wet and miserable weather may lower your resistance—making it easier for the cold virus to gain entry.

Q What is the difference between a cold and the flu?

A The main difference is that the flu is produced by a specific virus; colds are produced by many different ones. As with colds, upper respiratory (breathing passage) symptoms are also part of the flu—but this illness is more severe.

The common cold affects millions of people every year, particularly in the winter months. Research continues, but so far no cure has been found.

The common cold is not one disease, but many. They all have similar symptoms, all of which are caused by viruses (see Viruses). These viruses are transmitted to other people by breathing or sneezing.

Causes

There are at least 20 different types of viruses that are known to produce the common cold. Antibiotics are of no use in treatment, nor are there yet any effective antiviral drugs.

Not only is the body faced with a bewildering variety of different viruses, but in any one group of these there are many hundreds, and possibly thousands, of variations. A suitable protective vaccine would have to prime the cells of the body to recognize thousands of different types of viruses, and up until now, no practical solution has been found to this very complex problem.

People at risk

The sick, the elderly, or the undernourished are not as good at fighting infection as healthy people, and so they are more susceptible to the ravages of the common cold. Young children, whose immune systems have not come in contact with so many viruses, can suffer 20 or more such infections each year—as often happens when children start school.

The common cold is caused by many viruses (inset), and its symptoms are aggravating for those who suffer from them.

Symptoms and dangers

The symptoms of the common cold are, unfortunately, only too well known. The first sign is a feeling of being under the weather, which lasts a few hours. This is usually characterized by aching of the joints and a cold, shivery feeling. The body temperature is commonly subnormal at this stage; within the next few days—and sometimes hours—the body temperature goes up. A person may have a sore throat and generally feel miserable. As the throat begins to clear, the eyes and nose begin to stream, and there are bouts of repeated sneezing (see Sneezing).

For most people the common cold is a trivial illness, lasting only a few days. However, it can be a serious matter for the person who suffers from bronchitis, especially if he or she is also a smoker.

Treatment

Unless complications like bronchitis develop, there is no need to call a doctor. The best plan is to make the patient as comfortable as possible. Acetaminophen or aspirin can help reduce a fever. Aspirin should not be given to children with viral infections—acetaminophen is safer.

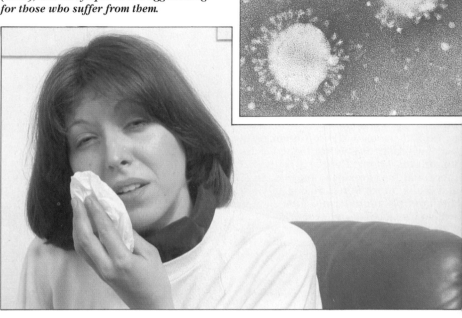

Complexes and compulsions

Q Is avoiding the cracks in paving stones always an example of compulsive behavior?

A In children it's more of a game, but if the child believes too strongly that something terrible will happen if he or she steps on the cracks, the resulting anxiety may cause the game to become a compulsion. In adults it is a pretty harmless compulsion.

Q Do short men always have inferiority complexes?

A By no means. But they may tend to have them more than tall men simply because they get pushed around more, especially when they are younger. It would also be true to say that small men with a natural tendency toward anxiety are more likely to have an inferiority complex than others who are both taller and more relaxed in disposition. But a tall man can also have an inferiority complex.

Q Are children of one-parent families more likely to have a complex of some sort?

A Not particularly. Of course, since one-parent families are often under greater stress than two-parent families, the children can be more susceptible to the formation of complexes. On the other hand, such families also have more practice at coping successfully with stress and may also be better at growing out of any complex that rears its head.

Q Is there any way that I can stop myself from overeating? Could this be some kind of compulsive behavior?

A Sometimes overeating is not due to a compulsion, but to an upset metabolism. If this is not the case, your behavior may be a compulsion in its own right, or it may be a displacement activity in which you compensate for a feeling of insecurity, of not being loved, or being neglected by others. A visit to the doctor, and perhaps to a specialist, must be the first step to determine the best treatment in your particular circumstances.

What exactly is a complex or a compulsion? And what should a person do if he or she suffers from one?

In psychology, a complex is a set of memories and emotions that are strongly linked together. They are often frightening and have their origin in childhood, when the world seemed fearful. If they last into adulthood, they may produce compulsive behavior. This is an attempt to relieve the buildup of anxiety that is the result of the complex, which is why the two words are often linked. Excessive handwashing is a common example of compulsive behavior, which can become a problem in its own right.

Complexes

The psychiatrist Carl Jung called his psychoanalytical approach "the psychology of complexes." He regarded a complex as a set of ideas containing strong and perhaps frightening emotions that may be repressed (stifled) and therefore barely remembered. A mother complex, for example, is one in which a boy becomes overwhelmed by the fear of a dominating mother and cannot form relationships in adulthood with women he perceives as overbearing or bossy.

Fortunately the misery produced by these problems can be lessened. Compulsions can be removed, and complexes can be treated by psychotherapy.

Psychiatry has given names to a large number of these bundles of associated memories, beliefs, attitudes, and acts, many of which have passed into everyday use.

Almost everyone, for example, has heard of the Oedipus complex, regarded by Sigmund Freud and his followers as a young boy's wish for some form of sexual relationship with his mother and the consequent wish to kill his father out of jealousy. Freud was of the opinion that every male child possessed this complex for some period during infancy and that it had to be resolved (grown out of) before further adult emotional development could take place.

The castration complex, according to Freud, follows the Oedipus complex. It represents the young boy's fear that his father will cut off his genitals in revenge for his designs on his mother. However, there is a great difference between these ideas and reality. Very few boys show these tendencies or the behavior linked to them.

Another well-known complex is the inferiority complex. This was made popular by the psychiatrist Alfred Adler. Adler

Constant, excessive handwashing is a common compulsion.

Brian Nash

A person with an inferiority complex may lack the courage to make friends.

believed that the universal tendency in humans to succeed and to achieve is partly colored by the feelings of inferiority that are the inevitable result of the pressures of childhood.

The complex builds up something like this: as small children, we were helpless; we had to do what our parents and other figures of authority told us without argument and whether we liked it or not: very often we had to do what they told us, solely because they were bigger and stronger than we were, not because they were necessarily right.

It is no wonder that many people have collected highly emotional ideas and memories of being inferior to those around them. For some people the memories persist into adult life.

Two reactions can occur as a result of inferiority complexes. The victim may take on an attitude of excessive humility and obedience to the will of others, in an endeavor to escape their criticism and the anxiety it produces.

Alternatively he or she may behave in an excessively superior fashion, with an exaggerated sense of his or her own importance, so that no one should ever remind them of the inferiority once felt and thus release the feared emotions.

Treatment

Not everyone acquires complexes, and some will quickly grow out of them. But for those naturally anxious people who are prone to complexes, good treatment is available.

Complexes are learned. There is no evidence to show that a person is born with them. This is important, because it implies that any problem that an individual may have from such complexes can be solved, or at least minimized, by behavior therapy, whereby debilitating anxiety can be unlearned and a happier, more positive attitude adopted.

Some common complexes

Remember that the majority of complexes can be effectively treated by psychotherapy.

- **Anxiety complex:** excessive anxiety over an object or in general
- **Cain complex:** strong rivalry between brothers and/or sisters
- **Castration complex:** a male child's fear of castration by his father
- **Electra complex:** a daughter's wish to seduce her father
- **Inferiority complex:** excessive feelings of inferiority leading to humility or its opposite, arrogance
- **Jocasta complex:** excessive attachment of a mother to her son
- **Lear complex:** excessive attachment of a father to his daughter
- **Oedipus complex:** a son's wish to seduce his mother, which causes hatred of his father
- **Persecution complex:** a belief that one is being hounded or victimized

---

Compulsions

A compulsion is an act that is carried out, usually repeatedly, to reduce anxiety. It may have developed from a pattern of behavior that was once perfectly normal. For example, an individual may feel a compulsion to go around locking all the windows in his house. Originally this may have been a very sensible precaution against burglars. But with the development of the compulsion, the individual feels the necessity to check over and over again that windows and outside doors are locked and that even inside doors, cupboards, and boxes are locked.

Alternatively a compulsion may result from a superstition. An example of this is the childish game played by the fictional character Christopher Robin, who would never step on the cracks between sidewalk slabs because of a belief that there were bears waiting around the corner to eat him if he did.

Almost everyone has minor compulsions that are hardly noticeable. Humans are creatures of habit, and a change easily raises the level of anxiety. This is because thought is required for awhile, instead of letting automated programs of behavior run unhindered.

Small rituals are therefore performed, such as tidying the pencil cup before leaving the office or plumping up the sofa cushions (which have not been sat on) before going to bed. All are harmless ways of lowering arousal levels and relaxing. But just occasionally, excessive tidying, checking, handwashing, overeating, or avoidance of certain situations can interfere with the smooth running of a person's life. Then the compulsion should be treated, and the anxious person may need some moral support from a partner or a friend to seek outside help.

Curing compulsions

Treating compulsions is seldom difficult. One of the most effective methods is the process called systematic desensitization. It is initially carried out in a clinic. The patient learns to give him- or herself an instruction to relax, repeating a word like *calm* until a tension-free state is achieved. The situation producing the compulsive behavior is then called up, either in real life or in the imagination.

When the compulsive behavior begins, the patient gives him- or herself the *calm* command and almost immediately senses his or her anxiety decreasing. As the fear lessens, so does the need to behave compulsively.

This strengthens the faith of the patient in the relaxing process he or she has learned. Soon the vicious circle is broken, and the obsessive behavior is eliminated altogether or at least made manageable.

Conception

Q We would like our next child to be a girl. Is it possible to predetermine the sex of our child during intercourse?

A No. The sperm defines whether the child is female or male, and there is nothing a couple can do to make sure that either a female- or male-chromosome-carrying sperm gets to the egg first. It has been suggested that the acid/alkali balance of the female's vagina and cervical canal has some influence on sperm and that an acid or alkali gel inserted into the vagina before intercourse may make it possible for the couple to choose a boy or a girl. This method has not yet been fully tested for either safety or reliability. There would also be dangerous social implications if such a choice became a possibility.

Q How long is the period of time during which conception is possible?

A The egg lives for less than 24 hours after ovulation, which takes place in the middle of a woman's menstrual cycle, and it is during this time that conception is possible. Sperm can live in a woman's body for up to 48 hours, so the egg may be fertilized by sperm ejaculated into the vagina as many as 48 hours before ovulation.

Q My husband has been told he has a low sperm count. What can be done to help men with such a problem?

A The number of sperm in a single ejaculation is what is called the sperm count. If a couple is having difficulty conceiving, the male will be asked to give a sample of sperm, which will be analyzed to see how many sperm are present and whether they are healthy. Sperm cannot survive in high temperatures, so hot baths, tight underwear, or being overweight can result in a low sperm count. Too much alcohol or tobacco can also be the cause. A male may be advised to take two cold baths every day and to try to protect his testicles from heat. If the low sperm count is caused by an inflammation or infection in the testicles, this can be treated by a doctor.

Knowing what happens during conception can help a couple to understand this complicated process and to plan their family.

Conception is a great deal more complicated than the simple joining of a sperm and an egg. It is a complex process in which a variety of conditions have to be right to insure that it is successful.

Menstrual cycle and ovulation

Every time a male ejaculates he produces sperm, but a female is physically ready to conceive only once during each menstrual cycle. Approximately 14 days before her period, she produces a single egg from one of her two ovaries, which is then drawn into the fallopian tube. The egg lives for 12 hours, and if it is not fertilized during that time, it dies and is absorbed into the cells that line the tube.

This is followed 14 days later by the menstrual period, and the cycle then begins again. The average menstrual cycle lasts 28 days, although some females find that their cycles are longer or shorter than this. Most females release approximately 12 eggs per year, assuming they have a regular 28-day cycle.

How an egg is fertilized

The sperm and ejaculation

If intercourse takes place around the time of ovulation, conception is very likely. A male produces around 400 million sperm in each ejaculation. These are surrounded by seminal fluid, which protects the sperm from the acidity of the vagina.

Once deposited in the vagina, the sperm immediately start their journey up the vagina, through the cervix (neck of the womb), and into the uterus. They move by vigorously lashing their tiny tails. Some of the sperm do not make this journey successfully and wither and die in the acid conditions of the vagina. This is nature's way of insuring that damaged or unhealthy sperm do not manage to fertilize the egg.

Fertilization

The millions of sperm that have reached the uterus are nourished by the alkali mucus of the cervical canal. Then they travel up into the fallopian tubes. This journey of about 8 in (20 cm) takes

An egg is released from one of the two ovaries, is fertilized by a sperm, and then implants itself in the wall of the uterus.

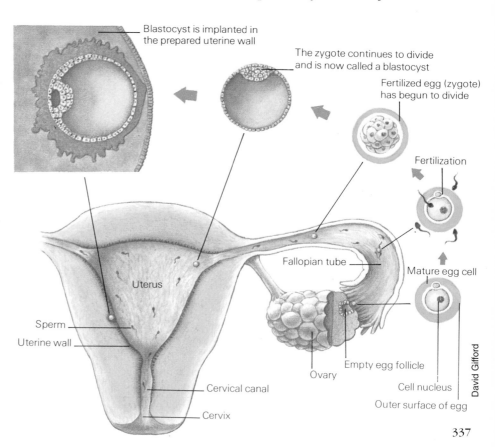

Blastocyst is implanted in the prepared uterine wall

The zygote continues to divide and is now called a blastocyst

Fertilized egg (zygote) has begun to divide

Fertilization

Fallopian tube

Mature egg cell

Uterus

Sperm

Uterine wall

Empty egg follicle

Ovary

Cell nucleus

Cervical canal

Outer surface of egg

Cervix

David Gifford

approximately 45 minutes—only about 2000 sperm may actually survive. The sperm will stay alive within the fallopian tubes for up to three days, ready to fuse with an egg if ovulation takes place. If an egg is already present within the tube, fertilization will take place immediately.

Fertilization is accomplished when a sperm penetrates the surface of the egg. Each sperm carries an enzyme (a substance responsible for causing life-supporting chemical processes) that helps liquefy the outer surface of the egg to make penetration of a single sperm easier. Once the egg is fertilized, the rest of the sperm die.

The egg and sperm (which has now discarded its tail) then fuse together to form a single nucleus (center), which then begins to divide into two cells. Within 72 hours, the cells divide 32 times to produce a 64-celled egg.

The fertilized egg then travels down to the uterus within approximately seven days (day 21 of a 28-day cycle). During this time it grows tiny projections that help it to burrow into the lining of the uterus, where it can be nurtured and a pregnancy can start. This process is called nidation, and once it has occurred, conception is complete.

The egg can now be nourished by the rich blood supply present in the uterine lining. From the moment of fertilization, the egg produces a hormone called human chorionic gonadotropin (HCG), which informs the ovary that fertilization has taken place and maintains the blood flow to the lining of the uterus so that the egg can continue its development. (Pregnancy tests work by detecting this hormone in blood or urine.) The body

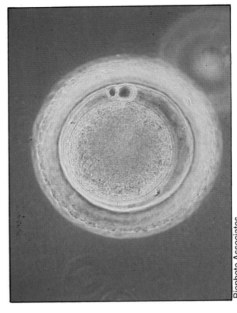

This photograph of a living egg, a few hours after fertilization, has been magnified 200 times.

therefore knows that the menstrual cycle must not continue, since a period would remove the fertilized egg.

Twins

Not every conception occurs in this way. If the fertilized egg begins to divide and the two cells produced separate, they will go on to form two embryos. They will be identical twins because they originated from the same egg and sperm. Nonidentical twins occur when two separate eggs are released at ovulation and are fertilized by two separate sperm.

Multiple births (three or more babies) occur for the same reasons, and though the use of fertility drugs has increased their number, they are still rare.

Difficulties in conceiving

Although most couples conceive within six months, it can take up to two years to become pregnant. Even after two years some still find difficulty in conceiving. The cause of the problem may lie either with the male or the female, or both.

The ease with which a woman becomes pregnant depends on her age and the age of her partner and the state of their health. Females are most fertile up till the age of 25; from 35 onward their chances of becoming pregnant decline rapidly until menopause. A male's decline in fertility is more gradual; at 60 he is still fertile, though to a lesser degree.

In spite of modern sex education, sexual intercourse for some couples may be unsatisfactory; but sex manuals and clinics may be helpful. Other couples have difficulties because they are unsure of the best time in the menstrual cycle to conceive; and when this is combined with infrequent intercourse, the chances of conceiving are low.

Emotional factors such as stress, anxiety, tiredness, or overwork can play a large part in conception. Intercourse may be less frequent, or the male may be incapable of maintaining an erection or of ejaculating during intercourse.

Females with infrequent periods ovulate less often, but they are still fertile, though their chances of conceiving may be reduced to only three or four times a year. A failure to ovulate, caused by thyroid problems, drastic weight loss, or premature menopause, is another common cause of infertility. There is sometimes a delay in the return of a female's fertility after she comes off the Pill.

Damage to the fallopian tubes, arising from an infection in the tubes themselves (salpingitis) or other causes, will prevent them from functioning normally. Adhesions may form, which prevent the egg from passing down to the open end of the tube.

In males difficulties may arise when the testicles are not working satisfactorily. A low sperm count is another possible cause of infertility. Diseases such as mumps may cause an inflammation of the testes, or there may be a testicle failure or a blockage in the vas deferens (down which the sperm travel) or epididymis (where sperm mature). There are many techniques available to discover the cause of infertility and to help circumvent it.

Identical twins occur when one egg is fertilized and then splits in two.

Congenital disorders

Q I am going to be a grandmother soon, and although I don't want to scare my daughter-in-law, I would like to know if there are any blood tests for congenital diseases in newborn babies?

A All babies have a blood test between the 6th and 14th days of life, called the Guthrie test, where blood is taken by pricking the child's heel. The test is used to detect a disorder of the body's chemistry called phenylketonuria, which can be treated with a special diet, but would otherwise cause a mental handicap. As it only occurs in one in 12,000 babies, this is only a precaution. The test is also sometimes used to detect a lack of the thyroid hormone.

Q I have just learned that I am pregnant. Should I avoid taking any drugs or medicines in case they damage my baby?

A It is wisest to avoid taking any drugs at all during pregnancy. The most vulnerable time for the growing baby is when it is an embryo, in the first two months of pregnancy; you should particularly avoid taking any medicines then—not forgetting that conception occurs two weeks before you first miss your period. Therefore, it is a good idea to stop taking any medicines if you think you might have conceived —even though many are perfectly safe. If you are taking a drug prescribed for a particular reason, consult your doctor. He or she will know if it could harm the embryo.

Q Someone once told me that if I was frightened by an animal during pregnancy, the baby could be deformed. I am pregnant now and have had terrible dreams that my baby will be crippled. Is this possible?

A Stop worrying! There is no evidence that a frightening experience during pregnancy can produce an abnormal baby. Many women have nightmares like this while they are pregnant—but if someone who has had such dreams does have an abnormal baby, it is purely a coincidence.

Many newborn babies have slight physical defects that are hardly noticeable or can be easily corrected. It is the serious ones that cause great distress, so it is vital to take the preventive measures available.

Everyone hopes that a baby will be normal at birth. Unfortunately some are born with an abnormality of some part of the body, or the internal chemistry does not work as it should. The word *congenital* simply means that it is present at birth; it does not mean the same thing as inherited, although some of the problems do run in families. Congenital disorders are still surprisingly common, occurring once in every 50 births, but many of these are quite mild in nature and cause very little trouble.

Types

An example of a mild congenital disorder is the extra finger seen on some people, mainly from the West Indies. This defect is passed on from parent to child and is usually removed soon after birth.

More serious disorders can often cause a baby's death shortly after it is born. This is particularly likely to happen with disorders of the heart and brain, which are relatively common (8 babies in 1,000 are born with congenital heart disease).

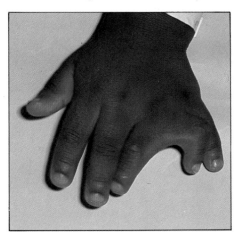

Webbed fingers (above), often accompanied by an extra finger or the presence of a double thumb (right), are fairly common deformities easily dealt with by surgery.

Another medical riddle is the fact that some congenital disorders are regional, with a higher incidence in some parts of the world than others. Abnormalities of the brain and spinal cord are found in one birth in every 2000 in the United States; the most serious is anencephaly, where the brain is incompletely developed and exposed. Spina bifida is a very similar type of condition, where the covering of the spine is not complete. Unlike these defects, cleft lip and cleft palate are not as common in the United States as in Japan and China.

Causes

In general there are two main groups of known causes: genetic or inherited problems, where there was already an abnormality in the fertilized egg; and those where something has damaged the fetus in the womb during the earliest stage of its development.

Some inherited problems, such as extra digits (fingers or toes), are actually seen in one of the parents as well as the child. In another type, each of the parents appears to be quite normal but has a gene that is passed on to the child, producing the problem. Cystic fibrosis (a serious malfunction of the glands) is an example of an inherited genetic problem.

Both drugs and infections are known to damage the tiny, growing fetus. A tragic example of a manufactured drug that caused serious damage was thalidomide, which was originally prescribed to pregnant women to combat morning sickness, but which prevented proper growth of the baby's limbs and caused a whole range of other disorders.

Rubella (German measles) can damage the heart, eyes, and brain of the fetus if the mother catches the disease—or has been exposed to the possibility of catching it—during the first three months of her pregnancy; even after that time, it may be the cause of deafness in an otherwise normal baby.

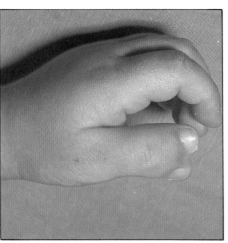

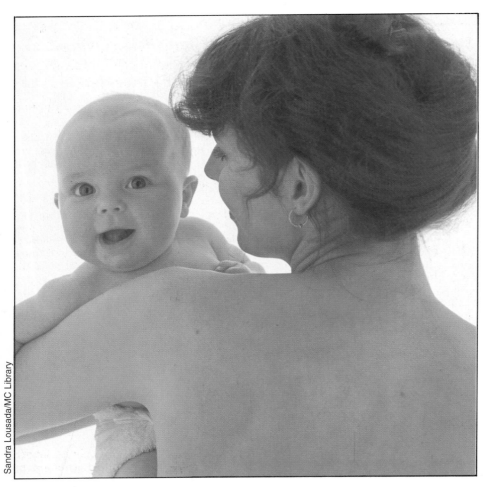

Sandra Lousada/MC Library

Although a few babies are born with congenital deformities every year, the majority of births result in perfectly healthy, normal babies.

Very often a combination of factors leads to abnormality. Spina bifida is undoubtedly more common in some families, but something else may help cause it, such as poor diet.

One special condition is caused by the presence of an extra chromosome in each of the cells in the baby's body; this is known as Down's syndrome. It is more common in babies born to older women, occurring once in every 1000 babies born to 20-year-olds, with the occurrence rising to one in every 50 babies when the mother is over the age of 45. Other chromosomal abnormalities have also been found.

Symptoms
In many cases the condition is obvious, but there may be internal problems resulting from the abnormality, as in spina bifida. Some internal conditions are recognized by their symptoms; a blocked gut, for instance, will cause vomiting within the first few days of birth and requires surgery. Breathlessness and a blue color to the skin known as cyanosis are often results of heart conditions.

Sometimes a special test reveals the problem, as with dislocated hips. Since this condition is a recognized congenital disorder, each and every newborn baby is very carefully examined in order to make sure his or her hips are normal and cannot be put out of joint.

Treatment
The way a defect is treated very much depends on the nature and severity of the disorder. Some congenital disorders, such as the webs sometimes found between the second and third toes, need no attention at all. Others are relatively uncomplicated to deal with. Dislocated hips, if discovered early, can be treated with a splintlike support that has to be worn for a few weeks; if the condition is found as late as the child's first birthday, an operation becomes necessary. The conditions of a blocked intestine or cleft palate can also be dealt with fairly easily by means of corrective surgery.

Abnormalities of the heart and brain are obviously far more serious, though heart operations are becoming more and more successful every day. It is also possible to close the skin over the bare spinal cord of a baby with spina bifida, but a child born with an exposed brain is, unfortunately, still a hopeless case.

When an abnormality, such as spina bifida, that can be improved with surgery arises, there is usually a discussion between the parents and the doctors to determine whether or not the surgical procedure should be carried out. It is not simply a question of saving the baby's life, but also of considering the amount of physical and mental handicap the child will have to live with throughout the rest of his or her life.

Outlook
Some conditions may improve with time, and some allow a totally normal life. For instance, the hole-in-the-heart condition (ventricular septal defect) is really a muscular window between two heart chambers. In the past this was thought to be permanent, but doctors now know that in over three-quarters of these cases, the hole closes by the time the child is eight years of age. Many other children can be restored to normal by means of open-heart surgery techniques.

However, many congenital disorders severely handicap the sufferer's life. Therefore it is important that new ways should be found to prevent the abnormality from happening in the first place.

When a couple knows that there is an inherited illness on either side of the family, they should consult a doctor, and possibly a genetic counselor, before planning to have a family. Sometimes a test can be done during pregnancy that will detect an abnormality in the fetus, such as the test for Down's syndrome, which is generally offered to all pregnant women over 40.

To avoid the damage done by rubella, no woman should reach childbearing age without being protected by vaccination against the disease. In the case of spina bifida, there is some evidence that an improvement in the expectant mother's diet can reduce the number of babies with this defect. This is, therefore, an additional reason why balanced eating, with plenty of protein and vitamins—and not too many carbohydrates, such as sugar or chips—should always be an important part of any conscientious expectant mother's prenatal personal care program.

If a child is born with a congenital disorder, there are numerous people who can help advise the family concerned. In addition to the family doctor and any specialists, there are physiotherapists, nurses, and health care workers who will be able to help parents deal with any problems that may arise.

Conjunctivitis

Q I want to buy contact lenses but have heard that they may give me conjunctivitis. Is this true, and does it apply to both hard and soft lenses?

A When contact lenses are first placed in the eye, they are like a foreign body, such as a speck of dust, and many people get an initial conjunctivitis. Usually it is not severe, but some people are particularly sensitive, and they find it is best to stick to glasses. The softer lenses cause less trouble, but you need to weigh up the advantages and disadvantages of hard and soft lenses.

Q I have just had a bout of conjunctivitis. How can I avoid catching it again?

A It depends on the type. Bacterial conjunctivitis will only come back if the source of the infection still exists: for example, if there is a sore elsewhere on the body. So the answer is to try to eliminate the infection. The cure for allergic conjunctivitis depends on finding the cause of the allergy in the patient.

Q My seven-year-old brother has conjunctivitis, and his eyes are sticky with pus when he wakes up in the morning. Will the rest of the family catch it?

A The infection can be passed on if pus from the infected child gets onto the skin of another child. You must make sure that nobody else uses anything that touches his face, such as a towel or washcloth.

Q I know someone who has recently had Bell's palsy and now has to wear special glasses to prevent conjunctivitis. Why?

A Bell's palsy is paralysis of the nerves controlling the muscles of the face. The muscles that keep the eye tightly closed become weakened or paralyzed, and the eye cannot shut properly, even during sleep. It is therefore easy for dust to blow into the unprotected eye, and the chances of getting conjunctivitis are high. So to prevent this, special dust shields may be worn with glasses.

Usually known as pink eye, conjunctivitis is a common complaint among young children and babies, who constantly rub their eyes while playing. It usually responds quickly to treatment.

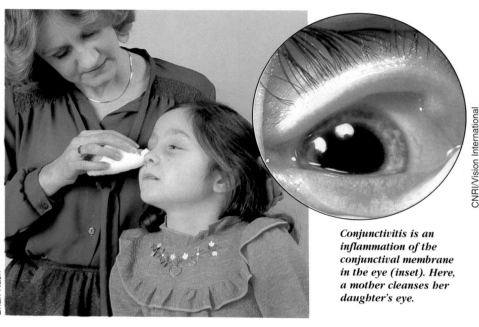

Brian Nash

CNRI/Vision International

Conjunctivitis is an inflammation of the conjunctival membrane in the eye (inset). Here, a mother cleanses her daughter's eye.

The thin, delicate membrane that covers the white of the eye and the underneath of the eyelids is known as the conjunctival membrane (or conjunctiva). Conjunctivitis is any inflammation of this membrane. The condition causes inflammation of underlying blood vessels, which become large and pink as a result.

The type of conjunctivitis common among children is not serious, but there are other, more severe types, including one called trachoma—found mainly in the East—that can cause blindness. Thus, conjunctivitis needs to be seen by a doctor so that he or she can diagnose the type and whether it is infectious.

Causes
Usually conjunctivitis is caused by a virus or a bacterial infection. Viruses are the smallest-known type of germ; bacteria are larger organisms. The viruses are spread by droplet infection in the air breathed out by an infected person, or by contact with an infected object, such as a towel. The bacterial infections are usually caused by bacteria settling in the eye—perhaps from another infected area.

Any irritation in the eye, caused, for example, by a speck of grit, could also cause conjunctivitis. Too much strong light can have the same effect. Wind, dust, or smoke can also produce a temporary case of conjunctivitis.

Symptoms
The common signs of the complaint are painful, red eyes; unusual irritation in strong light; and either pus or a watery discharge, which makes the eyes stick together first thing in the morning. Although the eye may itch, vision is quite normal. In many cases the eyelids may swell up, too.

Treatment
Antibacterial creams or drops, such as those containing chloramphenicol or neomycin, are frequently used to kill the bacteria or prevent damage from a virus. Antibiotics may be used for a recurring infection. Pus should be gently removed with salt water and clean cotton swabs. If it is infectious conjunctivitis, the person's washcloth and towel must be kept separate. If there is severe itching, the doctor may prescribe antihistamines. Dark glasses will give some relief from discomfort.

Outlook
The majority of cases clear up completely within a few days. With trachoma there may be damage to the eyelid and scarring of the cornea, and these must be corrected by surgery. With allergic conjunctivitis, the cure is more difficult. The cause has to be identified and, if possible, removed. For this, the help of a doctor or possibly a specialist will be required.

Constipation

Q Why do I always get constipated on vacation?

A Many people blame vacation constipation on a change in the water, but it is much more likely to be due to an alteration in your daily routine or to the stress of traveling. Even using a strange lavatory can make you constipated, especially if it is a different height from the one you are used to or has an odd smell that makes you reluctant to obey your body telling you to defecate. Lack of exercise is also a cause of constipation, so the next time you take a vacation, try to make sure you have a good walk every day in addition to resting and relaxing.

Q Is it true that constipation can give you blood poisoning?

A No, this is not true. Constipation cannot cause blood poisoning, but it can make you feel drained of energy and generally off kilter.

Q Why have I become so constipated since giving up smoking?

A The drug nicotine in tobacco smoke tends to speed up the movement of food through the digestive system and stimulate defecation, so it is the withdrawal of the drug that has made you constipated. Don't be tempted to take up smoking again. Instead follow the usual home treatment for constipation: a high roughage diet, plenty of fluids, and regular exercise sessions.

Q My sister goes on and on about how dangerous laxatives are and how you should always treat constipation naturally. Is she right?

A Yes. Too many laxatives can harm your digestive system. The best remedies for constipation are bran, fresh fruit, and vegetables. These contain the type of naturally occurring substances that encourage the bowels to move regularly, without harming them. And, of course, they are more pleasant to take than medication.

Constipation is usually easily cured by a sensible diet and plenty of exercise. If it persists, never take a laxative—see the family doctor for advice.

A person is constipated if he or she has long, often irregular, gaps of up to a week between bowel movements. These gaps are accompanied by an enlarged, uncomfortable abdomen and often by a furred tongue, flatulence (gas), bad breath, headaches, and pain on defecation (the passing of movements, or feces, during a bowel movement).

Everyone has his or her own particular pattern of bowel movements. This pattern can vary from three times a day to once in every two or three days. People who defecate at long intervals should not assume that they are constipated. Worrying itself can cause constipation.

How it happens

Food is normally passed along the intestines—the passages from the stomach to the rectum—by rhythmic waves of

Fresh fruit, vegetables, and bran are the natural cures for constipation.

muscle action called peristalsis. Constipation is simply some interference with this process in the large intestine or colon. Among the several causes of such interference, food itself is probably the most common.

The digestive system can break up and extract the goodness from most substances eaten as food, but there is one substance it can't cope with. This is plant cellulose, which in its common form occurs in the outer husk of grains of corn (known as bran), and in fruit and vegetables. The everyday names for plant cellulose are *bulk* or *roughage,* and while it doesn't provide nourishment, cellulose does form a vital part of the diet, for undigested cellulose in feces stimulates peristalsis.

Some foods contain no roughage at all. As might be expected, if they are eaten alone and in large quantities, they usually cause constipation. The most common such foods are eggs and cheese. A simple lack of food in the intestines is another

Causes of constipation

Cause	Additional symptoms	Treatment
Persistent ignoring of signals telling the brain that the bowel is full	Headache, gas; abdomen distended and may be painful	Try to set aside a regular time for defecation each day; increase roughage content of diet
Excess use of chemical laxatives	As above	Stop taking the laxatives, and change to a diet with plenty of bran and other roughage; drink more fluids and get more exercise
Muscle weakness in old age or after having a baby	As above	Change to a diet as above, but if the problem persists, see a doctor
Reducing diet, anorexia nervosa; low food intake due to mental or physical illness	As above, plus symptoms of underlying cause of illness	If due to reducing diet, take two tablespoons of bran daily (it contains few calories); otherwise, see a doctor for treatment of the underlying cause
Obsession with bowel movements, anxiety or stress about constipation	May be accompanied by furred tongue, gas, and the other symptoms of constipation	Try to ignore bowel movements, and change to high-roughage diet; drink more fluids and get more exercise
Damage to anus, hemorrhoids	Painful defecation, hard motions; possibly bleeding from anus, causing tendency to resist defecating	See a doctor, as drugs and possibly surgery may be needed to treat the problem
Intestinal obstruction due to twisting or constriction of intestine	Vomiting, acute pain in abdomen	A medical emergency; get to a hospital as quickly as possible
Diverticulitis—formation and inflammation of small extensions from the colon	Pain in lower left abdomen; temperature may be raised	See a doctor as soon as possible; long-term change to high-roughage diet

cause of poor peristaltic movements, which is why some people on diets become constipated. For the same reason, people with illnesses that cause loss of appetite are also likely to suffer.

Two diseases of the colon, colitis and diverticulitis, cause constipation. Pregnancy can cause it, too, because the hormones produced at this time tend to interfere with the intestinal muscle movements, as does pressure exerted by the enlarged womb. Weakness of the muscle in old age or after childbirth are also possible causes.

The psychological cause
Peristalsis, like breathing and heartbeat, is controlled by that part of the nervous system (called the autonomic nervous system) that works without our direct control. From toddlerhood on, people can control the time that they defecate. However, this ability to hold back a bowel movement may cause some trouble. For if the brain can indicate when it is time to defecate, it can also overlook signals from the intestine that the bowel is full and a visit to the lavatory is due.

If constipation is accompanied by pain on defecation, it tends to create a spiral of problems. The pain, which is commonly due to damaged veins (hemorrhoids) or cracks (fissures) in the anus, causes reluctance to defecate.

Constipation can be caused by bad eating habits or an unbalanced diet.

This makes the feces pile up in the passage, causing water to be absorbed from them into the bloodstream—making them harder and more painful than ever.

Treatment
Except when constipation is caused by a mental or physical illness, the best treatment is a commonsensical one. It is best to eat plenty of roughage and drink lots of fluids (especially water) which softens the feces. Adequate exercise is required to tone up the abdominal muscles and provide relaxation from stress.

The worst thing a person can do is to take laxatives. These work by irritating the nerves of the intestine and, therefore, speeding up peristalsis. They can cause griping pains and the passing of semiliquid feces.

After the intestine has been cleared out in this way, it tends to hold the next supply of food longer than normal, causing what seems like yet more constipation. The sufferer is likely to take another dose of laxative at this stage and possibly several more when the process is repeated. This creates a real danger, because the intestinal nerves may become so conditioned to the artificial stimulation that they fail to work when it is withdrawn.

If a laxative is taken at all, it should be as a last resort. The best ones to choose are those such as bran tablets. If constipation occurs along with some obvious illness, such as appendicitis, a doctor should be consulted—self-treatment could be dangerous.

Should constipation remain after the commonsensical treatments described here have been tried, a doctor should be consulted. It might be a symptom of an underlying disease.

Contact lenses

Q Can anyone wear contact lenses?

A No. Some people simply cannot tolerate them—particularly the hard type—because their eye tissue is too sensitive. Other people have a medical condition that prevents them from wearing contact lenses with any ease. This group includes people with allergies, hay fever, sties, or other disorders, such as excessive watering or bloodshot eyes. People with arthritis or tremors will have difficulty inserting the lenses, a procedure that requires some manual dexterity.

Q If my daughter is fitted with contact lenses, will they stop her from becoming more nearsighted?

A Unfortunately not. If her nearsightedness is hereditary and her eyesight is very poor, contact lenses will not prevent any further deterioration. If she feels embarrassed about wearing glasses, however, contact lenses might be advisable for cosmetic purposes.

Q Can I sleep while wearing my contact lenses?

A Most people remove their lenses at night for cleaning and reinsert them the following day. Napping while wearing the lenses is not uncommon, but while some people can tolerate it, others cannot. Certain types of lenses may be worn over a three-month period, including during sleep, but because they can cause complications, many ophthalmologists will not prescribe them.

Q My soft lenses once caused abrasions on my eyes that required medical treatment. Why did this happen?

A Soft lenses require extra maintenance and a very high standard of hygiene. Sometimes a film can build up on the surface, causing pain and severe swelling in the eye. Hold your lenses up to the light: if they appear cloudy or speckled, it is probably best to replace them.

Many people prefer contact lenses to glasses because they feel that they improve appearance and boost their self-confidence.

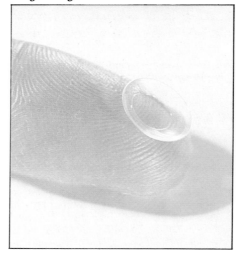

A contact lens is, as the name implies, a lens that fits over the front of the eye and is used in place of eyeglasses. Contact lenses are usually made of plastic or glass and come in many colors.

Many people wear contact lenses for cosmetic or professional purposes or for sports, though they may also be worn for other optical, medical, or surgical reasons. People who have had cataracts removed, who have corneal disorders, or who are very nearsighted can also wear them.

Contact lenses can also be used to help in cases where the iris has been lost through an accident or operation, because they can be custom-made to stop too much light from entering the eye. Similarly cases of albinism—a rare condition where the skin and hair are white and the irises red, making a person oversensitive to light—can also be aided by the use of special contact lenses.

Who can wear them?

Any age group—from small babies up to the elderly—can wear contact lenses, depending on their state of health. They are most advantageous for the nearsighted, and farsighted people or those with astigmatisms (defects of the cornea causing distorted vision) can also wear them.

However, not all eyeglasses wearers can actually tolerate contact lenses. They are unsuitable for people who have allergies, such as hay fever, which causes the eyes to run or recurrent sties or other eye disorders; which the lenses might aggravate. Those who suffer from tremors, or severe arthritis, will have some difficulty controlling their hands sufficiently to insert contact lenses.

Choice available

Contact lenses are usually prescribed by an ophthalmologist (eye specialist) in either a hard or a soft variety. Each has advantages and disadvantages.

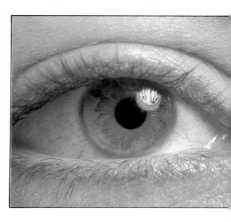

Before insertion, a hard contact lens is held on the fingertip (left). In the eye (above), it can only be detected by experts.

Hard lenses, made of an inflexible piece of plastic, are smaller, last longer, are less likely to cause infection, give excellent vision, and are less expensive than soft lenses. However, it takes longer to build up a tolerance to them.

Soft lenses, which are more pliable than hard lenses, are easily fitted to the eye. They can be tolerated more quickly and are infinitely more comfortable, even when first put in, but the vision achieved is not as fine. Eye infections occur more frequently, and soft lenses are liable to tear and do not last as long.

Most hard and soft lenses should not be slept in, but there are some soft ones now available that can be worn all the time for three-month stretches; however, even these can cause complications in some wearers, and many ophthalmologists do not recommend them.

Contact lenses can be harmful if they cause abrasions of the tissues. Prolonged wear or wearing dirty lenses can result in eye inflammations. Such complications occur in only a few patients and are more common in the first two years.

Care and maintenance

Hard lenses, which are inserted into the eye with a lubricant wetting solution, must be cleaned daily. Soft lenses require a special nonirritant soaking solution.

Contraction

Q If I have an IUD (intrauterine device) fitted by my doctor, how long will it take before it starts working?

A An IUD is effective as soon as it is in place. But for the first three months, you must check the string once a week, because this is the time the IUD is most likely to be expelled—and then you would not be protected.

Q I am 21 and getting married soon. I would like to have an IUD fitted, but I've heard it is not suitable for women who have not had children. Is this true?

A IUDs are not a first choice method of contraception for women who have not had children. The uterus and cervix have not been stretched by having a baby, and this makes it more difficult and more painful to insert an IUD, and there is more chance of the uterus expelling it. There is also a higher chance of side effects like painful periods, bleeding, and pelvic inflammatory disease (PID). Your doctor may, however, agree to fit you with an IUD in spite of all this if you have considered all other methods and are particularly eager to use this method of contraception.

Q I am pregnant and want to have an IUD fitted after the baby is born. I plan to breast-feed my baby: do I need to have it fitted during this time?

A Some doctors like to fit an IUD soon after the baby is born while others prefer to wait six to eight weeks. Ask your doctor, and if he or she wants you to wait six weeks, you must use other contraceptive measures in the meantime. Just because you are breast-feeding does not mean that you will not get pregnant.

Q Can using a condom during intercourse really stop you from catching venereal disease?

A A condom does give considerable protection to both the man and the woman, but it cannot be relied upon to give total protection from venereal disease.

Some contraceptives prevent pregnancy by creating a barrier between the sperm and egg; others either stop the fertilized egg from developing, or convince the woman's body that it is already pregnant. A couple should think carefully and ask for advice about what is best for them.

For thousands of years all kinds of ideas have been tried to prevent women from getting pregnant—ranging from crocodile dung put into the vagina to standing up after intercourse, sneezing, drinking something cold, and jumping backward seven times.

Fortunately nowadays the reproductive system is better understood, and far more reliable methods are available. The Pill is one of the best known (see Oral contraceptives), but not every woman can use it. Here we will deal with the other very effective contraceptive methods available. Choosing which one to use can be totally confusing unless you know how they work and what they do. Only then can you decide which sort will best suit you and your partner.

Some methods are safer than others, but may have side effects. Other methods require forethought and are more difficult to use and therefore have a higher failure rate because they are not used correctly. Some women are allergic to rubber, so for them most forms of the diaphragm and condom would cause too much irritation. Others have extremely heavy and painful periods, so an IUD (intrauterine device) would be unsuitable for them, because it can accentuate period pains and cause heavy bleeding.

A female should ask her doctor which methods are most suitable. If she goes to a birth control clinic, the clinic should be advised of her medical history. Whichever type of contraceptive she chooses, she should make sure she understands exactly how it works before using it.

In certain countries the use of contraceptives is barred or discouraged for religious and moral reasons. In these places the only method sanctioned is the rhythm method. Religion is another reason why some couples must give careful thought to all factors involved before deciding on their contraceptive method.

Spermicides

Spermicides contain chemicals that kill sperm when they come into contact with them. They also inhibit the movement of sperm up the vagina and through the cervical canal (the passage into the uterus). Spermicides are not reliable when used on their own, so they are usually used with a condom or a diaphragm, either of which creates a barrier between the man's sperm and the woman's egg (the ovum). This means that if sperm some-

Spermicide, in the form of a cream, jelly, or pessary, should be used by the woman when her partner uses a condom.

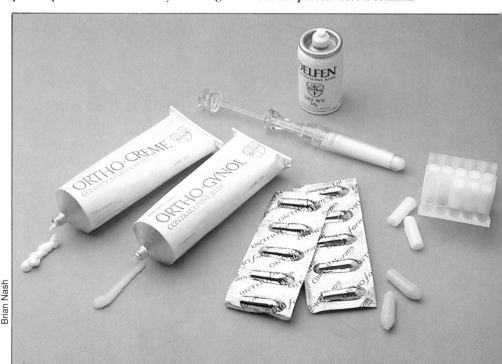

Brian Nash

how manage to escape contact with the spermicide, there is a physical barrier in place that will prevent them from reaching and fertilizing the egg.

Spermicides are readily available from drugstores without a prescription—and come in a variety of forms—aerosol foams (which are the most reliable), tubes of cream and jelly, pessaries, and foaming tablets (which break up in the moist environment of the vagina and release the chemicals). However, some spermicides have been found to be almost totally ineffective, while others can cause rubber to deteriorate. So before buying one it is wise to consult a birth control clinic to find out which brands they recommend.

The creams, foams, and jellies come with a syringelike applicator with a plunger. The applicator is filled with spermicide and put into the woman's vagina, with the applicator tip as close to the cervix (the neck of the uterus) as possible. This is to insure that any sperm that get that far will come in contact with the spermicide. The spermicide is released when the plunger is pushed down the applicator.

When to apply
Used with a diaphragm, spermicide can be applied up to an hour before intercourse. If a spermicide is used on its own, it should be applied not more than 15 minutes before intercourse takes place, but this is not an effective method of contraception. If intercourse takes place a second time, more spermicide should be applied, as there is only enough in one application to deal with sperm from one ejaculation. Spermicides should not be washed away earlier than six to eight hours after intercourse.

Pessaries or tablets should only be put in place two to five minutes before intercourse takes place, because they are not effective for very long. A finger can be used to place the pessaries as high up in the vagina as possible.

Condoms
Known by a variety of names—including *French letter*, *sheath*, *rubber*, *protective*, and *prophylactic*—a condom is a tube of fine rubber that is closed at one end. In its package, it is rolled up so that it looks like a flat circle with a thick rim. It unrolls as it is pulled over the erect penis. It can then catch all the semen that the penis ejaculates and stop it from reaching the uterus. In addition to being a method of contraception, condoms are also recommended as a barrier against AIDS.

The tip of the condom should be held between the forefinger and thumb of one hand while it is put on, because this keeps the air out and allows some space for the ejaculatory fluid. It also reduces the risk of the condom bursting.

A condom should be put on not only before the penis enters the vagina, but before it even touches the woman genitals, because semen can leak out of the penis throughout foreplay. One of the common complaints against condoms is that the couple must stop their foreplay to put the condom on. However, many couples overcome this problem by making it part of their foreplay.

There are condoms available that have been lubricated to prevent them from

Condoms are tubes of fine rubber of varying thickness and texture that are gradually unrolled to cover the erect penis.

tearing when they enter the vagina. If this type is not being used, it is a good idea to use spermicide as a lubricant (petroleum jelly should not be used as it destroys rubber). It is good practice to use a spermicide in any case, as an extra precaution, since there is always a chance of a condom being faulty. When the penis is withdrawn from the vagina, either partner should hold the condom at the base of the penis so that the penis does not slip out and allow sperm to escape.

Condoms are available in many countries in a choice of textures, sizes, and colors, without prescription, from drugstores, slot machines, and mail-order companies. They are the only method of contraception, apart from withdrawal and vasectomy (surgery that permanently prevents the presence of sperm in the ejaculation), in which the man takes total responsibility. They are 96 to 97 percent effective when used properly with a reliable spermicide.

Diaphragms
Diaphragms are round, dome-shaped contraceptives made of rubber. They are inserted into the vagina and cover the cervix, thus preventing any sperm from entering the uterus. There are three different types, but they all work on the same principle. Used correctly—with spermicide—they are 96 to 97 percent reliable.

The Dutch diaphragm is the largest, varying from 2 to 4 in (5 to 10 cm) across. It has a strong spring in the rim, and when it is in position, the front of the rim rests on a little ledge on the pubic bone and the back in a small crevice behind the neck of the uterus. Dutch diaphragms are the easiest to use and for this reason are the most popular. But they are not suitable for women who have poor pelvic tone, which means their muscles are not strong enough to hold the diaphragm in place. In these cases another type of diaphragm can be used.

The cervical diaphragm is much smaller than the Dutch diaphragm and looks like a thimble with a thickened rim. Some women find it is more difficult to handle, and men can sometimes feel it during intercourse because it is not as flat as the Dutch diaphragm.

The vault diaphragm is a cross between the other two types. Unlike the others, it can be made of plastic, so women who are allergic to rubber can use it. Like the cervical diaphragm, the vault diaphragm can occasionally be felt by the man.

Using a diaphragm
It is not possible to go to a drugstore and buy a diaphragm. A nurse or doctor must fit it to make sure it is the right size, as every woman is slightly different inside. A

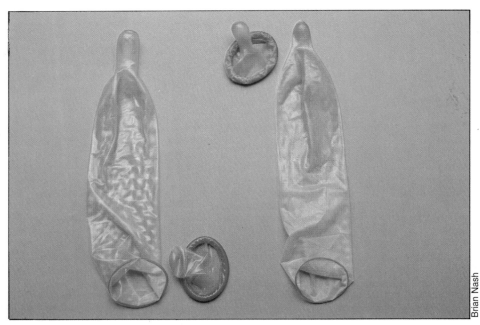

Brian Nash

How to insert a diaphragm

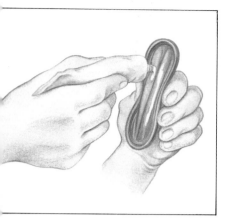

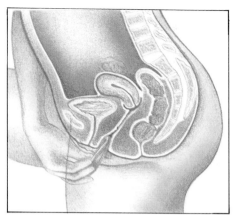

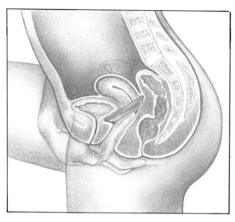

Place spermicide on both sides of the diaphragm, and smear more around the rim. Squeeze into a cigar shape with the fingers.

Squat or raise one leg, and after spreading the lips of the vagina, push the diaphragm deep into the vagina until in place.

Be sure that you can feel the cervix through the diaphragm. Leave in place at least six hours after the last ejaculation.

A properly fitted diaphragm should stay in place during intercourse without causing discomfort to either the woman or her partner. If it is uncomfortable or if it moves, then either it has not been fitted correctly or it is not the right type of diaphragm for the woman concerned.

A spermicide should always be used with a diaphragm, as a second line of defense, just in case any sperm get past it. A spoonful of spermicidal jelly or cream should be squeezed onto both sides. Then more jelly or cream should be smeared all around the rim. To insert the diaphragm, the woman squeezes it into a cigar shape using the thumb and finger. One hand spreads the lips of the vagina while the other inserts the diaphragm. It is usually easier to insert it if she squats down—this shortens the length of the vagina.

The woman can check the position of her diaphragm by making sure she can feel the cervix through it. The doctor or clinic will show her how to do this when the diaphragm is fitted. If intercourse does not take place until more than an hour after insertion, more spermicide should be applied without removing the diaphragm. The diaphragm should be left in place for at least six hours after the last ejaculation, since sperm can live this long in the vagina. To remove a Dutch or vault diaphragm, hook a finger over the rim and pull. Cervical diaphragms have a string that can be pulled to remove them.

After use, the diaphragm should be washed thoroughly in warm water and

checked for any small holes or faults, especially around the rim. If there are any, the woman should see her doctor about replacing the diaphragm and use an alternative contraceptive method in the meantime.

The diaphragm should be dried thoroughly and stored in the container provided away from direct sunlight.

A diaphragm should be checked by the doctor at least once a year to make sure that it still fits correctly and does not need replacing. This annual check is especially important if the woman has recently had a baby, has gained or lost an excessive amount of weight, or if she has just recently married or only just started having an active sex life.

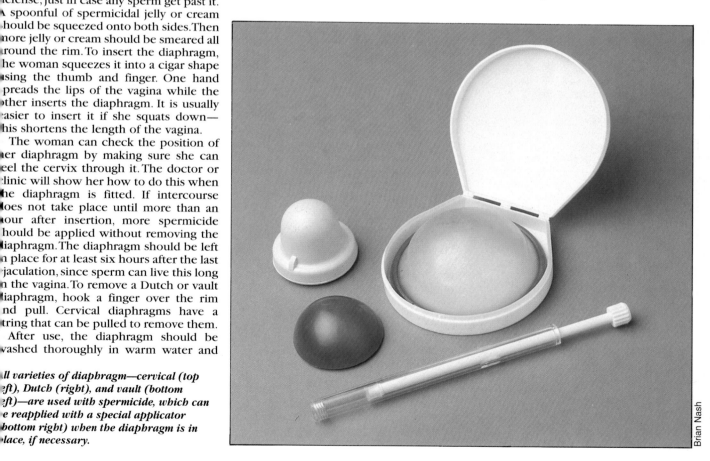

All varieties of diaphragm—cervical (top left), Dutch (right), and vault (bottom left)—are used with spermicide, which can be reapplied with a special applicator (bottom right) when the diaphragm is in place, if necessary.

Brian Nash

Q I have heard that there is a condom available that only covers the tip of the penis. Would this kind increase sensation for the man during intercourse?

A This type of condom is often referred to as an American tip. However, it is not reliable as a means of contraception, even if used with spermicide, because it can easily become dislodged and slip off.

Q I like the idea of having a Dutch diaphragm because, unlike other methods, it has no side effects, but is it a messy method to use all the time?

A It all depends on how squeamish you are—some women don't like to use tampons, for instance. A diaphragm does involve using spermicide, so it is messier than an IUD. It also takes a conscious effort to use it. On the other hand, there are fewer side effects, so it is really a matter of weighing all the advantages and disadvantages.

Q I have just been fitted with a Dutch diaphragm, but the clinic said I must use a spermicide with it. I don't see why this is necessary if the diaphragm is a good fit.

A Even though the diaphragm is fitted for your size and has a strong spring to make sure it stays in place, sperm are very tiny and there is always the possibility that they could swim around the edge of the diaphragm and into the uterus. However, if spermicide is used around the rim of the diaphragm and on the side nearest the uterus it will kill any sperm that do manage to get past.

Q Can I use a diaphragm during my period?

A Yes. All that happens is that the diaphragm holds back the menstrual flow until it is removed. Keep it in for six hours after intercourse, and then use a pad or tampon as usual. Intercourse during a period can be less messy, and therefore more pleasant, if you do use a diaphragm.

Benefits

The most important benefit of the diaphragm is that it has virtually no side effects. Occasionally it may cause a slight vaginal irritation, and some women find it brings on an attack of cystitis (inflammation of the bladder; see Cystitis). These conditions are, however, relatively minor, and after diagnosis by the doctor, they can be treated easily and effectively.

A few women find they cannot use any type of diaphragm. This may be because their muscles are too relaxed for it to stay in place. Some young women may have a vaginal opening that is quite small, and they have difficulty inserting it, while other women just find it too distasteful. Not all contraceptives are suitable for every woman. Doctors will help each woman to find one that is right for her.

Intrauterine devices

Intrauterine devices—commonly known as IUDs—work in a different way from condoms and diaphragms. They are inserted into the uterus, and rather than forming a barrier between the sperm and the egg, they prevent a fertilized egg from implanting in the uterus. Doctors are not sure why they work, but they are known to prevent the lining of the uterus from thickening—so the right environment for an egg to develop is not created. An IUD is the only form of contraception available—apart from the Pill—that does not require any pre-intercourse preparation.

The reliability rate of IUDs is 98 percent, which is slightly higher than that for diaphragms and condoms.

IUDs have been made in many shapes and sizes, but the only kind now used in the United States is Progestasert. This is a hormone-releasing IUD that is thought to be more effective than earlier IUDs and less likely to cause excessive bleeding. There is, however, still a risk of ectopic pregnancy (where the fertilized egg lodges in the fallopian tube).

Insertion

Most IUDs are supplied to the doctor or clinic in sterilized packs with a fine, plastic tube, about 0.08 in (2 mm) in diameter, for insertion. An IUD is usually implanted during or just after menstruation, because the cervix is more relaxed at this time. The depth of the uterus is checked by passing a small probe through the neck of the cervix. This shows the doctor how deep to insert the IUD. The IUD is straightened out inside the tube, and the tube is inserted through the cervix. When the correct depth is reached, the tube is detached and the IUD springs back into shape inside the uterus. The whole process is simple and takes only a few minutes.

The rhythm method

The rhythm method of contraception relies on the fact that a woman is only fertile for a few days in each menstrual cycle. By determining which days these are, she can avoid pregnancy by avoiding intercourse on her fertile days.

The two or three days just after ovulation are the fertile days, so to avoid conception, no intercourse should take place during these days. Because sperm may live for up to 48 hours in the female reproductive tract, it is also wise to avoid intercourse for the few days prior to ovulation.

In order to determine when she will ovulate, a woman needs to become aware of, and monitor, her temperature, the condition of the lower part of the uterus, and the production of fertile mucus (which keeps the sperm alive and guides them to the entrance of the uterus).

To follow this method successfully, it is essential to find a teacher. There are some natural birth control clinics that teach this method, or it may be possible to find a private teacher.

The insertion may be a little painful for some women, especially if they are nervous and tighten up their muscles. If the pain, however slight, continues for more than a couple of days, a woman should see her doctor.

Disadvantages

Some women may find they have heavier periods than usual for the first two or three months after having an IUD fitted, and sometimes there may be slight spotting between periods, backache, or stomach cramp. These symptoms normally disappear within a couple of months, but anyone who is having a lot of pain should see her doctor.

Occasionally an IUD may be expelled from the body for no apparent reason other than a woman's internal anatomy being unsuitable. If this does happen, it is usually within the first three months and can be during menstruation, when it may pass unnoticed. All IUDs have a fine nylon string attached that hangs down into the vagina, and it should be possible to feel this with a finger. If the string cannot be felt, or if it seems longer than usual, the woman should consult her doctor. Another method of contraception should be used in the meantime.

The string should be checked once a week for the first three months. After this

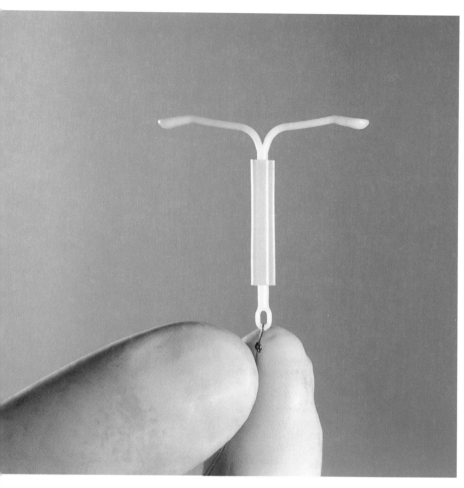

The IUD currently used in the United States is a hormone-releasing device. As with all IUDs, the fine plastic string at the bottom hangs through the cervix into the vagina, making removal easy.

Depo-Provera shot: This is an injection of the female hormone progesterone, which is given two or four times a year. It is as reliable as the Pill (which is 99 percent-plus reliable), but because it does not contain estrogen (see Estrogen), many of the dangers and side effects of the Pill are absent. It is especially good for women who have difficulty in remembering to take the Pill on a regular basis.

Silastic ring: This is a flexible ring, impregnated with progesterone, that fits inside the vagina in the same way that a diaphragm does. It releases the hormone into the body in the quantities normally present during pregnancy. The body is fooled into thinking it is pregnant and does not release any new eggs. The ring is worn for 21 days and then removed to allow menstruation. After seven days a new ring is inserted by the woman herself.

Hormone pellet insert (Norplant): Another method that fools the body into thinking it is pregnant is a slow-releasing hormone pellet the size of a grain of rice. It is implanted under the skin behind the neck and slowly dissolves, releasing hormones into the body. It is easily removed by making a small incision.

Nasal spray: This is a fine mist that is sprayed directly into the nose. The spray contains hormones that act on the gland that controls the release of hormones into the body.

t should be checked once a month after menstruation, as this is the time the IUD is most likely to become dislodged.

Some men complain that they can feel the string during intercourse, and if this bothers them, it is possible for a doctor to shorten the string. Tampons rarely get caught up in the string, but if a sharp pain is felt when a tampon is removed, the string should be checked.

Staying in place
An IUD can be left in place for some years, but the woman should have a medical checkup at least once a year.

A woman is unlikely to get pregnant with an IUD in place, but if she suspects she has conceived, she should see her doctor immediately. The IUD must be removed, because it could cause a miscarriage.

Morning-after IUD
If a woman has had intercourse at the midpoint of her cycle—her most fertile time—without using any contraceptives, some doctors will fit an IUD afterward. This must be done within 72 hours of intercourse. It can be removed at the next menstruation and is considered more of a safety measure than a contraceptive.

Douching
It used to be thought that semen could be flushed out of the vagina with hot water or a mild solution that is hostile to sperm. A syringe with a rubber bulb at one end is inserted into the vagina and the contents squeezed out. This method is not only totally unreliable, it can also be dangerous—it is possible for a dirty syringe to cause an infection.

Vaginal sponge
Usually made from polyurethane foam, this fairly recent contraceptive device fits over the cervix in the same way as a diaphragm. It is impregnated with spermicide that is released gradually over a 24-hour period. The sponge works in three ways: it blocks the entrance to the uterus, thereby preventing sperm from entering; it absorbs sperm; and the spermicide kills sperm on contact. The sponge must be left in place for at least six hours after ejaculation has occurred.

New methods
There are a few other methods that are available only as clinical trials but, nevertheless, deserve some mention. These methods are not in common use.

The vaginal sponge is a fairly new development. The loop aids removal.

Brian Nash

Convalescence

Q My mother has always believed in taking a good tonic after an illness. Is there any value in this?

A The idea of a tonic or pick-me-up has gone out of fashion, although they may still be prescribed, perhaps more as a psychological boost than for any medical value. Most commercial tonics either contain some vitamins and minerals or are simply glucose drinks that are easily digested to give instant energy. They are not strictly necessary but do no harm. A nourishing diet is the best tonic.

Q Why do medical staff always make a person take sleeping pills after an operation?

A Sleep aids recovery, and discomfort may sometimes cause an individual not to sleep as well as usual after an operation. For this reason a short course of sleeping pills may be advised by the doctor. A good diet can also help sleep. A natural substance called tryptophan, which is found in milk, eggs, cheese, and meat, is thought to encourage sleep. So a hot, milky drink at bedtime makes good sense.

Q In old-fashioned stories, you always read about people being sent to the seaside for convalescence. Is sea air really good for you?

A The idea that the seaside air provides beneficial effects in convalescence is now known to be a myth. The only good thing about sea air is that it is less likely to be polluted and therefore good for those with lung complaints.

Q My friend can afford to stay at a health spa regularly, and it makes her feel really fit. Is this a good idea after an illness?

A It depends on the health farm. Make sure that the place is well-established, that there is medical supervision, and that it is geared to the convalescent's needs. If so, it could do some good. But a short vacation in a pleasant climate may seem equally inviting.

A patient's attitude, together with care and attention, all help toward a speedy recovery.

Anyone who has spent a few days sick in bed will know the feelings of weakness and fatigue that accompany the early days of recovery. These sensations affect those who have had a serious illness or operation in an even more extreme way.

Aftercare
Discharge from the hospital depends not only on the speed and degree of recovery, but also on the kind of care available afterward. Older people living alone are not usually discharged until arrangements have been made for help and care at their home.

Caring for any convalescent can be an enormous strain, and people often take on more than they can cope with rather than face the possibility of feeling guilty or disloyal, thus risking stress for themselves as well as for the patient. It is far better to be realistic about taking on this task and to ask for any necessary help at an early stage.

A few hospitals offer special rehabilitation programs where patients return on an outpatient basis to learn, for example, how to walk after a stroke, or to adjust to arthritis. Relatives are sometimes invited to take part so that they know what type of help to offer the patient.

Diet and supplements
The modern approach is to forget a special diet except perhaps for the first few days after an operation or when a specific diet is necessary. A normal diet should consist of light, nourishing meals with plenty of fruit and vegetables, milk, cheese, eggs, meat, and fish. Extra vitamins may be suggested, and even if not, a general multivitamin supplement from a drugstore will do no harm—though a doctor's advice should be sought.

Often there is a dramatic drop in weight after an illness, which causes more weakness. If the patient's appetite is poor, small meals at shorter intervals may be more inviting.

Exercise and activity
In the hospital it is common to see postoperative patients tentatively making their way around the ward as part of their exercise routine. Once home, daily activity is advised in most cases, along with any specific exercises. There may be instructions to avoid lifting heavy objects or indulging in active sports, but otherwise patients are usually allowed to set their own pace.

Postoperative depression
Early recovery often seems fast and dramatic, particularly if the patient has been in intense pain. Sudden relief from this can seem miraculous, and there may be an unrealistic surge of optimism. But depression due to fatigue may follow, and if this persists for any length of time, it may need treatment.

A family's attitude can make all the difference to a young patient.

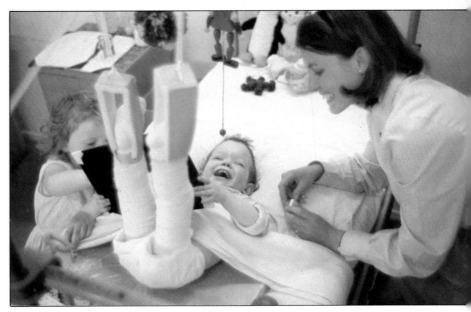

Convulsions

My brother spends a lot of his free time at a disco. Can convulsions be brought on by the flickering lights?

A Yes. Many people cannot tolerate the strobe lights in discos, since the frequency of the flicker induces a type of temporary short circuit in their brains. This causes the brain to assume a particular frequency of brain wave, which brings on a seizure. However, if your brother was susceptible, he would have been affected by now.

Q **My toddler has terrible temper tantrums. Could these bring on convulsions?**

A Convulsions can be triggered by a severe temper tantrum. Breath-holding is a sign of this—the child gets so agitated that breathing stops, resulting in unconsciousness and convulsions. Despite appearances, it is rarely serious, and you must simply wait for the symptoms to abate. Do not give in if the child is using this to get his or her own way.

Q **I suffer from convulsions. Is it safe for me to drive?**

A Aside from the possibility of a seizure while driving, the side effects of some drugs slow reactions and reflexes. For these reasons people who still need drugs to control convulsions should neither drive nor operate potentially hazardous machinery. Two seizure-free years without medication is generally recognized as an adequately controlled case, but laws concerning driving with seizures vary from state to state.

Q **Is it true that some foods and drugs can bring on convulsions?**

A Strong allergies to certain foods may bring on a form of convulsion—although reactions of this nature are rare. Convulsions may also be a symptom of food poisoning. Certain drugs may cause convulsions if given in improper doses or to patients susceptible to convulsions.

Convulsions can have a number of causes. Staying calm and performing simple first aid can do a lot to help.

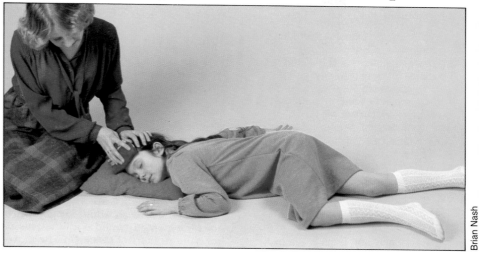

Brian Nash

Convulsions (seizures) can be very distressing to witness. They require immediate care and attention, but simple first aid can do a lot to help.

Causes
The most common cause of convulsions in infants and young children is a fever or sudden rise in temperature. The tendency to react to a high temperature with convulsions runs in families. But a resistance gradually builds up in those who suffer from them, so that this type of convulsion is unlikely to occur after the age of five. In a newborn baby convulsions may be caused by brain damage or central nervous system disorders. Epilepsy is a likely cause. Convulsions can also arise from accidental poisoning, alcoholism, or occupational hazards such as poisoning from lead or mercury.

Symptoms
A convulsion that occurs because of fever usually starts with the child becoming unconscious and falling down. He or she usually twitches uncontrollably and writhes and shakes. The eyes roll upward, breathing becomes labored, and there is sometimes frothing at the mouth. The teeth may be clenched violently, and if the tongue is in the way, it may be bitten through. Spontaneous emptying of the bladder or bowels may also occur.

Afterward the sufferer falls asleep, perhaps after coming to for a very brief period, and he or she may snore, with a peculiar facial expression. Convulsions such as these only last for a few minutes. Epileptic convulsions can affect either specific parts of the body or both consciousness and muscle function.

When the seizure stops, place the person in the recovery position, and then get help.

Dangers
Aside from the possibility of biting the tongue, injury can result from falling onto a hard object or striking furniture while writhing on the floor. Serious complications and possibly death can arise if the person vomits and chokes, or inhales vomit into the lungs. If a convulsion occurs when a person is driving or operating machinery, the consequences could be disastrous and possibly lethal.

Treatment
A person suffering from a convulsion should never be left in order to call for help. The attack will only last for a few minutes, and it is best to stay nearby.

Kneel beside the person on the floor and, if possible, place a small pad, for example, a folded handkerchief, between the teeth. If the teeth are clamped shut, avoid trying to force them open. Fingers should be kept out of the person's mouth to avoid being bitten.

Loosen clothing, especially around the neck and waist. Try to prevent the sufferer from hitting limbs or head against nearby objects or a fireplace—pull him or her gently away from such hazards. Never forcibly restrain the person or try to arouse him or her by slapping. If there is vomiting, turn the head to one side so that the vomit comes out of the mouth. When the writhing stops, move the patient into the recovery position, and when he or she comes around or falls asleep, contact a doctor immediately. If the patient has a fever, sponge them with tepid water while waiting for the doctor.

Coordination

Q My son has suddenly become very clumsy. Will he grow out of this?

A Lack of coordination in a child can happen for various reasons. At different stages of growing up, such as at the start of puberty, children may seem more clumsy because they are not concentrating as well as before; any emotional upset will have the same effect. However, if the clumsiness has occurred out of the blue, it would be worth consulting your doctor.

Q My uncle has lost an eye in an accident. Will this affect his coordination?

A Probably not. Each of the two visual centers in the brain receives information from both eyes, so the loss of an eye does not affect someone as badly as the loss of one field of vision (that is, the left or right half of each eye's sight). The brain is also able to compensate for the loss of vision in one eye, so coordination is hardly affected. However, if the visual centers of the brain are damaged through a stroke, and one half of the visual field is lost, then the patient does have difficulty in judging distances, particularly gaps like doorways, and often bumps into the side, thus appearing to be clumsy or lacking in coordination.

Q There's a man in our neighborhood who always staggers around as if he were drunk, but his wife says this is because he has an ear disease. Could this be true?

A Ear diseases can sometimes affect a person's coordination because of a delicate gravity detector located next to the part of the ear that detects sound waves. This gravity detector gives the brain information about which way the head is tilting. Many ear diseases involve this area and so are often accompanied by symptoms like vertigo (a spinning sensation) or unsteadiness of the limbs, since the brain is receiving the wrong signals about the orientation of the head. A similar effect happens when a person is spun around rapidly for several seconds.

Why are some people natural athletes or dancers, while others are less gifted? The answer lies in the complicated processes of coordination that begin in the brain.

The supple movements of a champion gymnast reveal, in their flowing patterns of motion, how delicately the human brain (see Brain) can control the hundreds of muscles in the torso and limbs. To achieve such intricate sequences of action, the human brain has evolved a complex system of control and guidance that makes even the most sophisticated computers look primitive.

Babies are born with many reflexes (muscular responses that occur without conscious thought). To visualize these reflex actions in an adult, imagine how quickly a person would withdraw his or her hand from a hot saucepan. The movements that are directed by the brain (voluntary movements) are superimposed onto these simple reflex actions. For every action that is performed, some muscles will contract, others relax, and still more will maintain their contraction to stabilize the rest of the body. The process by which all the individual muscle contractions are carefully synchronized to produce a smooth order of activity is called coordination.

A game like soccer requires a great deal of coordination between feet and eyes.

How coordination works

To understand this process, consider an everyday action like leaning over a table to pick up a cup of coffee. How does the brain direct this apparently simple task? Before the cup of coffee can be picked up, a series of events must happen.

First the person must know where the cup and his or her hand are and the relationship between them. This means that the brain must be able to generate a "map" of the space for necessary movement to be planned. This is called spatial perception. This "map" of the outside world must then be interpreted by the brain so that the problem of getting the coffee cup from the table to the hand can be solved. The plan of action must then be translated into a detailed set of instructions to the muscles so that they will contract in the right order.

During the movement, started by the planning parts of the brain (the premotor area), continuous streams of information pour in from all the sensors (nerves) in the muscles and joints. This information, which has to be organized and relayed back to the brain, provides the positions of the mucles and joints as well as their states of contraction.

How the brain enables us to pick up a cup of coffee

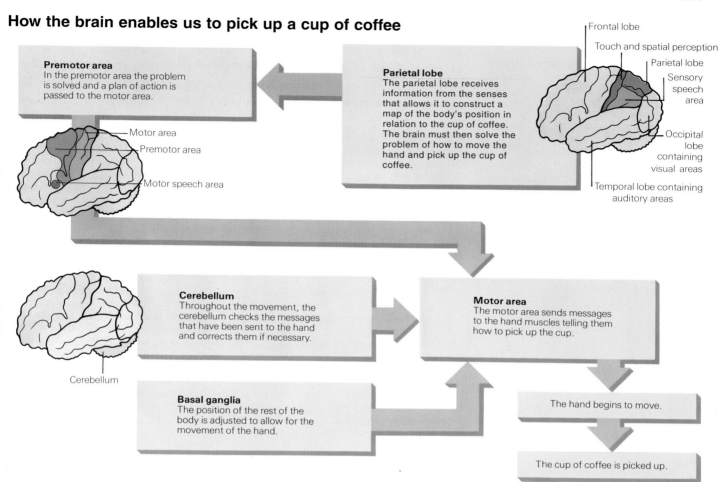

Premotor area
In the premotor area the problem is solved and a plan of action is passed to the motor area.

Motor area
Premotor area
Motor speech area

Parietal lobe
The parietal lobe receives information from the senses that allows it to construct a map of the body's position in relation to the cup of coffee. The brain must then solve the problem of how to move the hand and pick up the cup of coffee.

Frontal lobe
Touch and spatial perception
Parietal lobe
Sensory speech area
Occipital lobe containing visual areas
Temporal lobe containing auditory areas

Cerebellum

Cerebellum
Throughout the movement, the cerebellum checks the messages that have been sent to the hand and corrects them if necessary.

Motor area
The motor area sends messages to the hand muscles telling them how to pick up the cup.

Basal ganglia
The position of the rest of the body is adjusted to allow for the movement of the hand.

The hand begins to move.

The cup of coffee is picked up.

In order to move the hand to pick up the cup of coffee, the person also needs to lean slightly toward it and this alters the center of gravity of the body. All the reflex balance mechanisms must be controlled to insure that the correct changes in muscle tone are made, thereby allowing the movement across the table that the brain has ordered. This means that the background tone of many other muscles has to be monitored and coordinated.

First stages of coordination

All intentional movements need to be practiced before they become coordinated. Even such ordinary actions as walking were once major problems for every developing child. As a baby's brain matures and its interconnections increase, the primitive reflexes with which he or she was born (such as the startle reaction, causing the hands to be outstretched when the baby feels he or she is falling) are overlaid with progressively more complicated ways of moving.

A toy might attract the baby's eye, because its bright color causes a strong signal in the visual centers, but the baby finds that reaching out is not enough to arrive at this object, so he or she is impelled to move toward it. The first attempts to move are not coordinated: the limbs just thrash around. But these initial attempts enable the necessary brain connections to develop for the set of actions that make up a coordinated crawl. Once crawling has been achieved, the messages sent from the brain to the muscles can be improved upon until nothing at ground level is safe from the child's grasp.

When the baby discovers that he or she can get into an upright position, the cerebellum (the part of the brain responsible for coordinating voluntary muscular activity) has to analyze new instructions coming from the balance centers in the brain stem. Walking is another new skill to learn, requiring many attempts during which the cerebellum cooperates with the motor area to develop efficient messages to send to the muscles.

The separate parts of each action learned in this way are preprogrammed into the spinal cord, but they must form a coherent pattern to produce a coordinated movement, in the same way that an orchestra must have a conductor before it can produce a tuneful sound from all its instruments. Once these "simple" skills have been perfected, the brain has been programmed so that no concentration is necessary—the premotor area says "walk," and the right set of instructions go into action to produce the complicated mechanical actions that are involved. The cerebellum monitors the progress of the action, but this is less and less a conscious event. If a "problem" is introduced into the system, such as the change in the foot's posture caused by wearing high heels, some reprogramming is necessary, and concentration is needed while the motor cortex learns this new "tune."

Advanced coordination

In complex movements, the movement of the eyes is coordinated with the visual receptive centers of the brain and then with the movement of the rest of the body. This coordination is the last to mature. It forms the basis for learning the type of complex movements that are needed in sports or in skills such as playing a musical instrument.

Some brains seem better equipped from birth to develop in particular ways. However, to a large extent, abilities in complex types of coordination depend on how much the individual can concentrate to build up these "programs."

Cornea

The cornea—the eye's main lens—is the shining, transparent bulge at the front of the eye. If it is scarred or damaged, sight is impaired, but a graft operation from a donor eye can sometimes be performed to improve vision.

Q My father has to have an eye graft. Will it be painful?

A The eye may feel a little bruised after the operation, but there is almost never more than mild discomfort. Taking out the sutures (stitches) involves an overnight stay in the hospital—the procedure, lasting about half an hour, is performed under a local or general anesthetic. The eye may be sore, but usually the patient is too happy with the improved sight to notice any discomfort.

Q Will my eye look different in shape or color if I have an eye graft?

A If the eye needing the graft is scarred, a white area will show up on the cornea. After a successful graft, your eye will look much more normal than before, since the operation will bring back the color of the iris. The scar from the eye graft operation is only visible at very close range.

Q Can I become a donor for corneal grafting?

A Anyone can become a donor, so long as their eyes are free from disease or injury. Contact your nearest eye hospital and tell them—they will be delighted. Don't forget to tell your doctor and your nearest relatives of your intentions.

Q How can I best take care of the corneas of my eyes to keep them clean and functioning well?

A Ideally, let nature do the work. The tears contain a natural antiseptic, which can be washed away by eye baths. Do not use drops or put anything in the eye unless the doctor prescribes it. If you get grit in your eye, wash it with a mild salt and water solution.

Q I have heard that a disease of the cornea can cause blindness. Is this true?

A Unfortunately, yes. A viral infection, trachoma, is still very common in underdeveloped countries, and this can cause blindness, even in children.

The cornea forms the powerful, fixed-focus lens of the eye. The optical power of the cornea accounts for about two-thirds of the total eye power. Yet the cornea measures only 0.02 in (0.5 mm) thick at the center and 0.04 in (1 mm) thick where it joins the white of the eye, the sclera.

Structure of the cornea

The cornea consists of five layers. On the outside is a five-cell layer called the epithelium, which corresponds to the surface skin. Underneath this is an elastic, fiberlike layer called Bowman's layer. Next comes the tough stromal layer, made up of a protein called collagen. This stromal layer is the thickest part. The stroma contains various infection-fighting antigens that help to keep the cornea free from infection. It is also thought to help control inflammation in the cornea.

After the stroma comes a layer called the endothelium, which is only one cell thick. This thin layer keeps the cornea transparent and maintains a balance of water flow from the eye to the cornea. Once formed, the cells of this layer cannot regenerate, and so injury or disease to the endothelium can cause permanent damage to sight. The final layer, called Descemet's membrane, is an elastic one.

The epithelium is covered by a tear film. Without tears the cornea would have no protection against bacterial microorganisms, pollution, or dust. The tear film is also essential for vision, because without tears the epithelium would lose its transparency and become opaque.

Corneal grafting

This operation is done on diseased or injured corneas where the central portion is scarred or the curvature is deformed. Where the cornea is deformed, there is a thinning of the cornea, eventually forming an irregular cone shape.

The eye to be treated has a disc cut out from the cornea, removing the diseased area or scar tissue. Most corneal grafts done to restore sight are around 0.35 in (9 mm) in diameter. There are two procedures. One is to cut the full thickness of the cornea. Only part is cut in the other procedure. The latter operation, which is called a lamellar graft, is usually done to replace diseased surface tissues, when the deeper tissues are still in good shape.

The donor eye has a similar-sized disc cut from it, and this is placed in position over the living eye. The graft is sewn into place using an operation microscope and fine nylon or collagen thread mounted on a curved needle 0.16 in (4 mm) long.

In most instances the patient is allowed to leave the hospital within a few days, and many notice an improvement in their sight, even in this short time. If the graft starts to be rejected, then anti-inflammatory drugs are used, and in many cases the graft survives.

The stitches will be removed several months later, and then, provided that the graft is clear, the sight is corrected by glasses or contact lenses. At this point, if the operation has gone well, the patient should notice a great improvement in his or her sight. The graft will leave only a faint scar.

Before a corneal graft operation, the diseased cornea has lost its transparent quality, affecting the focus of the eye.

The same eye five weeks later. Note the very fine, zigzag line, holding the clear grafted cornea in place.

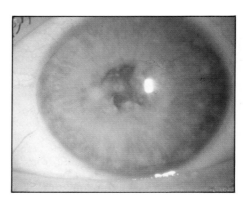

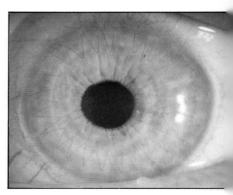

Corns

Q Why do corns ache if they are just dead skin?

A Microscopic sections of corns show there is an area of mild inflammation in the skin below the corn. Corns will ache if pressed, because the hard corn is applying pressure to the soft tissue.

Q I have very soft skin. Is there anything I can do to prevent blisters and corns on a hiking vacation?

A The best protection is to make sure you have a pair of very comfortable walking shoes and soft, woolen socks. If the shoes are new, be sure to walk several miles in them before going on a really long trek. Sometimes soaking the skin with rubbing alcohol helps to harden up areas that might blister, but if you are susceptible to corns, this should not be done, since it may encourage them.

Q The skin on my feet is hard and thick. What can I do to prevent it from becoming painful?

A Aside from making sure your shoes fit properly, you should pare the hard skin on your feet down to a minimum, since a hard area of corny skin will produce a blister beneath it if the rubbing or friction is severe enough.

Q Can corns turn malignant and become cancerous?

A This is so rare that it is virtually impossible. Although skin cell formation increases in corns, this is never malignant. A corn that bleeds, spreads unduly, or does not behave like other corns is probably not a corn and should be seen by a doctor.

Q I once picked at a corn that was over my bunion, and a plug came out. Should I have left it alone?

A In rare cases a corn may become infected and a small abscess may develop. This can happen when a dirty instrument is used to pare dead skin. In your case you probably picked at skin containing the plug of an abscess.

Corns are so common that most people have them at some time in their lives. They can usually be treated at home or, if severe, by a podiatrist.

A corn is a localized area of hard, horny skin that has formed as a result of repeated rubbing or pressure. Dead skin cells build up and create a thickening of the keratin (protein) in the skin. As this piles up, the deeper skin cells underneath become inflamed, causing pain and discomfort. There is only one type of corn, although those that are very large are usually called calluses.

Causes

Corns are likely to occur whenever there is excessive wear on the skin. Manual laborers and barefoot walkers develop pads of hard skin that are quite normal, never painful, and, therefore, not true corns. In other people, such as violinists (who are continually rubbing their chins against wood) and those wearing a new pair of tight shoes, pads of skin may form at the site of the rubbing, causing considerable pain. These are true corns.

Badly fitting shoes and high heels tend to cause corns. The most common sites are on the ball of the foot, the sides of the toes between the joints, and sometimes on the heel.

Corns frequently form over bunions, although there is no special association between the two. The reason is simply that the bunion, being a swelling on a prominent bone, presses against the side of footwear, causing pressure.

Corns invariably appear over the bony prominences, where the hard skin protects delicate structures underneath. Some people are more susceptible to corns than others; this is particularly true of the elderly.

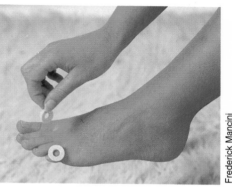

Frederick Mancini

Corn plasters (top) contain an acid that softens the hard skin so that it can be removed more easily. Corn pads (bottom) can be used to protect corns from rubbing.

Calluses can also develop where artificial limbs or appliances rub on the skin. They are a normal response to excessive wear. In some cases they can be useful, because they take the brunt of pressure and impact and protect the skin; but occasionally they may become uncomfortable and need trimming.

Symptoms

A corn can be recognized as an area of hardened, thickened skin that often looks yellow in comparison to the surrounding skin. It can be conical in shape. Corns between the toes can be soft.

Corns may first be noticed because they cause aching at the end of the day or because they feel tender under pressure. When chronic or severe, the surrounding area may be slightly red, and the corn may be extremely painful, even when the patient is at rest.

Symptoms vary considerably, and it is sometimes difficult to tell a corn from a verruca (plantar wart). In general,

---

Section through a corn

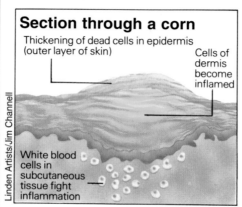

Thickening of dead cells in epidermis (outer layer of skin)

Cells of dermis become inflamed

White blood cells in subcutaneous tissue fight inflammation

Linden Artists/Jim Channell

A corn is an area of hard, thick skin, underneath which the skin cells have become inflamed.

Causes and treatment of corns

Type of corn	Cause	Treatment
Simple corn (on ball of foot, on side of toes between joints, on heel)	Excessive pressure on the skin. Occurs primarily through wearing tight shoes, but corns can also appear where there is a wearing away of the skin over a bone	**Remedial action:** Wear soft, good-fitting shoes with pads or arch supports on areas likely to rub
		Self-treatment: Small corns: Soak in warm water, and rub pumice stone over corn
		Well-developed corns: Gently pare off skin with a clean scraper or corn-paring knife. Or apply a corn plaster containing a chemical softener directly over corn; leave for 24 hours; lift off corn with pumice stone or corn-paring knife. Or pad corn with a ring of foam rubber surrounding the corn
		Treatment by a podiatrist: People suffering from persistent corns, or those with arthritis or who suffer from diabetes or circulatory disorders, should consult a podiatrist
Calluses	Same as above, only calluses are larger and can arise when artificial limbs or appliances rub on the skin	Same as above. The best remedy for calluses is to alleviate the cause of the rubbing
Corn on bunion	Bone of bunion pressing against the side of footwear	Same as above. The best form of treatment is to have the bunion removed surgically

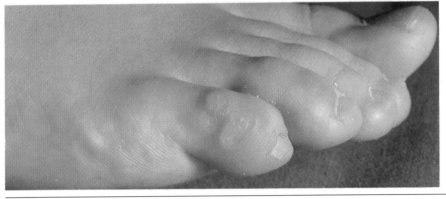

verrucae are initially small and painful under pressure. When the top skin is rubbed off, tiny black roots will appear as dots; the area may then look like a wart.

Dangers

Corns are uncomfortable and painful, but only rarely dangerous. The chief danger of corns is that, as the skin is pared off as part of treatment, infection may occur due to the use of unclean instruments. For this reason it is important to pare a corn very carefully.

This is especially necessary on the foot of a diabetic, who is likely to have poor circulation and in whom any infection can so easily turn gangrenous. Treatment is best undertaken by a qualified podiatrist (chiropodist or foot specialist).

Treatment

Because corns are merely made up of hard skin, they can usually be treated by removing the excess skin. After a good soaking in the bathtub, a pumice stone should be rubbed over the corn. This is enough to keep some people's corns at bay. For more well-developed corns, scraping off the skin with a scraper or paring the corn with a safety knife is often necessary.

The tools used should be kept scrupulously clean. The fine slivers of dead skin should be removed until soft, pliable skin is felt beneath the corn. Care should be taken not to pare away too much skin:

this could cause bleeding or introduce infection. Other tools may also be used to remove corns, including a clean file or an emery board.

Corn plasters work by removing the skin by softening it with chemicals: a 40 percent salicylic acid solution is soaked onto a plaster. The plaster should be applied directly over the corn and left for 24 hours. The skin should then be lifted

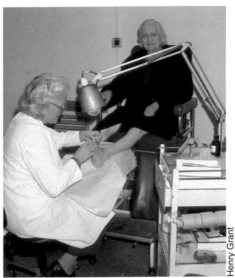

A podiatrist should be seen if there are recurring corns over the bones of the feet or between the toes.

Henry Grant

off with a pumice stone or corn grater. If the corn persists, further applications of the plaster may be used.

Some older people become so accustomed to tolerating their corns that they cease to take care of them, simply padding them so that they are not as painful. A variety of products are available for this purpose, the simplest being a ring of foam rubber on a sticky base with a hole in the middle.

Calluses can also be treated by applying a special solution containing salicylic acid on a plaster and then paring down the callus.

It is essential that diabetics and those suffering from circulatory disorders have regular professional podiatry (chiropody) to minimize the risk of infection.

Outlook

An isolated corn that has occurred because of a change of footwear or activity can usually be treated easily and should not recur. Calluses tend to need regular, permanent attention and will only disappear if the cause is removed.

Recurrent corns over the bones of the foot or between the toes will require regular, professional treatment. Wearing correct footwear can sometimes help, but such corns tend to be chronic.

Pain and aching should never be accepted as part of having corns: corns can usually be treated, although they do tend to recur.

Coronary arteries and thrombosis

What actually happens when someone experiences a coronary thrombosis—in other words, a heart attack? And what are their chances of leading an active life again? Advances in medicine can do much to help sufferers, but prevention is always better than treatment.

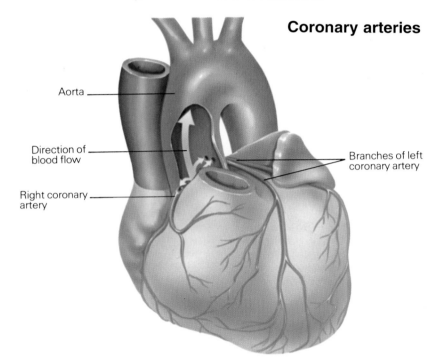

Coronary arteries

Aorta

Direction of blood flow

Right coronary artery

Branches of left coronary artery

Advertising Arts

The coronary arteries are the vessels that supply blood to the heart itself. They are particularly prone to partial or total obstruction by atheroma—the process of fatty buildup that is caused by many factors, but principally by excessive stress, sedentary living, smoking, and an unhealthy diet. Obstructed coronary arteries are the cause of heart attacks; and disease of the coronary arteries is the most common cause of death in the majority of Western countries.

The three arteries
The heart (see Heart) is a muscular bag that pumps blood around the body. Like any muscle, it has to be supplied with oxygen and food to continue working. This supply is carried in the right and left coronary arteries, which are the first vessels to leave the aorta (the body's main artery) as it emerges from the heart.

Almost as soon as it branches off the aorta, the left coronary artery splits into two big branches. So there are, in effect, three coronary arteries: the right plus the two branches of the left. They go on to completely surround and penetrate the heart, supplying blood to every part of it.

The coronary arteries supply the heart muscle with oxygen and nutrients. There are essentially three main arteries—the two branches of the left coronary artery, and the right coronary artery.

The coronary arteries are particularly affected by the disease because, like the heart itself, they are always in motion and the resulting strain on their walls hastens the buildup of atheroma.

Except in a tiny proportion of cases, the disease process is always the same. Fatty deposits build up on the wall of the artery, narrowing the whole artery and creating the risk of a total blockage.

Heart attack
If a coronary artery becomes completely blocked, the blood supply to an area of heart muscle is shut off. There is an intense, heavy pain, often lasting for hours or even days, and described by the patient as resembling a viselike grip. There is also shortness of breath, cold sweat, palpitations of the heart, and the patient looks very pale. Eighty-five percent of those who have a heart attack recover, but in some patients there is

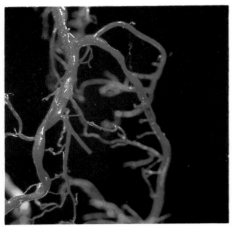

John Watney

Heart attacks are caused by blocked coronary arteries like the ones shown here.

obstruction. A heart attack is therefore often referred to as a coronary thrombosis or a coronary for short.

Angina

The other problem caused by coronary artery disease is angina. In this case there is a partial block that allows the heart to function normally at rest but does not allow the extra blood flow necessary in response to exercise. In some patients the pain of angina is caused by intense spasm of the coronary arteries rather than actual physical blockage. This type of pain manifests itself at rest rather than during periods of exercise.

This relative lack of blood flow produces pain. The typical type of angina chest pain spreads to the arms, shoulders, or neck. It is usually brought on by exertion or excitement and lasts only a few minutes. Patients who have angina may develop a full-blown heart attack, and, conversely, patients who have had a heart attack may get attacks of angina.

Treatment

Angina can be a crippling disease, even when the patient has not suffered a heart attack. At his or her worst, the patient

another, sometimes disastrous, attack in the first hour. After the attack, the area of heart that was affected eventually heals into a scar. That particular part of the heart muscle will never work again. But with careful treatment the patient will, in most cases, be able to lead a healthy, active life once more.

The blockage itself usually comes about as a result of what is known as a thrombosis (blood clot). The artery, narrowed by atheroma, restricts the flow of blood to such a slow pace that its natural tendency to clot or thicken begins to operate. This clot makes the final

may not be able to move more than a few yards without pain. Fortunately modern drug treatments that temporarily widen the coronary arteries are now available.

Patients can carry these drugs with them. When slipped under the tongue, they quickly stop attacks but are not very good at preventing them, because their effect only lasts for a few minutes.

Beta blockers, however, have been a more lasting treatment for angina since their development in the mid-1960s—a great medical advance. These drugs block some of the effects (the so-called beta effects) of adrenaline. In doing so they also reduce the amount of work the heart has to do and, therefore, its need for oxygen. Taken regularly, not just when there is pain, they reduce the number of angina attacks and help prevent heart attacks.

For people who cannot take beta blockers because they suffer from asthma, there is an alternative treatment with calcium channel blockers, which interfere with the movement of calcium (see Calcium) through cells to help reduce the work load on the heart.

Surgery

There have recently been considerable advances in surgery for the treatment of coronary artery disease. In bypass grafting, the surgeon removes a length of vein

Symptoms of heart attack and angina

	Heart attack	Angina
Type of pain	Dull, crushing, or heavy pain, "a tight band around the chest." Patient often describes the pain by clenching a fist. A sure sign is that nitrate drugs will not relieve the pain, as they do the pain of angina	May be heavy or dull pain, or may be sharp
How long the pain lasts	More than half an hour, often much longer	Minutes only
What brings it on	May come on at rest or during sleep, but may be precipitated by exertion, excitement, or a heavy meal	Almost always brought on by exertion or excitement, but also by sudden exposure to extreme cold
What stops it	Usually nothing	Stopping the exertion; glyceryl trinitrate or trinitrin under the tongue
Sweating	Usual	Rare
Nausea or vomiting	Usual	Rare
Breathlessness	Common	Uncommon
What the patient looks like	Often very ill with grayish skin	Most patients know they have angina and may not give any signs of pain or distress

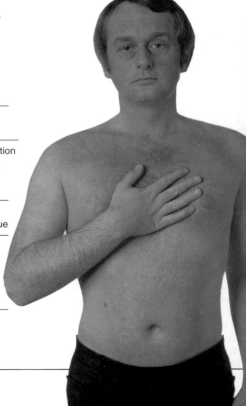

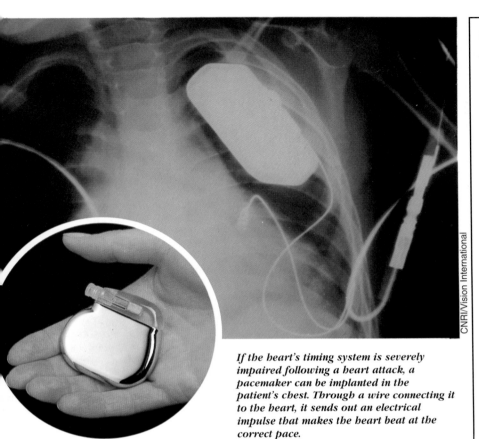

CNRI/Vision International

If the heart's timing system is severely impaired following a heart attack, a pacemaker can be implanted in the patient's chest. Through a wire connecting it to the heart, it sends out an electrical impulse that makes the heart beat at the correct pace.

from the leg and uses it to connect the diseased blood vessel directly to the aorta so that blood bypasses the obstruction. Successful bypass grafting depends upon very sophisticated surgical techniques. The joins must be able to withstand high pressures, and the blood vessels are only a few millimeters wide. There is no doubt that such surgery can be effective at relieving angina pains. It is also possible to attach an artery from the chest wall to the blocked artery.

Treatment problems

The reason why blood flow in coronary arteries becomes obstructed is still being extensively investigated. But one fact seems clear: blockage nearly always occurs when there is atheroma.

Death from heart attacks occurs for two basic reasons. First, the death of an area of heart muscle, caused by the blocked artery, causes a major disturbance of heart rhythm, which reduces the efficiency of the heart so severely that it may stop working.

Second, if too much heart muscle is destroyed, the heart is simply not powerful enough to pump an adequate amount of blood around the body. In contrast, relatively minor disturbances of heart rhythm—known as arrhythmias—can usually be treated with drugs or by giving

electrical shocks. If the timing sequence becomes totally interrupted, however, and the heart slows or even stops—known as a heart block—it may be necessary to use a pacing system.

A wire is passed into a vein and threaded in the direction of the blood flow, until it becomes lodged against the wall of the heart. The other end of the wire is connected to a pacemaker implanted in the chest. This sends out a regular, electric impulse that drives the heart at the correct speed.

Recovery

After one or two days in a coronary care unit, heart attack patients usually spend about ten days to two weeks in the hospital. During this time they gradually regain their strength and resume normal activities as much as possible.

After leaving the hospital and returning home for a period of recuperation, most people can go back to work within two or three months of a heart attack. In general, patients are encouraged to resume an active, and in every way, normal life. There is no need for family and friends or the patient him- or herself to protect the heart as though it were a permanent invalid, since a lack of exercise was probably a major cause of the heart attack in the first place.

Preventing coronary disease

- **Exercise regularly:** swimming, walking, or jogging are ideal, but don't suddenly start doing vigorous exercise if you have been sedentary for a long time. Build up gradually, and if in doubt, ask your doctor's advice. When you exercise, think about the exercise, not personal or work problems. If you are forced to sit at a desk all day, walk as much as possible instead of driving; take the stairs, not the elevator; and seek medical advice about an exercise progam that can be done at your desk

- **Eat a sensible diet:** cut down on potentially harmful substances such as animal fats. Replace butter with certain types of margarine and use, say, sunflower or corn oil for cooking. Cut down on sugar and starch, and avoid large, heavy meals

- **Reduce mental stress:** stress is part of living, but the body is not designed to put up with it constantly—so slow down!

Coronary disease—are you at risk?

- **Smoker?** Ten cigarettes a day doubles your chances of a coronary, because nicotine in the bloodstream causes the arteries to go into spasm, thus narrowing them and making thrombosis more likely

- **Overweight?** Anyone more than 20 or 30 percent above the proper body weight for their age, height, and sex is two to three times more prone to heart disease than a person of average weight

- **Stress?** If you have been under work or family pressures for a long time, a coronary is a definite risk

- **Desk-bound?** People in desk jobs who do not exercise are certainly more at risk than active people.

- **High cholesterol level?** If you eat large amounts, especially of dairy foods or animal fat, you are at risk and should adjust your diet

- **Family history?** If heart disease runs in the family, make sure you exercise and eat a healthy diet

Cosmetic surgery

Q I've been saving up to have the bags under my eyes removed, and I finally have enough money to pay for cosmetic surgery. Where should I look for a reliable surgeon?

A The best way to find a surgeon is to get a recommendation from someone who has had successful surgery. Alternatively your regular doctor may be able to recommend one. Check with the American Board of Plastic Surgery to make sure that any specialist you go to is trained and accredited in this area—not all surgeons offering cosmetic work are.

Q I've tried dieting without much success, and I'm tempted by the idea of liposuction. Is it the answer to my weight problem?

A If you are generally overweight, liposuction will not solve your problem. It works best on limited pockets of fat that do not respond to dieting. Lipectomy can yield better results in remodeling your body, but it's not an alternative to eating less. Try to get down to your ideal weight first, because losing or gaining pounds afterward will distort the results of lipectomy. And surgery will not give you the health benefits of diet and exercise.

Q I'm planning to have my breasts enlarged, but a friend told me that silicon implants can cause breast cancer. Is this true?

A The silicon gel filling of older implants sometimes breaks down and leaks out. It has been claimed that this can lead to autoimmune diseases, where the body is attacked by its own defense system, but this has not been proved. This may be what your friend is thinking of. In any case, the Food and Drug Administration banned these implants for use in cosmetic surgery in the United States in 1992 (they are still allowed in reconstructive surgery). Implants used now are filled with harmless saline solution. Neither type of implant has been shown to increase the risk of breast cancer.

Not all operations are performed on medical grounds: some perfectly healthy people choose to undergo cosmetic surgery to make their appearance more attractive.

Cosmetic surgery is a branch of plastic surgery that is carried out to change the shape of the body or to reconstruct or repair soft tissue. Cosmetic operations can have psychological benefits by improving the patient's body image and self-esteem and may also have some medical benefit, even if this is not the main reason for the treatment.

Cases for treatment

A badly shaped nose, or one that is too big or too small, can be improved with rhinoplasty—a nose job—which involves reshaping the nasal bone and sometimes the cartilage, the stiff tissue at the end of the nose. Rhinoplasty can be done on cosmetic grounds and also to correct breathing problems caused by a broken nose or misshapen cartilage between the nostrils. Less common is surgery to build up cheekbones or to alter a weak or oversized chin or jaw; the latter is sometimes performed together with orthodontic work to correct badly aligned teeth.

Rhytidectomy—better known as a facelift—is used to tighten the skin of the face when it starts to sag and wrinkle and may also involve reducing a double chin. Puffy eyelids and bags under the eyes are corrected by blepharoplasty, sometimes called an eyelid-lift. Eyelid surgery is also done to lift drooping upper lids that can interfere with normal eyesight.

Ears that stick out, either because the middle part of the ear is too big or because the upper fold is badly formed, can be pinned back by otoplasty. This is a common operation and is usually a straightforward procedure.

Skin scarred by acne, or disfigured by stretch marks or birthmarks, can be treated by dermabrasion, which rubs away the top layers of skin, or by chemosurgery (also called chemical peels), which dissolves the surface layers with a form of acid. Thread veins or spider veins—harmless red marks caused by blocked capillaries near the surface of the skin—can be treated with laser therapy or sclerotherapy. Both treatments close off the veins, which then shrivel up.

Synthetic implants can be used to reconstruct breasts that are considered too small or are misshapen after injury or surgery for breast cancer. Breast reduction is sometimes done to relieve back and shoulder pain or breathing problems, as well as for purely cosmetic reasons. Mastoplexy—an operation that lifts drooping breasts—is sometimes done when the breasts are reduced or enlarged.

Removing fat

People with areas of fat that remain even after they have lost weight can have liposuction, a technique used to remove fat by suction through a special tube. Fat concentrated in large areas such as the stomach, for example, can be removed by lipectomy, a more serious operation. This involves surgery to remove the fat and cut down and tighten the excess skin left behind. A similar operation may be performed to reduce bags of skin left after rapid, extensive weight loss.

What is involved

Cosmetic operations may involve cutting and repairing flaps of skin and muscle; grafting an area of skin from another part of the body; removing or implanting cartilage, bone, or tissue; or implanting a synthetic substance. They range from relatively simple treatments done on an outpatient basis to major surgery requiring weeks of convalescence.

Because there are always potential problems with any kind of operation, anyone considering cosmetic surgery should consider the pros and cons carefully. The surgeon should take time to discuss exactly what the operation involves, including the hazards and recovery time, and should find out if the prospective patient has any health problems that could increase the risks. It is important that the cosmetic surgeon should not

In a delicate cosmetic operation, a laser beam is used to remove superficial blood vessels around the nose.

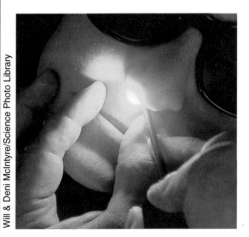

Will & Deni McIntyre/Science Photo Library

encourage unrealistic expectations of miracle improvements. Sometimes the patient can be shown a computerized image that gives an impression of what they will look like after surgery—for example, with a face-lift—but this must not be taken as an exact guide.

Even simple surgical procedures can produce swelling and a bruised look for several days around the area treated; serious surgery requires weeks to recover.

Surgical procedures

Rhinoplasty may be done under general or local anesthetic. The surgeon makes an incision, usually from inside the nostrils to avoid leaving obvious scars, separates the bone and cartilage that give the nose its shape from the tissue holding it together, and breaks the bone so that it can be set in a different shape. The cartilage may also be cut or shaved, or cartilage or bone from another part of the body may be implanted. Occasionally a synthetic implant is used. After the operation, the nose is stuffed with gauze, and may also be held in shape with a splint for a week or two.

Breast enlargement may be done under general anesthetic, but often needs no overnight hospital stay. A small incision is made, either under the breast, in the armpit, or around the outside of the nipple. This enables the surgeon to insert an implant, or prosthesis, made of a synthetic pouch containing saline or silicon solution. This is tucked behind the breast tissue and muscles, pushing the tissue outward to make the breasts larger. The breasts may be sore and bruised-looking for a while after the operation, and there may be some loss of normal feeling—but this usually recovers after healing. Breast-feeding should not be affected.

Breast reduction is a more complicated and more drastic operation than enlargement. An incision like an upside-down "T" is made from the nipple downward and along the underside of the breast, and breast tissue is then cut away.

In some cases the nipple and the areola, the dark ring around it, stay attached to the underlying tissue and are put back higher up on the breast; in other cases, a special skin graft is used in place of the nipple and areola.

The patient will usually need to stay in the hospital overnight and will take several weeks to recover. She will not be able to breast-feed afterward if the nipple has been removed during the course of the operation.

A surgical team performs a cosmetic operation to reduce and tighten up the surplus skin on the patient's eyelids. Bags under the eyes can also be reduced.

Lipectomy to remove large areas of fat is another serious operation that usually needs at least an overnight stay in the hospital, and a convalescence period of several weeks.

One or more incisions are made where the fat needs to be removed so that the skin and fat can be loosened. Then the fat is taken out, and any excess folds of skin are cut away. Sometimes, as with abdominal lipectomy—a stomach tuck—the underlying muscle is also tightened with stitches. The skin and tissues are then sewn back together, leaving tighter skin and a slimmer shape.

Liposuction, which works on smaller areas of fat, is less severe and is often done on an outpatient basis. A small incision is made so that a tube called a cannula can be inserted into the layer of fat and tissue between the skin and the muscle. Fat cells and liquefied fat are sucked out through the cannula, which is then inserted through other incisions around the area, until the fat has been evenly reduced. The incisions are sewn up and the area is covered with a tight dressing to reduce bruising. Liposuction is sometimes performed with a lipectomy and may also be done as part of a face lift.

Face-lifts

Face-lifts vary greatly, but in the basic technique the surgeon makes an incision at each side of the face, loosens the skin and fat from the muscles beneath, and trims away superfluous fat before pulling up and stitching the skin to leave a tauter surface. A face-lift may include a forehead, or coronal, lift, involving an incision under the hairline and an incision under the chin to reduce a double chin.

Risks of cosmetic surgery

Some types of cosmetic surgery are more complex and serious than others and therefore have more potential complications. All operations, however, involve some pain and the risk of bleeding, scarring, and nerve damage—causing short- or long-term damage to feeling and responses in the skin or muscles—as well as the dangers associated with anesthesia. Smokers and people with diabetes may be advised to avoid some forms of surgery because of the increased risk of circulation problems.

Infection is a particular risk where artificial implants are used, and antibiotics are usually prescribed to counter this. Another problem with synthetic implants is that they do not generally wear as well as the human body and may need to be replaced after several years. Operations to tighten skin and muscle will not last a lifetime either—facial skin and breasts will eventually sag thanks to natural loss of elasticity and the action of gravity.

The other main risk is that of disappointment, sometimes because people hope for too much. While some people who are self-conscious about a particular aspect of their appearance—a hooked nose or large breasts—find their confidence boosted after successful cosmetic surgery, others may be disappointed to find that reshaping their body has not solved broader personal problems.

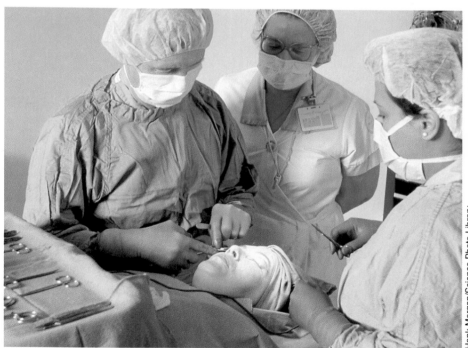

Hank Morgan/Science Photo Library

Cosmetics

Q My 13-year-old daughter is already using creams on her face. Won't this be damaging to her skin?

A Skin on younger people is easier to care for than the skin of older people, and creams are not usually necessary. Your daughter's skin is unlikely to be so dry that it needs a cream to soften it, and it will only benefit from the protection of a moisturizer when exposed to extreme weather conditions. If she uses a cream that is too heavy or applies it in the wrong way, she may damage the tissue. This would cause extra lines and wrinkles as she gets older.

Q I've started making my own beauty preparations, but they don't seem to last long. What am I doing wrong?

A Homemade beauty preparations, though often very effective, do not contain the preservatives found in manufactured cosmetics. You should make only small quantities of these at a time, and store them in the refrigerator.

Q My mother is in her 4Os, and her skin is very dry and developing a lot of lines. What is the best treatment for this?

A She should protect and lubricate her skin day and night with a rich moisturizing cream. This will make the lines less noticeable, although it will not slow down the rate at which they appear. At night she can use a special eye cream around the eye area. Cleansing with a rich cream cleanser should be followed by a freshener or diluted toner. The most important thing is to avoid long exposure to strong sunlight.

Q I have a young family and cannot afford to spend money on expensive creams, but I do want to take care of my skin. What do you suggest?

A Petroleum jelly, vegetable oil, and liquid paraffin are all effective weather barriers and will soften and smooth the skin in the same way as any other moisturizer.

The way cosmetics are applied is as important as choosing the right ones for a person's skin type. In addition, skillfully used makeup can disguise defects, such as scars and birthmarks, on both men and women.

Modern cosmetics are generally problem free, for there are strict controls on ingredients, labeling, and safety tests. Provided they are applied in the correct way, they can have a dramatic effect on the way a person looks and feels. Skin-care products form a large part of the cosmetics market and can be divided into two main categories: cleansers and moisturizers.

The importance of cleansing

Cleansing is the most important treatment for the skin, and there are products to cater to every skin type and need. Some people like to use cleansing lotions or creams, while others prefer plain soap and water.

So long as a gentle complexion soap is used, soap and water does not harm the skin. Makeup, however, must be removed with a cleanser. The face should not be cleansed more than twice a day.

Special cleansers

Many products are specially formulated to have a chemical affinity to the skin. When the face is cleansed with ordinary soap, it can take hours for it to return to its natural, slightly acidic state. But using a pH- or acid-balanced product means the skin will remain in this state even while being cleansed. Some cleansing products are medicated, but they should only be used with a doctor's advice, because their anti-bacterial agents can irritate.

Toning the skin

All cleansing lotions and creams tend to leave a filmy residue on the skin, so a toning lotion should be used afterward. These will remove the residue and also "plump up" the skin cells temporarily.

Toners are perfectly safe provided that the one used is of the strength appropriate to a person's skin type. Toners called fresheners are the mildest and they are suitable for dry skin, while astringents contain the most alcohol and are only suitable for oily skin.

Deep cleansing

One of the best cosmetics for cleansing deep down in the pores is the face pack or mask. Made of a sticky substance such as clay, rubber, or wax, it is applied to the skin, then either rinsed or peeled off.

1 Eye makeup should always be removed at night. A special eye makeup remover is best because it is designed to shift the most stubborn makeup, yet still treat this delicate area gently. Always use quick, light movements.

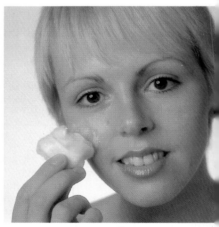

2 The rest of your makeup should also be removed, or pores will become blocked, leading to spots or even infection. Use either a makeup remover followed by soap and water, or a lotion or cream that cleanses as it removes the makeup. Use the same movements as for applying moisturizer (step 4).

The fresh, glowing look that masks produce is only temporary, but they are beneficial for cleaning out clogged-up pores. The peel-off types must be removed gently, and all face packs should be kept clear of the delicate eye area.

Moisture barrier

There are a vast range of moisturizers on the skin-care market, from the lightest lotions to the heaviest night creams. Their main contribution is to help seal in the skin's all-important moisture. Oily skin needs less help with this, since its oil content provides a natural moisture seal. But as a person grows older, the skin becomes drier and less efficient at keeping moisture in, and this is when moisturizers become useful.

Eternal youth

Some moisturizers are believed to keep the skin looking young by attracting moisture from the atmosphere; others contain supposedly rejuvenating ingredients, such as collagen (a protein substance that makes up the under layer of skin) and vitamin E. But there is little evidence to indicate that these additives have any substantial effect.

Handle with care

Many women believe that the more moisturizer they apply, the more they are keeping the wrinkles at bay. But wrinkles begin deep down in the skin and using more than a thin film of moisturizer can

Image Bank

If it is skillfully applied, makeup can disguise problem areas and enhance your best features for a glowing appearance.

damage this layer by its sheer weight. The key to preventing wrinkles lies in avoiding long exposure to intense sun and using protection if exposure is unavoidable. Also be careful when using cleansers and moisturizers; applying them too vigorously or with downward movements may strain facial muscles and result in extra lines.

Using makeup

While makeup does not actually do the skin any good, most of it does not do any harm either. There is no denying the psychological boost that makeup can give. Skillfully used, it can minimize or hide problems and highlight good features. Foundations and cover sticks are effective in covering red veins, pimples, and under-eye shadows, and can even improve skin tones. Green powder will tone down very red coloring.

Most skin troubles are caused not by the cosmetic itself, but by poor hygiene. Keep brushes very clean, and do not lend makeup to other people to use. Never spit on shadows or lick eye pencils, for this can lead to infection.

Caring for eyes

Eyeliner worn on the rim of the lower lid often leads to infection and is not advisable. Failing to remove eye makeup, especially mascara, each night can clog up the hair follicles, leading to infection. Always use quick, gentle movements in the eye area, whether applying or removing eye makeup. This tissue is delicate and extra wrinkles are easily created.

Allergies

If redness, itching, or swelling occurs, an allergy to one of the dyes, scents, or other ingredients is possible. Try a different brand or hypoallergenic cosmetics, which are free of the ingredients that most commonly cause allergic reactions.

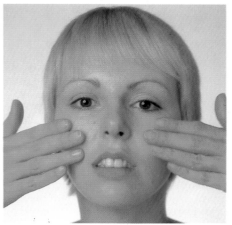

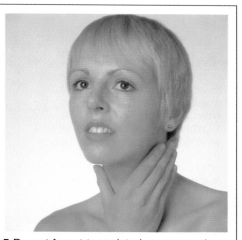

Frederick Mancini

If you have cleansed with a lotion or cream, you will need to follow it with toning lotion, which gives skin a tingly, fresh feeling and removes the residue left by the cleanser. It can also be used after soap and water but is not strictly necessary.

4 Moisturizer should be applied morning and night if your skin tends to be dry. Always use gentle, upward movements. Massage the cream in quickly and lightly, starting at the chin and moving up across the cheeks to the ears; then from the nose to the temples; and then across the forehead. Treat the eye area even more gently.

5 Do not forget to moisturize your neck and throat too, using long strokes from the collarbone to the jaw. In addition to being exposed to the elements, this area has a natural tendency to dry up. If neglected, it will be one of the first areas to show signs of age.

Cough syrup

Q I have some cough syrup left over from when one of the family had a cough a few months ago. Do you think it is still safe to use?

A It is unlikely to do any harm. However, it is best to buy a new bottle, checking the expiry date, since the mixture will be fresher. As a general rule, you should throw away any medicines left over after an illness.

Q Is taking a honey and lemon mixture as good as taking a proprietary cough medicine?

A Although honey and lemon mixture is pleasant and soothing, it is doubtful whether it can have any real effect on dampening down the cough reflex, which is how cough syrups work. A medicine containing codeine or dextromethorphan would be much more effective but should only be taken on a doctor's advice.

Q Someone once told me that a cough syrup is a medicine that should be licked off a spoon. Is this the way it should be given?

A In practice a cough syrup is often licked off the spoon because it may be too thick to run easily, and half the dose would otherwise be left behind. It is worth holding a cough syrup in the mouth for a few moments before swallowing, to get the benefit of its soothing effect on the throat. Once it is swallowed, the active ingredients will be absorbed into the bloodstream.

Q Is it safe to give cough syrups to children?

A Yes, provided that you are sure that it is a cough that ought to be suppressed and that the constituents and dose of the cough syrup are safe in terms of the child's age and weight. There are many cough syrups that are specially made for children; these can be particularly helpful in dealing with a cough that is causing a child distress at night. Your doctor can advise you.

Many people incorrectly refer to any cough medicine as a cough syrup. In fact, a cough syrup is a particular type of medicine used to soothe dry, irritable coughs.

Children who are suffering from a dry, irritable cough that is causing distress and preventing sleep should be given a specially formulated cough syrup.

Cough syrups are sweet, sedative syrups, with a honey, molasses, or similar base, which suppress, or at least soothe, dry, irritable coughs. It is always wise to consult the doctor if anyone has a cough. He or she can suggest the most suitable preparation to deal with the particular symptoms exhibited.

Composition
Cough syrups come in varying strengths, depending on their active ingredients and the proportions in which they are made up. The strongest and most effective cough suppressants are morphine and methadone (physeptone), but these are only used for very severe, unremitting coughs that sometimes occur in such conditions as advanced lung cancer. Less potent, but still effective, are cough syrups made from suppressants such as codeine or dextromethorphan.

Coughing as defense mechanism
Coughing is one of the body's most effective defense mechanisms. It is designed to force unwanted material, such as phlegm, out of the lungs and air passages so that it does not interfere with breathing or spread infection in the lungs. Therefore, when a cough is productive, it can be dangerous to get rid of it with a suppressant, because although this may succeed in eliminating a cough, the heavily infected sputum will stay down in the lungs where it may do a great deal of harm. Instead, an expectorant, which helps to bring up sputum, should be used.

When to use a cough syrup
If the cough is dry and unproductive, causing pain and possibly interfering with sleep, a cough syrup should be taken. However, if this sort of dry cough arises from irritation at the back of the throat, as in pharyngitis (sore throat), then sucking a cough drop or lozenge may be more effective.

Cough syrup is usually taken in doses of two 0.34 fl oz (5 ml) teaspoonfuls, up to three times a day and at night. Weaker preparations are suitable for children.

In some cases it is often sensible to take an expectorant during the day and then a cough syrup before going to bed and again, if necessary, during the night to quiet the cough and aid sleep.

Coughs

Q A friend told me that cough medicines don't really work. Is this true?

A Cough medicines do work insofar as they can either suppress or stimulate a cough, but there is much debate about whether they are necessary. Cough syrups containing codeine or dextromethorphan will suppress a cough. Specially formulated mixtures (called expectorants) will help to dilute and loosen the mucus that has gathered in the mucous membranes of the respiratory system, making coughing easier. Hot tea with honey and lemon, or even a shot of whiskey, are similarly soothing.

Q When I had a bad cold recently, I began to cough up yellowish phlegm. What does this mean?

A Phlegm is normally white in color and indicates that the secretions of the mucous membrane are normal. If the color changes to either yellow or green, it implies that an infection has set in. Clearly this is what happened to you, but since it cleared up by itself, it could not have been serious. For more serious infections, a visit to the doctor is necessary— he or she may prescribe a short course of antibiotics.

Q Does coughing spread infection?

A Yes. Although coughing and sneezing are reflex responses to outside stimuli, such as dust or gas, they can also transmit germs if a person has a cold or any other respiratory infection. This is why it is so important to cover your nose or mouth with a handkerchief and to avoid coughing or sneezing directly onto anyone nearby.

Q Why is it that I sometimes can't control my coughing?

A Coughing is the body's way of dealing with a foreign body in the upper airways or inflammation in the trachea. It is a reflex action— the messages to and from the brain are extremely rapid and not under voluntary control.

Infection will cause one type of cough, and smoking another, or a cough may simply be a nervous reaction. How is it possible to tell the difference?

A cough is the result of an explosive current of air being driven forcibly from the chest. It forms part of a protective reflex to insure that the air passages remain free of any obstruction. As soon as the obstruction has been cleared, coughing stops. Irritation of the upper airways by noxious gases such as chlorine, or inflammation by infections, causes coughing by a similar mechanism, but in this case the coughing is persistent.

Coughing is an essential protective mechanism designed to get rid of potentially harmful substances in the lungs and air passages. Using medicines to suppress a cough may do more harm than good.

Symptoms and treatment
Coughing in itself is not a disease, though it may be indicative of some respiratory problem. The most important symptom is not the cough itself, but rather the material that is coughed up, the frequency of the coughing, and whether there is any accompanying pain.

Coughs, particularly those due to colds, are not dangerous. However, persistent, exhausting coughs—accompanied by hoarseness, pains in the chest, breathlessness, fever, fatigue, and weight loss— should always be treated by a doctor.

In adults, a dry, persistent cough without any phlegm may be an indication that the patient is suffering from pneumonia or heart disease, though an inflammation of the trachea (windpipe) or bronchi (the large air passages in the lungs) is more likely. If the cough is productive, produces sputum (phlegm), and the color of the sputum changes from white to yellow or green, this is a sign of infection, as in acute or chronic bronchitis.

In asthma without infection, the sputum is white and frothy. Bloodstained sputum may be an indication of lung cancer, pneumonia, or tuberculosis. Coughing that becomes painful can indicate the development of pleurisy (see Pleurisy) but also happens when the chest muscles are strained by persistent coughing.

In children, if a cough is initially dry and then produces mucus and there is noisy, labored breathing, then croup is likely. Coughs that are strenuous and sound more like crowing, with heavy phlegm, might indicate whooping cough.

Diagnosis is dependent on the color of the phlegm and the other accompanying symptoms. Antibiotic drugs may be given to treat certain infections; bronchodilators, which are inhaled, are usually used to relieve asthma, and surgery may be recommended if cancer is suspected. Stethoscope examination of the chest, possibly followed by an X ray, will enable the doctor to decide on the cause. Minor coughs will get better on their own.

Outlook
Many of the diseases that have coughing as a symptom are treatable. However, coughing may last for months, especially after a viral infection.

Simple cough remedies

Symptoms	Remedy
Postnasal drip (mucus dropping down from back of nose)	Ephedrine or similar drops, 3 or 4 times a day. Consult your doctor after 5 days
Inflammation of the back of the throat or larynx	Inhalations of menthol or eucalyptus vapor, several times a day
Irritating, throaty cough	Cough lozenges
Dry cough or cough interfering with sleep	Cough suppressant or syrup, in doses of 2 teaspoonfuls, up to 3 times a day and at night
Thick, sticky sputum that will not come up easily	Expectorant cough syrup, as directed on the bottle

Melvin Grey

Counseling

Q What is the difference between counseling and psychotherapy?

A Psychotherapists tend to treat more deep-seated problems than counselors, and they may need to delve into your distant past—finding out about your childhood, for instance—or your internal world, asking about your dreams and fantasies. In practice, however, there is considerable overlap between the two and many counselors use psychotherapeutic techniques. Counseling can be very short-term—perhaps only one or two, sessions to help you through a difficult time.

Q How can I be sure that nothing I say will be repeated elsewhere?

A All counselors who belong to a professional body adhere to a strict Code of Ethics. This means that everything you say in a counseling session will be treated in strict confidence. However, if a counselor discovers through a counseling session that a murder or an act of terrorism has been committed, or is being planned, they are bound to inform the police.

Q How do I go about finding a good counselor?

A Many schools, colleges, hospitals, and workplaces have counselors on the staff. Specialist bodies that deal with particular problems, such as drug and alcohol abuse, HIV/AIDS, interracial conflict, or family breakup usually have highly trained counselors. Private therapists can be found through your doctor, natural health centers, advertisements, or by personal recommendation.

Q Is a course of counseling expensive?

A Counseling through your school, college, or place of work will normally be free. Some organizations ask for voluntary contributions only, but they may suggest an appropriate amount. Fees for private counseling will vary, but the most expensive is not necessarily the best.

Counseling is a way of helping people to understand their problems and to recognize and deal with their feelings. Through attentive listening, appropriate questioning, and sometimes by providing information, counselors enable people to find their own solutions to their problems.

Counseling is simply a formal way of having someone to talk to, but often it is more effective than just talking to a friend or relative. A trained counselor is able to listen in a more detached, unbiased, and honest way than someone who is involved in an individual's life. In addition, the client has the reassurance that whatever is said is kept in complete confidence and will not be repeated.

Who it can help

An individual may feel that he or she would like to try counseling because of a specific problem in life—bullying, difficulties with other family members or the opposite sex, examination nerves—or there may be just a general feeling of dissatisfaction or unhappiness. Counselors can also help at times of crisis—death of a loved one, rape, losing a job, etc.

Short-term counseling is sometimes provided when important decisions need to be made, such as whether to undergo a specific treatment at the hospital. In such cases the counselor will have specialized knowledge to help the person explore all the options. Counseling is also sometimes recommended for physical

In a counseling session, client and counselor may sit quite close together. The counselor focuses his or her attention exclusively on the client and the client's problems.

conditions that may have a psychological origin or be caused by stress, such as back pain or eating disorders. A person can be counseled alone, with a partner or other family members, or in a group.

Choosing a counselor

When counseling is provided as a service at a college, hospital, or workplace, it is not normally possible to choose a counselor. However, for long-term counseling it will usually be necessary to find a private therapist, and it is important to find the right person.

Counselors call the people they see *clients*. Some counselors receive clients in their own homes; others have more formal premises elsewhere. Some will have a couch for the client to lie on; others, a comfortable chair to sit in. It is up to the client to decide which sort of set-up suits them best and makes them feel most relaxed. Some people prefer to keep a distance between themselves and their counselor; others prefer to be closer.

The client also needs to decide what kind of counselor they will feel most comfortable with. Should he or she be the same sex—the same race—a specialist, or someone used to dealing with more general problems?

Some counseling is done on the telephone. This is ideal for clients who want to preserve their anonymity, for people unable to travel, or when immediate support is vital—perhaps when someone is contemplating suicide (see Suicide).

Seeing a counselor

In long-term counseling, the first session is likely to be exploratory, with the client deciding whether this is someone he or she feels comfortable with, and the counselor assessing whether he or she can offer the kind of help the client needs. The client has nothing to lose at this stage by being honest and expressing any misgivings about the whole idea of counseling, about the counselor, or anything else. The client may even find that this is the beginning of the unraveling process.

Counselors are trained to recognize serious mental problems, and if they think the client needs a different kind of therapy, they will say so immediately. On the other hand, a counselor would never dismiss a client's problems or concerns as trivial. This would go against the whole ethos of counseling.

At the first session the counselor will also give the client an idea of how many sessions he or she thinks may be needed.

When things go wrong in a relationship, it can be helpful to talk to a relationship counselor, who is trained to listen to both partners impartially.

Sessions are usually weekly, and counseling may extend over a couple of weeks or a year or more. The client need not decide at the outset how long the counseling will last and sessions are usually paid for one at a time.

What counseling is like

A counselor gives the client his or her complete attention. This in itself is therapeutic—how many people have the luxury in daily life of being properly listened to? In addition, this attention is uncritical. A counselor is not there to judge clients but to help them understand themselves. When someone else really listens, the client starts listening to him- or herself.

The counselor may prompt the client with questions, if he or she feels that this is necessary. These are not the sort of questions that friends ask, which are usually motivated by curiosity, but questions designed to help the client see things more clearly. They may be questions no one has ever asked before or questions the client has never asked him- or herself. In family therapy the counselor's questions may induce family members to say things that other members of the family never knew they thought or felt.

Another technique counselors use is that of "reflecting back" to clients the things they have said or feelings they have expressed, or only hinted at. The counselor may say something like, "So, when this happens, you feel such and such, and this leads you to . . ." This not only shows that the counselor has heard and taken in what the client has said, but makes the client feel that he or she is being taken seriously and that his or her feelings have been given validity.

In the course of counseling, the client may experience strong emotions—perhaps unexpected ones—and the counselor will encourage the client to explore and release these emotions. Because the counselor is not involved in the emotions, it is safe for the client to feel them without any risk of upsetting anyone or provoking anger in them. In the case of partner and group sessions, a counselor can act as a sort of referee, turning emotional conflicts into constructive events that offer insights into the relationships. Some counselors offer physical contact at these times—holding hands or hugging, for example—but this is a matter of personal style.

The aim of counseling is to increase a client's confidence and make him or her more at ease with life in general, and to enable the client to be more in control of his or her own destiny.

What can go wrong?

Unfortunately there may be a few counselors who are not as professional as they should be. Some of the problems that might be encountered are:
- Physical contact that oversteps the bounds of what is acceptable
- Confidentiality being breached
- A counselor who tries to dominate the client—if this is happening, the client will feel worse after a session rather than better
- A counselor who spends too much time talking about him- or herself. A certain amount of self-revelation is permissible in a counselor—it shows that sympathy is felt for what the client is saying—but this should be relevant and kept to a minimum

Types of therapy

Co-counseling In co-counseling, two people work together, taking turns to be counselor and client. Both need to be trained to do this, but once trained, people can work in pairs to develop their own understanding of themselves, at the same time helping the other person

Gestalt therapy This is based on the belief that we all have an innate ability to function in a creative, positive, and healthy way but that social conditioning can harm this. The therapy uses techniques, such as reenacting arguments, to put you more in touch with your own emotions. It can be done either on your own or in a group

Person (Client)-centered therapy This form of therapy aims to help people achieve their full potential. It is based on the belief that once people understand themselves better, they will be able to find their own way out of any difficulties they may have. The therapist relies less on theories and more on following what the client seems to want. The therapy was founded by US psychologist Carl Rogers. Most counseling is based on person-centered therapy

Psychiatry The treatment of mental illness with drugs or surgery. Psychiatrists are medically trained

Psychoanalysis An intensive form of psychotherapy, often lasting several years, with several sessions a week

Psychodynamic counseling Counseling that uses psychotherapeutic techniques

Psychology The scientific study of the mind

Transactional analysis This was invented by Eric Berne, a Canadian doctor who believed that we have three ego states (ways of behaving): parent, adult, and child. Treatment aims to make people aware of which ego state they are in at any time and ultimately to express all three at once

● A counselor who wants too much social contact outside the sessions. Social contact changes the nature of the counseling relationship and is not usually a good idea.

When things go wrong
The first person a client should complain to is the counselor. Whether or not this is easy to do is in itself an indication of the health of the relationship between client and counselor. If the counselor works in an organization, such as a college, the client should discuss the problem with someone in authority. The professional organization the counselor belongs to can also be contacted. Serious offenses should be reported to the police, but it is wise in these circumstances to remember that it will be the client's word against the counselor's.

A bad experience should not be allowed to deter someone from finding another counselor. Most counselors are dedicated and skilled. However, dissatisfaction with the counselor may be a sign that the therapy is coming to an end.

Saying good-bye
The client is in charge of the course of the counseling and should always be the one to decide when to end it. Some people may need the support of a counselor all their lives, but this is highly unusual. The aim of counseling is to empower the client, not to make him or her dependent on another person, in this case the counselor. Some clinics only allow a limited number of sessions anyway. In short-term therapy the ending will be in sight all through the counseling, and every counseling session will work toward this.

Organizations such as Alcoholics Anonymous offer a form of group therapy to help with specific problems.

It is vital to finish counseling properly, so as not to undo what has been learned or devalue the whole process. There will be difficult emotions—anger that the counselor cannot help anymore, sorrow at the parting, fear that one cannot manage on one's own. All these can be worked through in the final sessions.

Preparing to leave can take several sessions. One way to prepare for an ending is to space sessions more and more widely apart. The client can leave the door open at the final session: "I am leaving for now, but I can always come back if I need to." Some people return at times of stress throughout their lives.

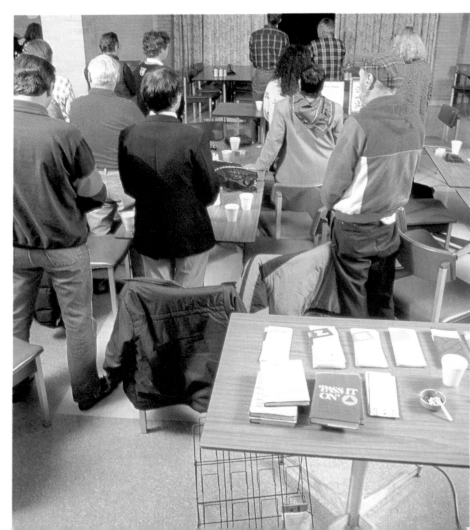

Cramp

Q My brother has to write a lot and says that he suffers from writer's cramp as a result. What is this, and is there a cure for it?

A Writer's cramp is also known as professional or occupational cramp, since it can affect anybody who uses their hands for delicate work, such as musicians, seamstresses, and artists, as well as writers. The muscles of the fingers, and even the forearm, seize up, so that work with the affected hand is impossible. Usually the hand can be used normally for anything else, which leads to the belief that it is a psychological condition. It is not linked to an organic or bodily disease. The best way to treat this form of cramp is to discover the underlying psychological cause and to treat that. Sometimes a rest from work is the best cure. In your brother's case, slightly altering the way he holds his pen may help.

Q I only suffer from cramps on my annual vacation in Mexico, although I exercise all through the year at home. Why does this happen?

A If you exercise vigorously in a hot climate—perhaps by playing volleyball on the beach—you will lose salt from your body along with the sweat. It is this lack of salt that causes heat cramps. Try taking salt tablets while you are on vacation.

Q I am pregnant and frequently suffer from cramps in my legs at night, which keep me awake for a long time. Why is this?

A Your muscles are under additional strain during the day, due to the unaccustomed weight of the developing baby, and as a result, they go into spasm at night when you are lying down and relaxed. Ask your partner to massage your legs when the cramp occurs, since you will not be able to reach them comfortably. Once you have had your baby, it is likely that the attacks will completely disappear.

Almost everyone has experienced muscle cramps— unexpected and agonizing pain, usually in the backs of the legs. But it is not usually a sign that anything is seriously wrong, and it can be relieved by self-massage.

A cramp is a painful and involuntary contraction of a muscle or group of muscles. Cramps in the limbs occur most commonly in the legs, affecting the muscles in the calf or the back of the thighs. They come on suddenly and without warning, sometimes when the person is deeply asleep. The muscle fibers contract into a hard knot during the spasm, which may last from a few seconds to a few minutes.

Causes
Cramps can be caused by poor circulation, which results in an inadequate supply of blood reaching the muscles in the limbs. Exposure to cold can also bring on an attack of cramps and, when combined with exhaustion, is sometimes a cause of swimmer's cramp. Athletes with slight injuries to the muscles in their limbs may also suffer from cramping in an affected muscle. Heavy sweating, which leads to a severe loss of salt, can also induce cramps, as can eating just before exercise.

Symptoms
The cramped limb seizes up with a sharp local pain, and ordinary efforts to move and relax the muscle are useless. People who suffer from persistent cramps should check with their doctor to be sure that it is not a symptom of a circulatory problem.

A cramp in itself is unpleasant but not dangerous. However, someone suffering from cramps while swimming in deep water is in real danger. When engaging in any type of physical activity, a person should stop and deal with a cramp rather than attempting to continue with the exercise while suffering.

Treatment
Cramps caused by circulatory problems, such as artery disease, can be treated by vasodilator drugs, which a doctor can prescribe. These open the narrowed arteries, and this improves the flow of blood to the muscles.

Young people and others involved in sporting activities should avoid eating shortly before physical exertion. If a cramp has been brought on by loss of salt from the body, as happens after prolonged sweating, then salt tablets taken with water will help to restore the balance in the body. An attack of cramps can be somewhat eased by massaging and manipulating the affected muscle.

Cramps that are caused by artery disease usually occur later in life, and although drugs may alleviate the symptoms, they do not cure the hardened arteries. Most active people find that their cramp attacks are temporary. Pregnant women who suffer from cramps usually find that the attacks disappear after they give birth. Some people, especially the elderly, may get severe cramps at night for no particular reason. These night cramps can often be prevented with a type of quinine pill.

Frederick Mancini

Cramps in the legs can be relieved by flexing the foot upward. Persistent cramps are often cured by pacing around the room for a while.

Creutzfeldt-Jakob disease

Creutzfeldt-Jakob disease belongs to a group of diseases, called spongiform encephalopathies, that affects the brains of both animals and humans. It is thought to transfer between species, and there is no cure at present.

Q **My friend's dad has CJD. Can I catch it from him?**

A CJD cannot be spread like a cold or the measles. It cannot be caught by touching a person who has CJD or by breathing in the same air. People who nurse, eat with, or live with a CJD patient are no more likely to develop the disease than anyone else.

Q **Do animals suffer from Creutzfeldt-Jakob disease?**

A CJD belongs to a family of diseases, called spongiform encephalopathies, that affects both animals and humans. In all these diseases, the brain becomes riddled with tiny holes and protein deposits. Sheep have a related disease called scrapie, so-called because affected sheep scrape themselves against trees and other objects. They become unsteady, stagger around, stop eating, and lose interest in everything. Cattle have a related disease called bovine spongiform encephalopathy (BSE), or mad cow disease, first described in Britain in 1986. The symptoms are similar, except that cattle may become aggressive or anxious, too. British cattle may have become infected after being given feed containing sheep remains infected with scrapie. Another theory is that cattle developed the disease after receiving feed that contained the remains of other cattle that already had "spontaneous" BSE. Laboratory mice injected with prions from sheep, cattle, and humans have developed spongiform encephalopathy. Researchers do not know how the disease transfers between animals.

Q **Can I catch CJD from the food I eat?**

A In 1996 there were ten unusual cases of CJD in the UK. Some scientists claimed that the cases, involving people aged 17 to 41, were linked to eating BSE-infected beef (such as spine or brain). Others argued that unusual cases of CJD had occurred before this epidemic but that patients had been misdiagnosed as having Alzheimer's disease.

Creutzfeldt-Jakob disease is a rare form of dementia (see Dementia). It is one of a group of diseases, called spongiform encephalopathies, in which the brain develops tiny holes and deposits of protein, resembling a microscopic sponge.

Creutzfeldt-Jakob disease (CJD) occurs worldwide and affects about one person in a million every year. People with the illness start to lose their memory, eyesight, and coordination. Normally the disease takes several decades to incubate, so it tends to afflict people from 50 to 75 years old. Once symptoms appear, the disease progresses rapidly and usually kills within six months.

Symptoms

Establishing exactly when the illness begins is difficult. The first symptoms are usually forgetfulness and unusual behavior such as losing interest in family and friends and becoming withdrawn. Simple tasks at work become hard. As a result, doctors may conclude that the patient has mild depression.

Within weeks, however, the symptoms become much worse. The patient becomes unsteady on his or her feet and starts losing the ability to see and speak. The patient may then develop incontinence, shakiness, stiff arms and legs, and jerky movements. In the end the patient cannot speak or move, and death usually follows within months. In a few cases, however, patients have lived for another two to five years after diagnosis.

Cause

No one knows for certain what causes CJD. But scientists believe that a protein normally found in the brain, called a prion, plays a key role in the disease. This protein seems to help electrical impulses to travel from one nerve cell to the next.

The prion protein comes in two forms. Both forms are made up of the same amino acids (the building blocks of life). What sets them apart is their different three-dimensional structures. The normal prion protein, which is found in all cells and especially on the surfaces of nerve cells, can be broken down by enzymes. The abnormal form, which only appears in the brains of people who have CJD (and other spongiform encephalopathies), cannot be digested by enzymes.

Scientists have found that once a tiny amount of abnormal protein appears in the brain, it forces the normal protein to

A cow infected with bovine spongiform encephalopathy (BSE), or mad cow disease. BSE-infected cows suffer from severe nerve damage, which causes glazed eyes, anxiety, and uncontrolled shaking.

change into the harmful, abnormal form. Some researchers believe that the abnormal protein alone causes CJD. Others say that the infectious agent is hidden inside a coat of abnormal protein and that once such a protein enters a cell, it removes its coat and starts to convert the normal protein into the abnormal form.

Some say the infectious agent is a virus. But a virus would trigger the production of antibodies to attack the virus, and no such antibodies have been found. A virus would also be visible under an electron microscope, but no virus linked to CJD has been discovered. Although chemicals, sterilization, and radiation can kill viruses, they cannot kill the agent that causes CJD.

How CJD may be transmitted

A person's genes give the code for making all the protein that the body needs to survive. If the gene is faulty, then the protein is not made properly. A few people have a mutation in the gene that codes for the prion protein, and this means they are more likely to develop CJD. But in most cases the disease developed after abnormal prion protein entered the patient's body.

In the past some children were given the human growth hormone to help them grow taller. A few of them then later developed CJD. The hormone was extracted from the pituitary gland, which is found at the base of the brain. Some of these hormones were taken from patients who had died from various causes, including, unfortunately, CJD. Doctors only discovered that the disease could spread in this way in 1985. Nowadays the hormone is made artificially. The risk from growth hormone treatment has, therefore, been eliminated.

In Australia some women who received human pituitary gonadotropin (a hormone that induces ovulation) during fertility treatment died of CJD. Again, some of the hormone came from people who had died of CJD.

There have also been a few cases of people developing CJD after receiving a cornea (the transparent coating over the eye) from dead CJD patients. Others have caught the disease after being operated on with surgical instruments that were used on CJD patients earlier in the day. Today steps are taken to insure that there is no risk to patients undergoing medical treatment.

British government scientists now believe that eating beef infected with BSE, a disease similar to CJD, can also cause CJD in humans. However, no such cases of CJD resulting from eating infected beef have been found in the US. Further research in this area continues.

Diagnosis

At present there is no hospital test that can diagnose CJD with absolute certainty. However, in 1996, US researchers found that two proteins (not the prion proteins) seem to be present in the spinal fluid of CJD patients. By developing a test that looks for these proteins, it should be possible to diagnose CJD reliably in the future.

At the moment, CJD can only be confirmed after death. This is done by examining the patient's brain for the tiny holes and protein tangles that are characteristic of the disease. While the patient is alive, doctors can perform tests to rule out other possible conditions.

The patient's brain may be examined by using a computerized axial tomography (CAT) scanner or a magnetic resonance imaging (MRI) scanner. Although these techniques cannot detect the tiny holes and protein deposits caused by CJD, which are minuscule, the scans can help doctors to eliminate the possibility of other illnesses.

Another test involves attaching tiny electrodes to the patient's scalp to obtain a trace, or electroencephalogram, of the brain's electrical activity. Different brain diseases cause different changes in the pattern of brain activity. A patient who has CJD may produce a trace that is characteristic of CJD. This would make the diagnosis more certain.

Treatment

There is no treatment for CJD. Therefore the aim is to help the patient stay as comfortable as possible. Once the patient can no longer move, it is important to change his or her position often to prevent pressure sores. Some patients find they can no longer swallow food. They must be fed either intravenously or through a tube that goes into the nose and down the food pipe. Sedative drugs will help patients who suffer from shakiness or jerky movements.

A section of the human brain showing Creutzfeldt-Jakob disease. The brown plaque in the center is produced by the abnormal protein particles that cause the rare and fatal disease.

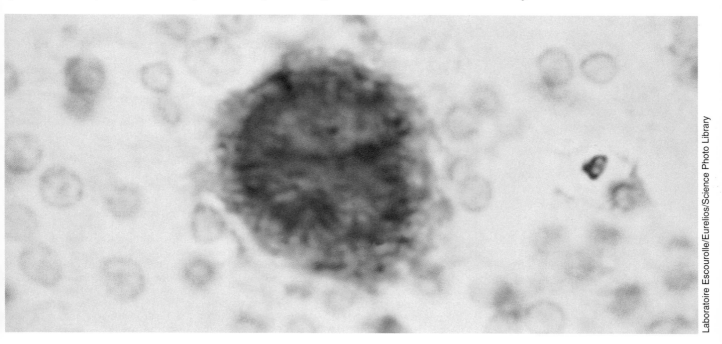

Crib death

Q One of my friends recently lost her baby. She was told this was a case of crib death. How can I prevent this from happening to my baby?

A All you can do is care for your baby as well as possible, and follow the basic safety measures. You can learn about baby care at prenatal classes. Once the baby is born, try to breast-feed, because this is usually advantageous to the baby's overall health. The baby should sleep in a room that is warm and free from drafts, and he or she should never be allowed to get too hot or cold. You can always check a baby's body temperature by feeling under the crib covers. If the baby is sweaty, he or she is too hot and will need a drink of cooled, boiled water. If you or your partner smoke, try to quit, or at least try not to smoke in the same room as your baby, because parental smoking is thought to have a link with crib death. Above all do not panic—crib death is rare, but always consult your doctor if your baby seems unwell in any way.

Q My sister lost her first child through crib death at the age of four weeks. She is now pregnant again. What is the risk of the same thing happening twice?

A The chance of this event repeating itself is very slight, although, understandably, many parents have a great fear of losing another baby in the same way. The chances of a second crib death in the same family are no greater than they are in a family that has not suffered a crib death.

Q I have been told that it is better not to put my baby on her stomach to sleep, since there is a remote possibility she might suffocate. Is this true?

A No one really knows what causes crib death. Doctors now advise that babies be put to sleep on their side or on their back. Traditionally newborn babies were put on their side to sleep, with the lower elbow a little in front of the body.

Despite continuing research, the cause of crib death remains a mystery. However, if a tiny baby is well cared for, any risk to his or her life and health will be reduced.

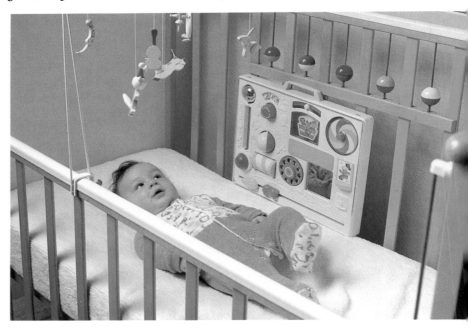

There is nothing more tragic and disturbing for a family than the unexpected and unexplained death of a young baby. An apparently healthy baby is put to bed in a crib or buggy. When next looked at, he or she is dead, and for no obvious reason. This sad phenomenon, known as crib death, or SIDS (sudden infant death syndrome), is one of the most pressing and perplexing problems facing doctors.

Crib deaths are most common among babies aged between four weeks and one year, and they occur particularly between the ages of two and four months. There are more cases among boys, twins, and babies whose birth weight was low. They also happen more during the autumn and winter (often coinciding with local epidemics of the flu), and more often to babies who are bottle-fed rather than breast-fed. There are no warning signs, and death can occur in the parent's bedroom, in hospitals, clinics—even while a baby is being nursed in its mother's arms.

Symptoms

Probably one of the most puzzling aspects is that there appear to be no warning signals of any kind. But subsequent examination does reveal evidence of unsuspected abnormality or serious disease, such as pneumonia or meningitis, in about one third of cases. However, recent research has shown that while some babies definitely do die quite inexplicably, the majority have had minor symptoms in the preceding week or 24 hours. These may include a cold, stuffed up nose, listlessness, drowsiness, or breathing difficulties.

These minor symptoms are the basis of the apnea, or cessation of breathing, theory. Periods of apnea alternate with active breathing as a normal occurrence during sleep. Some adults, and even more babies, naturally experience this. Usually a baby automatically changes to active breathing by taking a deep breath, but it is possible that some babies who have experienced these minor symptoms do not switch over to active breathing—with fatal results.

Crib deaths are not related to choking, smothering, child abuse, or neglect. Contrary to popular belief, many of these babies have been better cared for than those who survive.

Effects on the family

For the parents, profound shock is probably the first reaction, followed by feelings of guilt. Older children, who may have felt jealous or resentful of the baby, also suffer badly from guilt. It is essential for the entire family to talk to an understanding outsider. Comfort and practical help during this grieving time can be sought from close friends, the family doctor, a health visitor, a therapist, or a religious authority.

Crohn's disease

Crohn's disease is an inflammation of the gastrointestinal (digestive) tract. It usually attacks the walls of the small intestine, causing pain and swelling, but it can affect any part of the tract, from the mouth to the anus.

There are between half a million and a million Americans with Crohn's disease. The illness affects mostly young adults, but it can strike at any age. The disease may attack just once or twice, or it may flare up throughout the patient's life. Although drugs and surgery can help to relieve symptoms of the disease, sometimes for years, there is no known cure.

Causes

There are various theories about what causes Crohn's disease, but most researchers believe that the body's own defense system is to blame. If bacteria or a virus infect the intestine, for example, the immune system will produce immune cells to attack the invaders. If for some reason the immune system is not then "down-regulated," but instead continues to attack the cells of the intestine, the intestinal walls will become inflamed and swollen.

Other scientists argue that Crohn's disease is an autoimmune disease in which the body has been tricked into thinking that the intestine is a foreign body. As a result, it produces immune cells, such as T cells, that damage the intestinal wall.

Some people claim that diet plays a part in causing Crohn's disease, but researchers have found no significant differences in the diets of people with Crohn's and those who are unaffected by the disease.

Symptoms

The first signs of Crohn's disease are abdominal pain and diarrhea. The patient often develops a pain around or to the right of the navel after eating. Other common symptoms are a lack of appetite, weight loss, and fever. The patient's abdomen may also become distended, so that it becomes possible to feel the thickened intestine.

People with Crohn's disease may also develop various complications. They may find it difficult to digest certain foods, such as fats and dairy products. Other nutrients may also pass through without being absorbed, and the patient becomes malnourished.

Over time, areas where the gastrointestinal tract has become inflamed may develop fibrous or scar tissue. This hard tissue can build up to constrict the tract or block it completely. Moreover, any cracks in the wall of the gastrointestinal tract can tear open to produce tiny holes (perforations) in the wall. These perforations may allow blood to flow into the tract, leading to bleeding from the anus. The perforations may also become infected so that abscesses form.

A small intestine afflicted with Crohn's disease. The intestinal wall has become thickened and pitted with fissured ulcers, which can lead to obstruction, pain, and diarrhea, and may result in malnutrition.

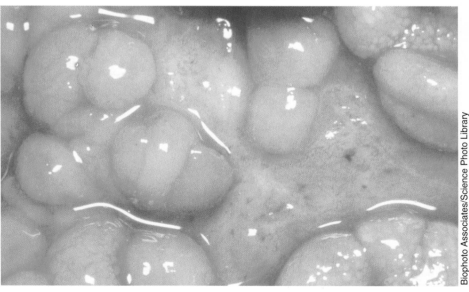

Some patients may develop abnormal channels, called fistulas, that run from the bowel to the anal area, vagina, skin surface, or other parts of the bowel. Other complications may include arthritis, ulcers, kidney stones and gallstones, skin rashes, cataracts, and glaucoma.

Diagnosis

As the symptoms of Crohn's disease vary from person to person and can often be confused with those of other illnesses, such as ulcerative colitis (an inflammatory bowel disease that affects the colon and rectum), diagnosing the disease can take weeks. Doctors start by testing the patient's blood and feces to rule out other possible illnesses.

The patient may then be examined using an endoscope—a lit, fiberglass tube that is inserted either into the mouth or the anus to study the inflamed digestive tract. This process can reveal ulcers, regions where the digestive track has narrowed, or the patterns of "cobblestones" that are seen where the intestinal wall has thickened and cracked. All these features are typical characteristics of Crohn's disease.

Doctors can also use endoscopes to perform a biopsy, a process that involves removing tiny pieces of the digestive tract and examining them under a microscope. If the biopsy shows that the whole thickness of the gastrointestinal wall is inflamed, with deep cracks and pockets where immune cells have collected (called granulomas), then the patient has Crohn's disease.

The patient may also be given liquid barium, either by mouth or by infusing it through the rectum. The barium will then show up on X rays and reveal certain abnormalities in the digestive tract, such as the particular regions where the tract has narrowed.

Treatment

Although diet does not cause Crohn's disease, some patients may be able to relieve their symptoms by changing the type of food they eat. Eating soft, bland foods, while avoiding dairy products, fats, wheat, and spicy and high-fiber food, may help. If the patient becomes malnourished due to the disease, however, nutrients should be given intravenously.

Drugs cannot cure Crohn's disease, but they can ease the symptoms. Sulfasalazine pills, which contain a sulfa antibiotic and a drug from the aspirin family, reduce inflammation and also help patients who have recovered from a flare-up to stay in good health. The drug has several side effects and may cause the patient to feel nauseous and dizzy. It can also trigger headaches, anemia, and

skin rashes. Patients may be able to moderate at least some of the side effects by first taking the drug in small doses and then building up gradually to the full daily dose.

If the intestine becomes very badly inflamed, doctors may prescribe corticosteroids. These drugs are given to patients only when their symptoms are severe, because the long-term use of such drugs can produce bad side effects in some patients.

Some patients respond well to azathioprine and 6-mercaptopurine, two drugs that suppress the immune system. However, these drugs should be used with caution, since it is known that in some patients the drugs can lead to nausea, fewer white blood cells, and an inflamed pancreas. Laboratory tests have also shown that high doses of these drugs (much higher than the doses patients receive) can occasionally cause cancer in animals.

Surgery

If none of these treatments is successful, or if part of the intestine becomes blocked, it may be necessary for the patient to undergo surgery.

In the United States, between 67 and 75 percent of Crohn's patients eventually need to have surgery to remove the diseased part of their digestive tract. Although this may relieve symptoms, sometimes for years, the disease usually returns to attack the the region close to where the two healthy ends of the digestive tract were sewn together.

People with Crohn's suffer physical and emotional stress during flare-ups of the disease. Therefore, support and encouragement from family and friends can be just as vital as medical treatment.

A barium X ray of the large intestine of a patient with Crohn's disease, showing the ileocecal region, where the large and small intestines join.

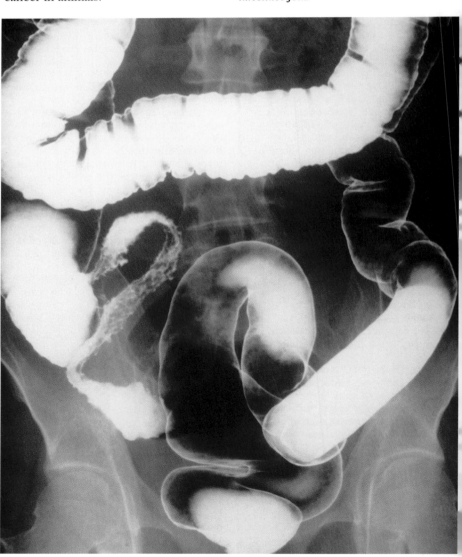

Crying

Q My relations keep telling me that I will spoil my son if I pick him up every time he cries. He is two months old now; should I leave him to cry?

A At this age the only way a young baby can get your love and attention is by crying. If you ignore this, it can only be more distressing for both of you. Small babies need plenty of physical comfort and contact, and it is impossible to spoil them during their first few months. As your son grows older, you may decide that he can sometimes be left to cry for a while. Many children develop a "testing cry" at bedtime. But at no age should a child be left to cry for more than five or ten minutes.

Q Both my friend and I have babies of similar ages. But mine seems to cry much more easily than hers. Is there any particular reason for this?

A It depends. Some babies are certainly fussier than others, and there may be various reasons. In some cases a baby may have colic. This shows itself as a sharp abdominal pain that recurs, usually in the evening. It is accompanied by uncontrollable screaming. The causes of colic are still uncertain, and it is notoriously difficult to treat, but it does wear off by the time the baby is three months old. Alternatively a baby may be hypertonic. Such babies are very tense, overactive, and difficult. They need a very calm environment and careful, slow handling. Doctors sometimes prescribe mild sedatives in these cases. Finally, a baby may just have a tendency to fuss for no particular reason. It is nothing to worry about and will pass.

Q Men never seem to cry as easily as women. Do women make more tears?

A From a physical point of view, crying operates equally in both sexes. Boy babies cry just as much as girls do. But rightly or wrongly, boys are usually encouraged not to cry, making girls and women appear to cry more easily.

Crying is a spontaneous and very necessary expression of human emotion. It is perhaps easier to respond to tears in children, but people of all ages are usually asking for love, understanding, and reassurance when they cry.

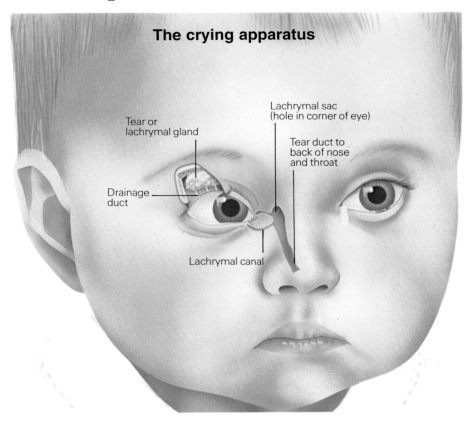

The crying apparatus

Tear or lachrymal gland

Lachrymal sac (hole in corner of eye)

Tear duct to back of nose and throat

Drainage duct

Lachrymal canal

Advertising Arts

All humans cry—in fact, it is often the first sound that a newborn baby makes. Usually it is a way of expressing grief or pain when words cannot be used; at other times it may be a natural and often involuntary reaction, caused by an emotional state or as a response to pain. In this case the purpose is to release tension.

How crying occurs

Tears, in the form of a watery, salty fluid, are produced continuously from the tear (lachrymal) glands, situated above the outer corner of the eye. This flow, medically known as lacrimation, serves to keep the eye clean and germ-free and to lubricate the movement of the eyelid over the eyeball. Every time the eyelid blinks, the fluid drains away into small holes in the inner corner of the eye, down the tear duct, and into the back of the nose and throat. But when a person laughs or cries, or if the eye is irritated by a foreign body, such as dust or grit, lacrimation increases, and there is an overflow of tears.

Tears from the tear glands, which normally lubricate the eye, drain into the tear duct. When crying occurs, the excess flow of tears pours down the cheeks.

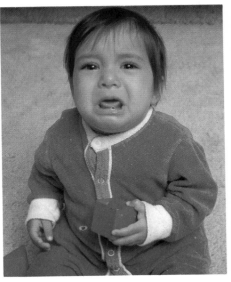

MC Library

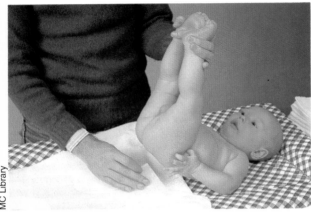

MC Library

Changing a baby's diaper can often cause him or her to cry.

The reasons for this are not fully understood, but the lachrymal glands are controlled by the parasympathetic nerve fibers of the central nervous system. These act automatically, without a conscious decision on a person's part. Under certain emotional influences, these nerves, which in turn are controlled by the brain, stimulate tear production.

When a person cries loudly, the face becomes flushed, the forehead wrinkles, the corners of the mouth may turn down, and there is a marked change in breathing. The rate of respiration gets much faster—a deep initial breath can be followed by a series of sobbing or wailing sounds. The length of time that anyone cries varies. Older children and adults can get their tears under control fairly quickly, but a younger baby may continue to sob long after it has been soothed.

Why babies cry

Infants spend a great deal of time crying, and during the first weeks of life, it is the only way in which they can communicate. The most common causes are hunger, wind, general discomfort, pain, teething, boredom, and loneliness.

A sudden change or unexpected noise can also set off crying, as can tiredness or overstimulation. Strangely, wet or dirty diapers are unlikely to produce much distress, but careless handling or being dressed or undressed can cause tears very easily. Other possible reasons may be the onset of illness such as a cold or an earache or what is commonly known as three-month colic, which causes stomachaches.

Soothing techniques can be used. Some babies like being swaddled tightly in a blanket or being rocked. Others relax to soft music or singing or enjoy being carried around a room. Pacifiers, too, can provide comfort, but they should never replace affection or physical reassurance.

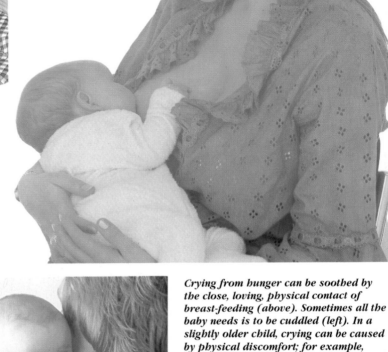

Luis Vaamonde

Crying from hunger can be soothed by the close, loving, physical contact of breast-feeding (above). Sometimes all the baby needs is to be cuddled (left). In a slightly older child, crying can be caused by physical discomfort; for example, taking a tumble.

Image Bank

Teething troubles cause a lot of tears; a plastic teething ring is comforting.

Crystal therapy

Q Are crystals safe to use in a therapeutic sense?

A Crystal therapy is generally considered safe, but it is sometimes held responsible for headaches, numbness, or upset stomachs. Therapists say that simply removing the crystal should stop the effect. Using a crystal for a short while each time is said to build up the body's ability to deal with the crystal's energy. It is often claimed that crystals can have a malignant force that will not help to heal a person. Therapists say that you should simply discard a crystal if it does not feel right to you.

Q Can crystals be used alongside other therapies?

A Yes, crystals can be used with both orthodox medicine and alternative therapies. In fact, crystal healers will advise you to seek orthodox medical advice for any serious health problem, while also suggesting a crystal to help your body heal itself. Many crystal therapists make use of other systems to complement their practice, such as color therapy. Some healers also use crystals as a way of focusing healing energy.

Q How can you tell a good crystal from a bad crystal?

A A good crystal is said to be one that makes the user feel comfortable, and a damaged or badly formed crystal will not work as well as a clear, well-cut crystal. The most common type of crystal used for healing is a six-sided length of quartz with a point at one end. Double-terminated crystals (those that have a point at each end) are said to be very effective.

Q Does a crystal have to be clear to work properly?

A Therapists believe that for a crystal to be "programmable" and tune into the body's vibrations, it must be a clear, quartz crystal that conducts electricity. A crystal with impurities will "short out" like an electrical circuit. But where crystals or gemstones are used only as a meditation tool, they may be completely opaque.

The use of crystals to improve health is an ancient tradition that has become popular again in recent years. But do crystals heal, or do their healing powers come from the beliefs of those who use them?

Humans have been fascinated by crystals and gemstones for thousands of years. Many of the ancient civilizations believed that crystals had magical or health-giving properties. For example, the ancient Egyptians ground up lapis lazuli to paint around their eyes, which they believed improved their extrasensory perception, or ESP. Many modern crystal therapists believe that the ancients used a highly sophisticated crystal technology for communication, the rediscovery of which is beginning to be seen in the shape of laser technology and quartz in clocks.

The word *crystal* is drived from the Greek word for ice, *krustallos*. This is because ancient civilizations believed that quartz crystals were made from frozen water that had been petrified over the ages. Rather than needing to be frozen, however, quartz crystal requires very high temperatures to form—up to 1120°F (600°C). In fact, crystals are made of regular atomic or molecular structures that repeat themselves over and over again to form a recognizable pattern. Crystals are not necessarily expensive—although diamonds are a crystalline substance, so too is common table salt.

Crystals used for healing are chosen for properties that may be beneficial to an individual. Vibrations emanating from a crystal may help physical energy flow.

John Glover/Images

Q Do people have to believe completely in crystal healing for it to work?

A No, practitioners say that crystals can help skeptics as well as those who believe in their benefits. But it is said that crystals may not, necessarily, help everyone. Instead a person may need to try a number of different therapies to see which one works best for them.

Q Can anyone be a crystal therapist?

A Anyone can set themselves up as a crystal therapist, but practitioners suggest that the occupation is more effective when an individual feels that he or she is particularly drawn to working with crystals. There is no single formal qualification in crystal therapy, although some organizations do offer training courses.

Q Are crystals especially good for any particular problem or group of problems?

A Crystals have been used to treat a wide range of symptoms, both physical ones, such as headaches or sports injuries, and psychological problems, such as depression. Practitioners use different types of crystals, depending on the problem. However, some practitioners seem to be very successful with a certain set of symptoms, such as sprains and bruising, whereas others specialize in using crystal therapy to help with psychological or mental problems.

Q Why is crystal healing regarded as an alternative form of therapy?

A Crystal healing in itself does not have a history of use by any single professional or medical group. There is little, if any, scientific research on the subject, and there is no generally accepted body of knowledge that is being formally studied and developed. These are not reasons in themselves to decide that crystal healing is not a useful therapy, but they do lead to its being classified as an alternative form of treatment.

Crystals worn close to the throat chakra are said to induce healing of all of the ailments associated with that energy center.

Although crystals have a very long history of use by humans, their use as a healing tool has only come into fashion again in the past 20 years or so as part of the natural healing movement. Crystal therapy is regarded as more of an alternative therapy by those close to orthodox medicine, but many crystal healers feel it will come to be accepted in the way that homeopathy and aromatherapy have been. However, there is little or no evidence that crystals work in a way that would indicate definite proof of their effectiveness to scientists.

Historical use of crystals
The use of crystals surfaces both in recorded history and in legends. Historically, many crystals were used in amulets to ward off evil spirits or to help cure a disease or injury. They have been found in the archaeological remains of many societies, including those of Egypt, India, the Middle East, Native America, and Europe.

Papyri from ancient Egypt detail the use of gems for healing, while formulas for using crystals appear in the texts of the Sumerians—people who lived in the region of what today is called the Middle East—thousands of years before the birth of Christ. Native Americans put a high value on quartz crystals: for example, the Apache claimed the crystals enabled them to locate lost or stolen ponies. Crushed gemstones were used in medical

concoctions in the Middle Ages, and it is now thought possible that such potions contained minerals that offered the patient some benefits.

The most popular myth tends to focus on Atlantis—the legend of an ancient and powerful civilization that was lost beneath the sea. Many books on crystal therapy tend to take the Atlantis legend as fact, and some claim that the abuse of the sophisticated crystal technology in use at the time led to the downfall of Atlantis. Although Atlantis often appears in crystal mythology, there is no evidence to confirm that the place ever existed.

Today's practitioners believe that crystals work by magnifying the healing ability the body already has. It is claimed that as crystals vibrate at certain frequencies—what scientists call the piezoelectric effect—they tune into the body's energy and help it to heal itself. Crystals do not store energy, as a battery does, but quartz crystals can conduct electricity. Scientists claim, however, that although crystals may be used in technological applications, it does not follow that they also have a healing effect.

However, it is possible that the process of focusing the mind on an object, in this case a crystal, is enough in some cases to encourage the body's immune system to begin the healing process. A sympathetic healer will also help patients to feel better about themselves and therefore help them recover from an illness sooner.

Placebo effect
Another possible factor of crystal healing is the the placebo effect, which could lead to a patient feeling "better." This syndrome occurs when a person feels unwell but believes that a treatment will improve health—and so it does just that. Many healers acknowledge the importance of this effect, which is a well-documented medical phenomenon.

Crystals are often used by therapists to improve people's mental well-being—to help improve their attitude about life in general or to make them feel more energetic, for instance. As no objective way has been found of measuring a person's state of mind, it is impossible to prove whether the treatment received has actually made any great psychological difference. But if a patient claims that he or she feels better, then a healer must assume that the treatment has helped.

Crystal and gem types
Over the centuries different types of crystals and gemstones have come to be associated with different healing properties, although crystal therapists tend to claim that if a crystal works for an individual, then he or she should keep using that

pe. Amethyst quartz is frequently used healers, since it is said to be good for haustion and stress. It is often worn by cople who need a general boost of ener for both mind and body. Garnet is said help improve circulation, while aqua arine is held to be good for asthma and y fever. Malachite is used to draw out inflammation, such as arthritis, and is so thought to be good for the teeth.

Sometimes the healing property of a one is connected with its color. The ue of aquamarine is said to have sooth g qualities, whereas red bloodstone, as name might suggest, is used to clear e blood of toxins.

There is a whole tradition connected to e color of stones and their supposed operties, and many crystal therapists so use color therapy to help their ients. In the same way that a person ay find it soothing to be in a pale green om rather than a bright red one,

crystal ball is the traditional tool of the rtune-teller—but crystals such as double ded quartz may also be used to heal the ind, body, or spirit of the individual.

crystal healers maintain that this sooth ing effect can be achieved with a green stone, such as emerald or jade.

Many crystals are also associated with a particular sign of the zodiac. For exam ple, rose quartz is associated with Virgo, and tourmaline with Pisces. Some are even associated with more than one astrological sign.

Crystal therapists use crystals and gems in different ways to help their clients, depending on what is deemed appropri ate. Gemstones or crystals that do not conduct electricity may be used as tools for meditation, or as part of a method of finding the source of ill health, by being moved over the patient's body.

The healing session

During a formal healing session, a crystal therapist may use just one crystal, or he or she may arrange a number of stones around the patient's body or on the part of the body that he or she wishes to treat. Different arrangements may be used, depending on what the healer is trying to accomplish. These have special names such as clusters, arrays, and chakra

arrangements. A chakra arrangement is designed to realign the body's "energy fields," to open up the chakras—symbolic points at which energy is said to pass from the immediate area around the body, into the body—and thus create a feeling of well-being. An array would be designed to balance a person's mental state by drawing the body's energy field in a particular direction, say from the head to the feet, in order to ground a per son in reality.

During the healing session, the patient is not necessarily touched by the thera pist, but his or her hands are used to redi rect the energy fields around the body. Sometimes, however, crystals are used to actually massage the body—the point or the base of the crystal is used. Another method is to apply a single crystal to the part of the body that is causing a prob lem. A single crystal may also be used to focus mental energy and to help visualize positive images of well-being.

A patient may wish to use a crystal without a healer present, although thera pists suggest using their services initially in order to find the process that works

Images

well. A crystal amulet, which has been "programmed," may also be worn in the traditional way. Such an amulet should be worn throughout the day.

Choosing a crystal

When crystal therapy begins, therapists claim that a patient should choose a crystal that holds a great attraction or that catches the eye. Before the stone is used, it should be cleansed. This can be accomplished either by performing a washing ritual, using saltwater or seawater, or by simply breathing on the stone and visualizing the clean crystal. It is also recommended that crystals used frequently for healing purposes should be cleansed at least every couple of weeks.

If a crystal is given as a gift, it should be programmed with the giver's good wishes—but these might not be attuned to the recipient's current needs, and it may need to be reprogrammed. It may take some time for a crystal to get used to its owner's vibrations, but if the crystal still makes the owner feel uncomfortable after a considerable length of time, it should be discarded.

A single crystal can be "programmed" for a specific task. This involves concentrating on the crystal, while visualizing the desired help. This could be, for example, the strengthening of a sprained wrist or the successful completion of a task at work. Various cuts of crystal are held differently in order to program them. Crystals with points at both ends, known as double-terminated crystals (which are said to be more powerful than single-pointed crystals), are held between the palms of the hand to form a bridge while they are being programmed.

Crystal tools

Some crystal workers weld their crystals into tools of various kinds, which they believe will make them more effective. Wands are popular tools, as they are believed to focus a crystal's power. These are usually made of copper with a quartz crystal imbedded in one or both ends.

Headbands can also be made with copper and a single crystal set on the forehead, or a number of crystals set at key points in the headband. Advocates of this system suggest that the headband works in a way similar to broadcasting radio and television waves—they suggest that humans are naturally telepathic and that crystals can enable people to focus and transmit thoughts more easily to other people. However, there is no scientific explanation as to why humans should be able transmit energy in this way.

Because quartz crystal can conduct electricity, it is said to be an excellent transmitter of life-giving energy, which may improve the energy flow of the individual.

Crystal growing

Most of the quartz crystal found in the United States today is from Arkansas although deposits have been found all over the country. Some types of crystal can be grown very easily. By dissolving say, copper sulfate in a jar of water, a super saturated solution results. If a piece of string is then left to dangle in the solution crystals of copper sulfate will form on it.

Quartz cannot be grown in the same way at home, as high pressures and temperatures are required. However, some commercial companies do produce high quality quartz to supply the electronic industry. This sort of quartz is greatly valued by those who believe in the therapeutic properties of crystals, as it is very clear and contains no impurities.

Outlook

Scientists are skeptical about the claims of crystal therapists. Crystal healers generally acknowledge that their methods will not work for everyone, and that any healing achieved in crystal therapy comes from within patients themselves.

Cyst

Q Is it possible to be born with cysts?

A One group of cysts, classified as congenital, are due to an abnormality in development which causes cysts to grow soon after birth. So, although babies can be born with cysts, this rarely happens; they are more likely to develop slowly afterward. Various cysts of the skin and the kidney (polycystic disease) arise in this way. However, the great majority of cysts arise later in life.

Q I suffer from chronic mastitis, and my doctor occasionally extracts fluid from the cysts. Does this mean I might have cancer?

A Patients with chronic mastitis (chronic fibrous and cystic inflammation of the breast tissue) do have an increased liability to breast cancer. So your doctor is checking for any potentially malignant changes and no doubt checking for new lumps regularly, too. Other tests may be used to spot areas of increased activity. Malignant changes are rare, but regular examinations will mean any change can be quickly detected and treated before it becomes serious.

Q Does a cyst stop growing, or will it keep getting bigger?

A The size to which a cyst will grow depends on the tissue where it is growing and its location in the body. Some, such as sebaceous cysts, grow very slowly and once they reach the size of a walnut, will stop; others, such as those in breast tissue, remain the size of a pea. The largest cysts are found in the ovaries. Before modern surgery, many of these inflated the stomach like a balloon and contained many pints of liquid.

Q My boyfriend has a cyst. Are they contagious?

A No. The only cysts that may be transferable are those caused by parasites. This rarely happens in the US, since they can only be passed to a human via another animal called a vector.

Cysts are very common growths. They may occur in any part of the body, and most are harmless. However, a doctor should be consulted, since many need to be removed.

A cyst is any abnormal sac within the body that contains fluid and sometimes solid matter. These sacs can occur in virtually any organ or tissue and they can be tiny or large enough to contain many pints of fluid.

Most cysts are benign—they expand but do not spread elsewhere or invade surrounding tissue. Others are malignant (cancerous) and will eventually spread and invade other tissues.

There is no self-treatment for cysts. In virtually every case the exact type and characteristic of the cyst must be determined by the doctor, just in case it turns out to be cancerous. Generally the cyst is removed surgically and then sent to the laboratory for tests.

The common cysts occur in skin, bones, breasts, eyelids, kidneys, livers, and the tissues of women's ovaries, and they vary in structure. When a cyst has two or more compartments, it is called a loculated cyst. When many small cysts are grouped together, the entire area is called polycystic.

Causes

In the majority of cases a tissue will suddenly develop a cystic growth or swelling

Where cysts commonly occur

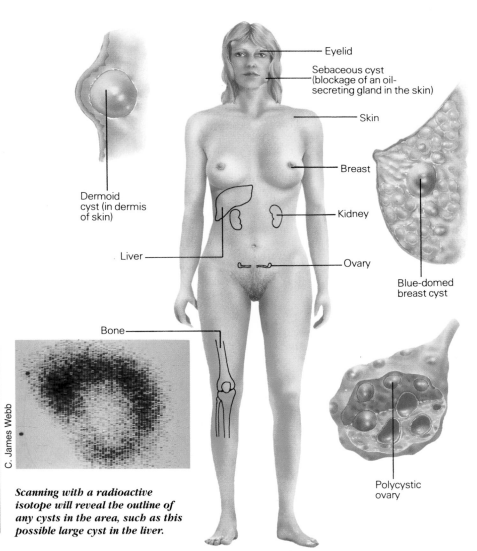

- Eyelid
- Sebaceous cyst (blockage of an oil-secreting gland in the skin)
- Skin
- Breast
- Kidney
- Ovary
- Dermoid cyst (in dermis of skin)
- Liver
- Bone
- Blue-domed breast cyst
- Polycystic ovary

C. James Webb

Scanning with a radioactive isotope will reveal the outline of any cysts in the area, such as this possible large cyst in the liver.

Linden Artists/Jim Channell

Treatment of cysts

Location and type	Symptoms	Treatment
LIVER Hydatid cysts, caused by dog tapeworm; large and central within the liver	A heavy, dragging feeling in the abdomen as the cyst enlarges. If it becomes massive, compression of the liver may cause jaundice	Surgical removal of the cyst and its linings
KIDNEY Multiple cysts may form within the kidney, as a result of its abnormal growth in the fetus	Kidney failure at birth or soon after; or progressive failure in adult life. High blood pressure	Control of blood pressure and treatment of the failure, eventually by kidney machine or transplant
BREAST Cysts form as a result of a blocked mammary gland or as part of chronic inflammation	Lump in the breast, often accompanied by tender and painful breasts, especially before menstrual periods	Surgical removal and microscopic examination. All such lumps are suspected of being cancerous until proved otherwise
SKIN Sebaceous cysts may form in blocked sebaceous gland ducts	Painless lumps beneath the skin, often with a small puncture hole	Removal by surgery if unsightly, painful, infected, or large
EYELID A meibomian cyst on the eyelid may form after a sty	Follows some days after a stye that has not discharged	Removal under local anesthetic
BONE Rare; a cyst may develop at the growing end of a large bone	In a child, swelling or pain in a limb. Cyst shows on an X ray	Cyst must be surgically removed. If benign, bone grows normally
JOINT Small, multiple cysts occur at joints in severe degenerative osteoarthritis	Multiple cysts show on an X ray	No surgery needed. Antiarthritic drugs may help
TESTICLE Cysts may form as a result of defects in the epididymis or in the seminal vesicle	Swelling of, or near, the testicle, rarely causing any pain	Surgical removal if painful. Diagnosis is essential, to see if the growth is benign or malignant
OVARY Cysts occur if the follicle fails to release the egg, causing swelling	Pain on intercourse and swelling of the lower abdomen. If the cyst is infected or twists on its stem (torsion), acute abdominal pain	Surgical removal to see if the growth is benign or malignant. Specialist treatment is essential

for no known reason. In other cases cysts form because of a small defect in the development of the body. A dermoid cyst is one that has arisen because some skin cells have been buried or closed beneath the skin. With the passage of time, the cells secrete fluid and the area swells to form a cyst.

In the case of a polycystic kidney, the tubules of the kidney do not join completely into the drainage channels. Swelling takes place, and the kidney becomes cystic as the urine is trapped and unable to discharge.

Blocked glands
For no known reason, some glands have their exits obstructed, and as the secretion continues, the gland swells and the cyst forms. A common example of this is the sebaceous cyst under the skin, where the sebum gland becomes blocked.

Cysts can also be caused by the formation of fluid in response to the presence of a parasite. Fortunately these parasites are rare in countries with proper hygiene and veterinary procedures.

Occasionally heavy blows can result in the formation of cysts within muscles. The blow ruptures a blood vessel, a clot is formed, and as it disperses, it attracts fluid from the blood. This forms a cyst.

Symptoms
The symptoms of a cyst depend on its situation and type. The patient will probably notice a lump or bump if the cyst is under the skin. Where the cyst affects an internal organ, such as the ovary, there may be some tenderness in the abdomen or just a generalized swelling, since the larger the cyst becomes, the less room is left for the normal organs.

In most cases the doctor is able to feel the cyst or to see its presence, either by X ray or by scanning the area with thermography or a radioactive isotope. Some cysts are painful when pressed, especially if they are already swollen. A cyst near the skin will fluctuate with pressure like a soft ball.

Some cysts occurring in the scrotum—known as hydroceles—contain fluid, and a light will shine through them clearly, as opposed to the dark shadow of the solid testes. This process is known as transillumination, and it indicates the precise position and size of a cyst.

Complications
Any new lump on the body could well be a cyst. Cysts are rarely dangerous, but you should always get a doctor's opinion. If there is any doubt, the earlier the cyst is removed, the better the outlook.

Infection is also a possible danger. A sebaceous cyst that becomes infected turns into a sebaceous abscess and may need to be opened.

An ovarian cyst that becomes infected is a potential cause of peritonitis (inflammation of the membrane lining the abdominal cavity), a serious condition. Like other large cysts lying free in the abdomen, it may twist on its stem, producing strangulation of its blood supply and subsequent degeneration. This may also occur if it bleeds into itself. In this case the patient will feel intense abdominal pain and be very tender in the area of the cyst. The cyst must be surgically removed immediately.

Outlook
Once removed, a benign cyst will not return. If new cysts develop in the same area, such as the breast, they must be checked by the doctor.

Where a cyst is found to be cancerous, the outlook depends on the degree of malignancy and whether or not spreading has already taken place. For this reason, surgeons removing cysts that are likely to be cancerous tend to remove surrounding tissue to prevent cancer cells coming into contact with other tissue and forming fresh growths.

Cystic fibrosis

Q Can I be a carrier of cystic fibrosis without knowing it?

A Yes. It is possible to be a carrier if there is a history of the disease in your family. But this will not matter, as long as you do not have a child with someone whose family also has a history of the disease. Because the effects of the disease are so serious, it is unlikely that you would not know if the disease was in your family.

Q Is there a test I can have to find out if I am a carrier?

A Yes, there is. Both men and women can be tested for the presence of the gene that causes cystic fibrosis.

Q I have been told that my child has cystic fibrosis. Is there anything I can do?

A Try and get your child into one of the units that specialize in the care of cystic fibrosis patients. These are attached to some hospitals. With the antibiotics available nowadays, doctors are able to prolong life by several years. You may also wish to investigate the possibility of participating in experimental gene therapy.

Q My first child died of cystic fibrosis. I was told there was a chance the same thing could happen again. Is this true?

A Unfortunately, yes. There is a 25 percent chance that your second child could also have the disease. There is also a 50 percent chance that he or she could be a carrier, though this would not matter unless he or she had a child with another carrier. The chances of the child being normal are 25 percent.

Q My cousin died of cystic fibrosis when he was in his teens. I am now 18—does this mean that I could get it as well?

A It is unlikely. If you were going to get cystic fibrosis, the symptoms probably would have appeared by now. However, the symptoms of cystic fibrosis can occasionally appear in adults.

This rare disease is inherited. People from families in which it has occurred can be tested to see if they are carriers of the abnormal gene.

Cystic fibrosis, also called mucoviscidosis, affects about one in every 2,000 of the Caucasian population in the United States. Although it is rare in itself, it is the most common genetic disease in the US. It is caused by an abnormal gene (a chemical carrier of hereditary features) in the body. This gene makes the glands (see Glands) secrete an excessively sticky mucus that gums up the lungs, liver, pan-

Inheritance of cystic fibrosis

If both mother and father carry a gene for cystic fibrosis, some sperms and some eggs will carry the abnormal gene. If a carrier sperm and a carrier egg unite, the child will have cystic fibrosis. A carrier sperm uniting with a normal egg, or vice versa, will produce a carrier child. If both egg and sperm are noncarriers, the child will be normal.

creas, and intestines. Usually people with the disease die before they reach their 20s.

Cause
Cystic fibrosis is only inherited if both parents are carriers of the gene. It cannot be passed on if only one parent is a carrier. It could be passed on if one parent was actually suffering from the disease, but this is unlikely to happen.

Symptoms
The disease usually becomes apparent soon after birth, when the baby becomes ill. Sometimes the first sign is an intestinal obstruction caused by abnormally sticky mucus. Later the pancreas becomes gummed up and fails to secrete the enzymes essential for normal digestion. This, in turn, can cause obstruction of the liver, which may lead to cirrhosis.

However, the most serious complication is in the lungs. The mucus produced blocks the bronchial tubes, and this causes repeated infections. Finally the lungs become filled with little cysts containing

pus, and the delicate elastic tissue in the air sacs is replaced by fibrin, which is much more rigid—hence the name cystic fibrosis. One unusual feature of the disease is the high level of salt in the body sweat.

Treatment
Pancreatic extract is given to overcome the lack of digestive enzymes, but a special low-fat diet is essential. Antibiotics and nursing care have made it possible for some patients to survive repeated pneumonia, and there are hospital units specializing in treatment. Modern medical science is approaching the day when the abnormal gene itself can be replaced with a normal one, offering a potential for cure.

Cystitis

Q I got cystitis for the first time a few days into our honeymoon, and the doctor said this was honeymoon disease. What did he mean?

A Those who are not used to sexual intercourse can often be overenthusiastic and forceful, and the entrance to the vagina and around the entrance to the urethra may become very bruised and swollen. Bacteria that normally exist on the perineum, causing no harm, are thrust upward into the bladder, where they begin to breed, thus causing an attack of cystitis. Hence the name *honeymoon disease* or *honeymoon cystitis*.

Q I am suffering from another bad bout of cystitis. But last time I went to the doctor, the tests were negative. Is it worth troubling her again?

A Although about half of patients with cystitis have a negative test result, they still improve with a course of antibiotics. It is, therefore, worth seeing your doctor again.

Q My doctor told me I had urethral syndrome. Is this the same thing as cystitis?

A In some cases of recurrent pain on urination, the urethra, the passageway leading from the bladder down to the front of the vagina, becomes chronically inflamed. This is thought to be due to a deficiency in the female hormone estrogen, and an oral supplement will usually cause the inflammation to subside. So urethral syndrome is not the same as cystitis.

Q My husband thinks he has cystitis. Is this possible?

A Certainly, but there may well be another reason for his discomfort. Cystitis in males tends to be less common, simply because their anatomical makeup protects them to a great extent; the length of their urethra prevents bacteria entering the bladder and setting up an infection there. Your husband should see the family doctor so that his problem can be correctly diagnosed.

Cystitis affects many people, especially females, but until recently, very little was known about it. Fortunately much can now be done to relieve the painful symptoms and to prevent attacks from recurring.

Cystitis is a common and distressing condition. It is an inflammation of the bladder, the organ responsible for urination, and has three basic symptoms: pain when urinating, increased frequency of urination, and sometimes blood loss in the urine. These symptoms vary in intensity from person to person.

Cystitis tends to affect females to a greater extent than males. The first sign of cystitis in a female is a stinging, sometimes knifelike pain when she urinates. Gradually this develops into a sharp lower abdominal pain, and as the inflammation spreads, she will get a dull backache, often with a temperature and a feeling of general sickness.

The urinary system

The blood is the body's transport system, carrying nutrients and waste products. It is the kidneys' function to select and remove unwanted products, then expel them. As the blood flows through the kidneys, the kidneys remove sugar, urea, and many other waste substances from the blood, and then remove these substances from the body.

The watery waste products removed by the kidneys pass down the ureters—tubes leading from the kidneys to the bladder. At the bottom of each ureter, there is a valve that allows the passage of the urine into the bladder. When the bladder is full, the nerves send a message to the brain telling it that the time has come to urinate.

As the person relaxes, the valve (sphincter) relaxes. The exit from the bladder also relaxes and opens, allowing urine to pass into the urethra and out of the body. The bladder then contracts, which helps to get rid of all of the urine.

Urination occurs normally between

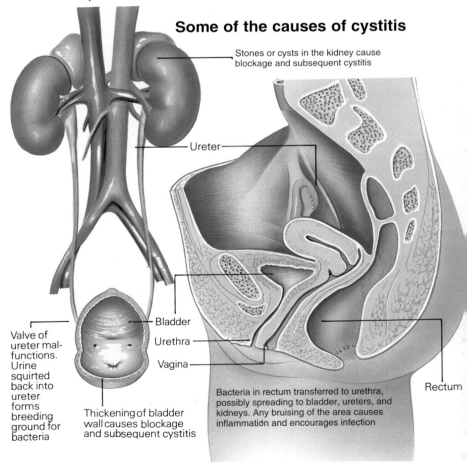

Some of the causes of cystitis

Stones or cysts in the kidney cause blockage and subsequent cystitis

Ureter

Valve of ureter malfunctions. Urine squirted back into ureter forms breeding ground for bacteria

Thickening of bladder wall causes blockage and subsequent cystitis

Bladder

Urethra

Vagina

Rectum

Bacteria in rectum transferred to urethra, possibly spreading to bladder, ureters, and kidneys. Any bruising of the area causes inflammation and encourages infection four and five times a day (but seldom during the night). Obviously the need to urinate will increase if a person drinks large quantities of liquid.

Causes

Cystitis is most commonly caused by bacteria called *Escherichia coli* (*E. coli*). *E. coli* live in the bowel and, like other bacteria that live in the body, are not harmful in this area. They are sometimes even useful. The problems arise when *E. coli* are transferred from the bowel

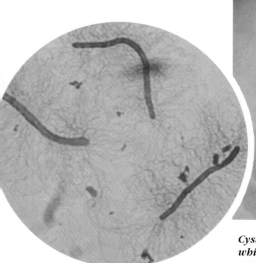

Cystitis may occur when bacteria (left), which normally live in the bowel, come into contact with the urinary organs.

The bacteria flourish in this acidic environment and can spread up into the bladder, ureters, and kidneys (above).

C. James Webb

and come in contact with the urinary organs. *E. coli* flourish in the urinary passages because they thrive in the urine's uric acid content. The design of the female body makes this accidental transference of *E. coli* a particular problem—the woman's anal, vaginal, and urethral openings are so close together that bacteria are very often transmitted from one to the other.

As *E. coli* multiplies, it causes an inflammation, which, unless it is checked, can spread from the urethral opening up into the bladder, ureters, and finally the kidneys. If the infection reaches the kidneys, it is called pyelitis, and unless a cure is prompt, the infection can do lasting damage to the kidneys. The earlier the infection is treated, the better.

Sex and cystitis

Cystitis is sometimes called the honeymoon disease, and for good reasons. Many females suffer their introduction to cystitis when they first make love, since having sex frequently can inflame the tissue around the vagina, including the urethral opening, and also introduce bacteria and encourage infection.

If the penis is inserted into the vagina before the woman is adequately lubricat-

ed, the vaginal skin can be broken, presenting another good breeding ground for bacteria and infection. And some males inadvertently carry harmful bacteria under the foreskin of the penis.

Hormonal changes can also promote cystitis. During her life, a female is subject to radical hormonal changes at times such as puberty, pregnancy, menopause, and after a total hysterectomy. But the complex hormonal system can be affected by a variety of factors, including stress, and changes can also occur at almost any time in a woman's life.

Sometimes certain methods of contraception can bring on cystitis. Some spermicides, for instance, may irritate the sensitive urethral opening. The hormonal effects of the Pill can occasionally trigger cystitis, although it has also been known to diminish attacks. Cystitis can also be related to blockages in the urinary system, such as kidney stones, cysts, or a thickening of the bladder walls; but these problems are less common, and they are usually corrected by surgery.

Sometimes cystitis attacks children, often because their daytime liquid intake is inadequate. When only small amounts of liquid are drank, the urine is more concentrated, resulting in a burning sensa-

tion during urination. This in itself does not constitute an attack of cystitis but, if left untreated, can inflame the urethral tissues and result in cystitis.

Treatment

When a person suspects he or she may have cystitis, advice and treatment should be sought as early as possible. This is because, once it takes hold, it may spread throughout the urinary system and be more difficult to cure.

Cystitis tends to recur in some people. Many females get it three or four times a year, and some have it as often as once a month. This seems to be because the tissues situated in a previously infected area are more susceptible to re-infection and because some females seem especially prone to attacks.

An attack of cystitis can be cleared up in the early stages by following the self-help instructions given here or with antibiotics, if it is already developed. A female can attempt to stop persistent cystitis by finding the cause. The doctor can help identify the cause and find a remedy. In a first case of cystitis, the doctor cultures the organisms from a urine sample. This is tested for sensitivity to antibiotics, and the correct one will be selected.

Another treatment is to alter the acidity of the urine to make it more alkaline. The bacteria that commonly infect urine thrive in acid surroundings; this means that the introduction of a substance that alkalinizes urine will alleviate the symptoms. Potassium citrate is most commonly used. In many cases it is prescribed as a daily preventive measure.

Creams seldom help, but those containing estrogen may be used if there is a local deficiency of this hormone. The cream is applied to the vagina over a period of days, and this makes it more difficult for infective organisms to thrive. Where the diagnosis is in doubt—in cases of recurrent cystitis, particularly in children—the doctor may order an IVP (intravenous pyelogram) or CT (computed tomography) scan. These show the outline and functioning of the renal system and reveal any possible physical causes of the problem.

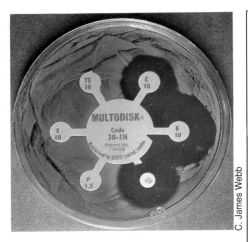

C. James Webb

By culturing the bacteria from a urine sample, a doctor is able to identify which antibiotic will be most effective against the particular cystitis; the most effective is shown by the largest red area.

Coping with cystitis

Times when a woman is most liable

Various events or stages in a female's life can trigger an attack. Here are some of the times when you will be most susceptible:

Puberty
● Cystitis can often be linked to the commencement of menstruation and an unsettled hormone balance, which can correct itself in time

Sexual relations
● The cervix, vagina, and urethra can be inflamed by frequent sex, incautious penetration, or clumsy hand stimulation

Pregnancy
● An irritating discharge can develop during pregnancy, and urine retention can cause discomfort

Childbirth
● Inflammation can result from careless stitching

Menopause/hysterectomy/old age
● Degrees of hormone imbalance often manifest themselves in females over 50, resulting in cystitis

Ways of reducing the risk

The most effective way to deal with cystitis is to minimize the risk of developing the problem by following these simple rules:

● Wash the vaginal area daily with warm water. Always wipe from front to back. Wear pads rather than using tampons. Do not use talcum powder or a vaginal deodorant

● Use a lubricating jelly to cushion the vagina. Afterward, wash the vaginal area with a good flow of cool, clean water from a bottle or a hand shower. r

● Wash the vaginal area (as described above). Empty the bladder completely. Do this by stopping the flow of urine by consciously tightening the muscles around the perineum (the area between the vagina and the anus), then bend over and release the muscles, pushing to help expel any residual urine

● Inform the doctor of any skin sensitivity. Take special care when washing the perineum after delivery. Relieve sensitive irritated skin with warm salt baths

● Ask your doctor to refer you to an endocrinologist, or go to the outpatient clinic of your local hospital for an examination and advice

Self-help for cystitis

Even the most unrelenting cystitis can be self-induced, and unsuitable, self-taught routines can often make things worse. The following hints can help prevent cystitis, in addition to bringing some relief:

● After passing a stool, soap the anus only and pour warm water from a bottle down the perineum (the area between the vagina and the anus) from front to back (or use moistened paper tissues). Dry the area gently but thoroughly. Always wipe from front to back
● Wash the vaginal area before and after making love. Pass urine as soon as possible afterward to flush out any traveling bacteria
● Your contraceptive may be causing recurring cystitis. Ask your gynecologist's advice
● Drink three to five pints of water-based drinks each day
● Wear cotton underwear, which should be boiled in plain water away from the family wash. Avoid pantihose and tight jeans or pants
● Never use chemicals—either in toiletry form or as a medication—on the perineum
● Avoid certain foods such as citrus and soft fruits; hot, spicy foods; and lots of black pepper seasoning—all of these can irritate the bladder. Cut down on sugar and starchy foods

If you still get an attack

Think back over the last 48 hours, and try to pinpoint any unusual occurrence or change in routine. See your doctor for an accurate urine check from an early-morning specimen

In the meantime, to get some immediate relief:

● Drink a glass of bland liquid every 20 minutes for three hours. Cystitis and kidney patients should watch their alcohol intake
● Take one level teaspoon of baking soda in water each hour of the attack (unless you have heart trouble or kidney stones). Or your doctor may prescribe potassium citrate
● Place a hot water bottle, wrapped in a towel, high up between the legs. This makes the skin around the urethral opening hotter than the urine and can bring relief when urinating

Dandruff

Q My brother has bad dandruff. Can I catch it if I use his comb?

A For many years, it was believed that dandruff was an infectious condition, but this has been disproved. Therefore, you cannot get your brother's dandruff.

Q Is it true that having dandruff is likely to make me bald?

A You can stop worrying. This is an old medical belief that was based on the idea that the constant rubbing and scratching of a severely affected person's scalp not only damaged hair, but also produced baldness. This is definitely not true. Dandruff has no effect whatsoever on whether someone goes bald or not.

Q My boyfriend has dandruff, and I think it gets worse if he doesn't shampoo his hair enough. He says if he shampoos it too often, it makes it worse. Who is right?

A Some shampoos may be unsuitable for a scaly scalp, and it is possible that your boyfriend has been using one of these, or he may even have become allergic to his shampoo. You are probably right, however; the correct shampoo should wash away excess grease, dirt, and all the old scales, leaving his hair greatly improved. Unfortunately severe dandruff recurs—sometimes within hours of washing. If your boyfriend suffers severely, he needs medical advice.

Q My doctor said my dandruff would disappear when I was a teenager; later he said it would go when I was over 25. Now I am 40 and still have the condition. Will I have it for life?

A Dandruff is a condition that can disappear as a person gets older, so your problem could have cleared up at any age. Your doctor was probably just trying to be helpful. However, the longer you have the condition, the less likely it is to disappear, although few old people ever complain of dandruff.

Although it causes little more harm than itching, dandruff can look unsightly and cause great embarrassment. Fortunately it is usually easy to treat.

Frederick Mancini

Dandruff is an excessive scaling of the dead skin of the scalp and other parts of the body. It forms part of what doctors call a seborrheic tendency: an overproduction of sebum, the natural oil secreted by glands in the skin. It affects all the areas where hair grows, most commonly the scalp and occasionally the eyebrows, the chest, and the groin.

Causes
In the great majority of cases of dandruff, there is no known cause, but there are indications that heredity, diet, or an upset in the body's hormonal balance may be contributory factors. Stress and severe emotional upheaval can make dandruff worse, while a good period of rest and relaxation while on vacation may virtually abolish the condition altogether.

If you have dandruff, it helps to wear your hair short and off your face. Brushing it regularly with a soft brush will prevent the flakes from accumulating.

In addition the excessive greasiness of an adolescent's skin is a well-known cause of the condition. Campers who are unable to wash their hair regularly may suddenly develop it, as may swimmers who bathe in saltwater without wearing swimming caps.

Symptoms
Dandruff appears as scales of skin resembling tiny white flakes on the scalp and, in some cases, other hairy areas of the body. The scaling is sometimes, but not always, accompanied by intense itching. In severe cases there may be excessive

greasiness of the skin and hair. Patches of scalp redden, and tiny openings appear, which ooze and form hard yellow crusts. The skin on the face, particularly on the forehead, cheeks, and eyebrows, becomes reddened, and scaling occurs in the skin of the ears, on the front of the chest, and over the breast and collarbone.

Complications

The only serious complication occurs if any cracks in the affected skin open and crusted areas become infected, leading to the development of impetigo, a contagious skin disease. Occasionally the condition can turn into eczema: the redness and inflammation worsen and the skin discharges a clear fluid. People with severe dandruff affecting the skin of the ears may develop otitis externa, an infection in the outer ear canal. This requires medical attention.

Dandruff should not be confused with psoriasis (isolated tiny patches of scaly

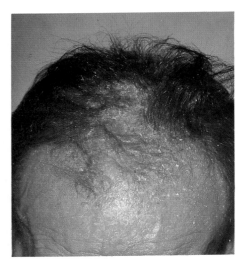

Dandruff—an excessive flaking of skin on the scalp and elsewhere on the body—is best treated by shampooing regularly with an antidandruff shampoo.

skin) or exfoliative dermatitis (scaling all over the body), which is a serious condition that needs hospital treatment.

Treatment

The mainstay of treatment for ordinary dandruff is regular shampooing with one of the many antidandruff shampoos on the market. Doctors recommend coal-tar-based shampoos, which are safe and relatively inexpensive. Shampoos containing sulfur, a special mixture of vegetable oil, fatty acids, and chlorophyll or selenium are also beneficial.

Only severe dandruff requires medical treatment, and this should be sought where there is scaling of the surrounding skin, severe itching, and cracking of the scalp, or signs of spreading elsewhere on the body. Bouts of dandruff can be treated with steroid lotions or ointments applied to the scalp. Where there is a secondary infection in the scratched or cracked skin, antibiotics will help.

Outlook

Medically there is no cure for dandruff. The condition may improve and then recur from time to time or disappear altogether at any age. But why this happens is not yet known.

Dandruff: helpful hints

- Find a shampoo that suits your skin by trying as many as possible
- Shampoo hair as often as it needs it. This may be twice a week, but in some cases it may be every day
- If you are using a medicated or selenium-based shampoo, follow the instructions on the bottle about method and frequency of use
- Keep hair as short as possible and off the face. Hair appears to irritate the skin, and dandruff often disappears after a radical haircut
- Brush out the scales every day with a soft hairbrush. Avoid hard brushes and sharp combs that can tear the scalp and lead to cracks and crust formation
- Try changing your diet and getting out in the fresh air
- Get over the embarrassment of dandruff. Accept that you have it, and carry a small brush for your shoulders before meeting people. If the subject arises, be knowledgeable
- Dandruff is not an infection, but a condition, and it is not your fault
- Wear light-colored clothes to hide dandruff scales

Deafness

Q My three-year-old brother is just learning to talk. When I call him from the backyard, he sometimes doesn't hear. Could he be partially deaf?

A A child who is slow to talk and appears deaf most definitely needs a hearing test. At least this will reassure you and your parents that all is normal. But children are famous for hearing only what they wish to, especially when deeply engrossed in play. So if your brother hears normally at other times, he may be ignoring your call.

Q I have worked in a foundry for 20 years but only recently have been offered ear protectors. Can loud noise cause deafness?

A Repeated exposure to loud noise greater than 90 decibels will damage hearing. The delicate sensory mechanism in the inner ear first becomes damaged at the high tone level and then at the lower tones. Industrial hearing damage is not something that simply happens to unlucky people. It can happen to all workers who work in a noisy environment and do not wear ear protectors. Hearing loss is inevitable, unless preventive measures are constantly used.

Q Why do some people go deaf when they have a cold?

A In the same way that a virus infection will make the nose run and water, a virus in the middle ear will cause congestion. This blocks off the eustachian tube, making the patient feel blocked-up and reducing the hearing. When the cold clears up and drainage from the eustachian tube to the throat returns to normal, the blocked-up sensation disappears, and hearing is back to normal.

Q My ears get very waxy. How can I clean them?

A Zealous attempts at cleaning can cause deafness, so be careful. Wash the outside with soap and water; dry thoroughly. Clean just inside with a Q-tip, but do not insert the Q-tip—or anything else—straight into your ear.

While few people are totally deaf, there are many degrees of hearing loss, resulting from infection, disease, heredity, or noise pollution. Fortunately much can be done to prevent and treat hearing problems.

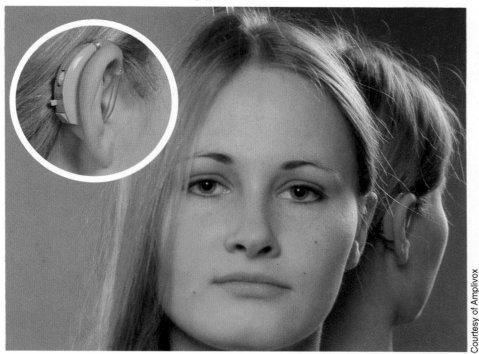

Courtesy of Amplivox

Some forms of deafness can be alleviated with a hearing aid, which fits neatly into the ear and is hardly noticeable.

Deafness is the inability or reduced ability to hear. It can affect one or both ears, and the onset may be slow or sudden. The causes are varied, and there are many forms of treatment and devices available to remove or alleviate the symptoms.

To understand deafness, it is necessary to know how the ear works. Sound is caused by vibrations occurring in waves within the air. Under normal circumstances, these sound waves travel along the outer ear to the tympanic membrane, or eardrum. The drum vibrates, and this vibration is transferred along three tiny individual bones in the middle ear: the malleus (hammer), incus (anvil), and stapes (stirrup). These are known collectively as the auditory ossicles. The mechanical vibration is then taken up as energy by the inner ear and is transmitted as electrical impulses along the auditory nerve to the brain, where it is interpreted as sound.

The ear is also the organ of balance. This is why some hearing diseases that cause deafness also affect balance and can produce vertigo (dizziness).

The middle ear is connected to the back of the throat by a canal called the eustachian tube. When ascending a steep hill in a fast car or leaving the ground in a nonpressurized airplane, a person often feels a popping sensation in the ears. This is because the outside pressure has dropped and the middle ear has expanded. Yawning or swallowing will equalize the pressure. Germs can spread along this tube from the throat or nose and lead to infection in the ear (otitis media).

Types of deafness

There are two main types of deafness: conductive deafness and perceptive deafness. In conductive deafness, sound waves are prevented from reaching the inner ear. This can be because there is wax in the outer canal, fluid inside it, or the tiny ossicles (bones) in the ear have seized up (otosclerosis). In perceptive deafness, although the sound can reach the inner ear, there is a disease of the nerves leading to the brain or a condition affecting the function of the inner ear.

In the majority of cases, deafness falls into one of these two categories. In some instances, however, the causes may be confused: for example, an old person may have excess wax, causing conductive

Q Why is deafness associated with loss of balance? My great-aunt has to wear a hearing aid, which she manages pretty well, but she still loses her balance a lot.

A There is a close connection between balance and hearing. The organ of hearing, the cochlea of the inner ear, is also part of the organs of balance, the semicircular canals of the inner ear. Both send information to the brain along the same auditory nerve. Therefore, conditions that affect one sensation easily affect the other. In the case of old age, the amount of information carried by the auditory nerve is reduced, so hearing ability decreases, as does the sense of balance. A cane may give your great-aunt more confidence when she goes for a walk.

Q Why do I need to have my ears syringed every six months? Other people seem to have no trouble.

A There are two explanations for this common condition. You either produce more wax than other people, so that your ear canal becomes blocked more quickly, or the shape of your ear canal is so narrow that wax becomes clogged. There is nothing you can do about either of these, so having the ears syringed professionally every six months is a good preventive measure.

Q I fly a lot for work. Why do I occasionally go a little deaf as the plane takes off?

A Whenever you climb quickly, whether on a plane or in a fast car going uphill, the atmospheric pressure drops, and this causes the air in the middle ear to expand. Discomfort is felt momentarily, but it disappears when you yawn or swallow. This equalizes the pressure by letting air out of the eustachian tube into the back of the throat. Hearing is affected because the eardrum bulges and moves the ossicle bones, thereby reducing sound. Try swallowing or sucking a candy to stop the feeling and return hearing to normal. People sometimes feel the same sensation when going up in an elevator.

deafness, together with a hearing loss affecting the nerve that carries sound to the brain.

Mild or partial hearing loss is extremely common. In children, deafness can slow down the general ability to learn as well as speak. In adults, the deafness caused by gradual hearing loss or old age simply increases feelings of isolation and loneliness. Deaf people have to take special precautions in traffic or crowds and tend to be more accident-prone because of their hearing disability.

Diagnosis

Deafness is a symptom of malfunction of the ear. The earlier it can be identified, the sooner treatment can begin. A person with normal hearing can easily hear words or numbers whispered softly from about 5 ft (1.5 m) away. A slightly deaf person will miss most of the words whispered at this distance, and a very deaf person will be unable to hear a conversation 6 in (15 cm) from the ear.

There are various methods of testing hearing. Voice tests are the first; another way is by means of a tuning fork. This produces a sound of constant pitch: the larger the fork, the lower the note. It is moved slowly away from the ear until the patient says he or she can no longer hear the sound, and the distance is measured. The process is then repeated with the other

ear. This makes it possible to plot hearing levels for different notes. Sometimes it is found that the patient hears best if the foot of the tuning fork is placed on the bone behind the ear. This is characteristic of conductive deafness, and the test is used to identify hearing difficulties affected by this condition.

With small babies, hearing tests are often performed at six months and one year by the doctor or nurse. One test involves shaking a bell or rattle to one side of the baby's head, out of his or her vision. If the baby turns to look at the

A baby's hearing can be tested using a bell or rattle. If a child is deaf, he or she can attend a special school, where staff are trained to develop speech.

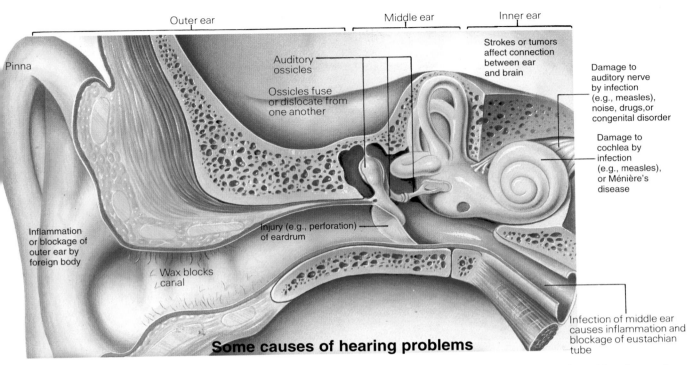

Outer ear | Middle ear | Inner ear

Pinna

Auditory ossicles

Ossicles fuse or dislocate from one another

Strokes or tumors affect connection between ear and brain

Damage to auditory nerve by infection (e.g., measles), noise, drugs, or congenital disorder

Damage to cochlea by infection (e.g., measles), or Ménière's disease

Inflammation or blockage of outer ear by foreign body

Injury (e.g., perforation) of eardrum

Wax blocks canal

Infection of middle ear causes inflammation and blockage of eustachian tube

Some causes of hearing problems

Conductive deafness arises from any problems that prevent the transmission of sound waves through the external ear canal and middle ear as far as the innermost auditory ossicle. Perceptive deafness involves damage to the cochlea and/or the auditory nerve, so that, although sound waves reach the inner ear, transmission to the brain is adversely affected.

Causes of hearing problems and their treatments

Condition	Cause	Symptoms	Treatment
Conductive deafness			
Wax	Excessive production of wax, sometimes from skin conditions like seborrheic dermatitis	Wax swells following a cold or after swimming, and deafness then develops	Medical attention is necessary. A few drops of wax solvent or olive oil are put in the ear for two or three nights, and wax is syringed using warm water. Dramatic relief of deafness
Eustachian congestion	Inflammation of eustachian tube, following a cold or throat infection, causes congestion, which blocks the tube	Periods of deafness that may clear on blowing the nose	Decongestant capsules. A tube may need to be unblocked by the doctor
Middle ear inflammation (otitis media)	Viral or bacterial. Follows repeated blockage of eustachian tube from congestion. Frequently occurs in children	Deafness, accompanied by pain in the ear and fever. Discharging of sticky fluid from the middle ear. Sometimes perforation of the eardrum and discharge of pus may be followed by deafness	Antibiotics and painkillers from doctor. Place a warm hot water bottle near the ear to relieve earache. Heals when infection is eradicated
Chronic middle ear inflammation	Viral or bacterial. Follows repeated blockage of eustachian tube with catarrh (inflammation of the mucous membrane). Frequently occurs in children	Gradual deafness, accompanied by repeated pain in the ear and fever. Perforation or discharge of pus is less common. Bulging eardrum	Surgery may be necessary. Perforation is made, a grommet is installed, and fluid is sucked out and then drains. In time, grommet falls out and tiny perforation heals
Inflammation of the outer ear (otitis externa)	Often associated with dandruff, greasy scalp, or eczema. Made worse by scratching or cleaning the outer ear with rough towels, paper clips or wooden matches	Itchy, red, swollen, painful ears. Debris of swelling blocks ears. Often recurs	Special eardrops and painkillers from doctor to treat initial stages. Hearing quickly returns. Steroid eardrops to prevent further skin irritations

Condition	Cause	Symptoms	Treatment
Foreign body in outer ear	Placing a bead, candy, or berry in the ear, usually done by a child	Discomfort and discharge of pus. Deafness sometimes unnoticed	Removal of the foreign body by a doctor. Antibiotic drugs are sometimes necessary
Injury to the eardrum—possibly puncturing it (perforation)	Skull fracture, shock from an explosion, slap on the ear, unskilled attempt to remove a foreign body or wax from ear with a wooden match, hairpin, or paper clip	Often sudden; painful at moment of injury. Deafness, occasionally dizziness, and ringing in the ear	Antibiotics from doctor. Gradual return of hearing
Otosclerosis	Fusion of the tiny bones (ossicles) of the middle ear. Frequently occurs in young adults, mainly females, and gradually worsens. Often hereditary	Slow onset of deafness and sometimes tinnitus (buzzing or ringing sound in the ear)	Surgical removal of tiny stapes bone and replacement by vein graft or plastic device. Usually successful, though sometimes a hearing aid may be necessary
Perceptive deafness Senile deafness (presbyacusis)	Aging	Gradual inability to hear, with high-pitched sounds affected first	Hearing aid. Amplifier and earphone. Learning to read lips and speak from memory
Infections damaging the hearing nerves	Bacterial infections damaging the cochlea (hearing organ). Virus infections attacking the hearing nerve to the brain. Can occur as a complication of measles, mumps, meningitis, and rarely, syphilis	Progressive deafness	Same as senile deafness
Congenital deafness	Abnormality of the growth of the hearing apparatus or damage to the hearing nerve from rubella; shortage of oxygen at birth or congenital syphilis	Extreme or total deafness. Speech difficulties	Special education. Hearing aid. Phonic ear (combined radio receiver and hearing aid). Speech therapy
Damage to the auditory nerve	Severe loud noise, noise from aircraft, loud machinery, and gun or bomb explosions	Gradual deafness	Wearing ear protectors to prevent damage. Hearing aid if damage already present
	Large dosages of streptomycin, quinine, or aspirin	Deafness occurs during or after a course of drugs	Avoid drugs concerned
	Growth on nerve between ear and brain (auditory neuroma)	Progressive deafness	Surgical removal of tumor
Ménière's disease	Rising pressure within cochlea of the inner ear	Dizziness and ringing in the ear, vomiting. Gradual deafness	Drug treatment to reduce the pressure of the fluid within the inner ear

sound on more than one occasion, hearing is considered to be functioning in a normal way. Modern otoacoustic emission devices test a baby's hearing by measuring a sound that bounces back from the baby's inner ear.

The only scientific method of accurately assessing adult hearing is to use an instrument called an audiometer. This machine emits standard notes at different volumes, and the patient signals when a sound is heard. Not only does it measure the air conduction from the sound emitted, which is heard in an earphone, it also tests what is known as bone conduction, when the sound is played directly into the bone of the skull.

Ears, like eyes, are precious. When deafness occurs, either suddenly or over a period of time, it is very important, after an initial assessment, to start treatment as quickly as possible.

Coping with deafness

Where treatment is of no avail and deafness is permanent, a suitable hearing aid may be fitted. If even this does not help, the patient has to learn to read lips and to speak from memory. Small children have to be taught to speak and can receive special schooling; most deaf people also learn sign language.

Although deafness is a handicap, it is possible for deaf people to lead a normal and useful life. However, they must be additionally careful when driving. Total deafness may be considered a hazard to driving, but provided that warning sounds can be converted into visual signals, deaf people can drive.

Since some forms of deafness can be caused by carelessness, some precautions can be taken. Never place hard and dangerous objects, like safety pins or paper clips, in the ear. Never syringe someone's ear unless you are medically trained, especially in the case of babies and small children. Never slap a child on the side of the face, since this may rupture the eardrum. Avoid continuously exposing the ears to loud noise, whether at the airport or in discotheques, and if employed in an industry where there is constant, loud noise, always wear ear protectors or plugs. Seek medical attention for a discharging or painful ear, and have regular hearing tests if there is any cause for concern.

Death

Q My father is terminally ill. Should he be told so that he can prepare himself for death?

A Much depends on the person involved. Some people might despair if they were told, while others would take it calmly. However, this is not something you can risk doing without talking to the doctor, other family members, and a religious adviser, if relevant.

Q Should a child be allowed to go to a funeral?

A Small babies and infants cannot really tell the difference between a funeral and any other service, but certainly a child of six or seven will understand. If the funeral is of a close relative, the child may benefit from being part of the family and sharing in the service, albeit in a child's way. The child may resent not going, especially if the person was close to them, and this could have harmful repercussions later on. However, if he or she shows a strong determination not to attend, it is probably wise not to push the matter any further.

Q How can I be sure I will really be dead before being buried or cremated?

A This is a common fear. However, these days the diagnosis of death is so accurate that there is little to worry about. Uncomplicated deaths are usually patently obvious, and the more complicated ones are tested by machines so there is no doubt left.

Q How do I leave my body to medical research?

A While you are alive, it is necessary to contact the institution of your choice, possibly a teaching hospital, and enter into an agreement with them. A note should be made in your will and your relatives informed of your wishes. After death, when a certificate of disposal has been granted, your body will be collected by the medical school. After the research is completed, the medical school will arrange for cremation or burial, according to your preference.

Facing death, whether one's own or that of a close relative or friend, is a distressing experience. Rather than being fearful of the unknown, it is better to become acquainted with this most basic process.

Redferns

Different cultures treat death in different ways. Here, Earl Turbinton pays tribute to celebrated saxophonist Professor Longhair in a New Orleans funeral parlor.

Death is the natural and inevitable ending of life within the human body. It can occur suddenly, as in a car or other accident, or more slowly, as a result of a fatal illness. In all cases it is accompanied by a complete loss of consciousness, which precedes or accompanies the actual stopping of the heart.

In the human body there is a constant turnover of cells as some die and others are replaced. In tissues like the skin, and in the blood, this is rapid and constant. When death occurs, the cells of the nervous system that lie in the brain perish. There is a loss of consciousness and, depending on the varying times that tissues can survive without oxygen, the other cells in the body also begin to die.

Causes
Death is caused by the failure of a vital organ to function. Although a person can manage without an arm or a leg, failure of an internal organ, such as the heart or a major blood vessel, can result in an instant loss of life. When the brain fails, for instance, from a hemorrhage, death is usually instantaneous. Similarly a heart attack will stop the heart from beating.

In the lungs, asphyxia (suffocation) may result from gas poisoning, strangulation, or a massive blood clot that prevents the blood from obtaining oxygen. This starves the brain and causes death to occur. If organs such as the liver or kid-

neys fail, medical support will keep the patient alive for up to a few weeks. Without support, toxic substances will build up in the blood, eventually upsetting the blood's chemistry so that the heart stops.

The causes of death vary in males and females. In males the main culprits are coronary heart disease (heart attacks), strokes, lung cancer, and then pneumonia. In females cardiovascular disease (strokes), heart attacks, breast cancer, and uterine cancer are most commonly responsible. Sometimes a secondary disease or infection can kill a patient suffering from a long-term illness of another kind. In many cases of terminal cancer, for example, the spread of cancerous cells so weakens the patient that he or she contracts pneumonia and dies. For this reason a death certificate may list not one, but several causes of death.

How to establish death
At the actual moment of death, the brain cells die, and all consciousness is lost. The heart may continue beating for a few minutes after breathing has stopped, but the beats will be weak and ineffective. Some cells take longer to die than others, for example, the cells of the eyes.

DEATH

How long can men and women expect to live?

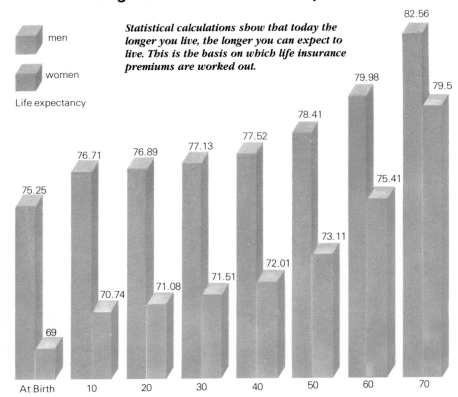

men

women

Life expectancy

Statistical calculations show that today the longer you live, the longer you can expect to live. This is the basis on which life insurance premiums are worked out.

John Hutchinson/HMSO Life Losses

	At Birth	10	20	30	40	50	60	70
men	75.25	76.71	76.89	77.13	77.52	78.41	79.98	82.56
women	69	70.74	71.08	71.51	72.01	73.11	75.41	79.5

In death the body is still: movement and respiration are absent; no pulse can be felt; heart sounds cannot be heard over the chest. The eyes are glazed. The pupils are dilated, and when light is shone into them, there is no response.

Within minutes the body begins cooling and soon feels cold. The skin turns pale as blood drains down to the lower extremities, and this causes a discoloration of the flanks and buttocks. Within a period of about four hours, the body becomes stiff as rigor mortis—a contraction of the muscles as stored energy is released—sets in. This may last for 48 hours but sometimes lasts far less.

After death many of the cell membranes break down, and within a short time, decomposition commences. For this reason, the undertaker will plug up the openings with cotton wool and may embalm the body with preservatives to await burial or cremation.

What to do
If you are uncertain whether a person is dead or not, call a doctor immediately. Where death is expected and obvious, then the doctor will not need to attend as an emergency.

Only the doctor who has been attending the patient can write out a death certificate. When this has been issued, a relative is required to register the death.

Providing all is in order, a certificate of disposal is given that allows for the body to be buried or cremated. The undertaker is familiar with the necessary arrangements and can give advice.

If there are suspicious circumstances, or the death is sudden and the cause is not known, or if the doctor is uncertain as to the cause, the coroner or medical examiner must be informed. The former is a lay person, with legal or medical training, or both, who works with the police to establish causes of death that are not immediately apparent. The latter is a pathologist. In such circumstances the body must not be touched or moved until the police have made an inspection and the coroner gives permission for its removal. In certain circumstances an autopsy may have to be performed, and sometimes an inquest is held before permission is given to dispose of the body.

How to cope with bereavement
The general trend in Western society is to treat death as a taboo subject. In other societies, death is accompanied by mourning, festivity, and ritual, which many regard as consoling.

It is normal for friends and relatives to mourn, but close relatives may react violently—even strangely—on bereavement. They may become overemotional, totally withdrawn, or experience hallucinations

where they feel they can touch or talk to their departed relative. Some people believe such reactions are less likely to be severe if the mourning is open, the body is touched or kissed, and the funeral arrangements are lavish rather than hushed and minimized.

In some cases mental depression follows bereavement, and when this is excessive or continues for long periods, then antidepressant drugs may be prescribed, or the bereaved may consider seeing a psychiatrist.

When a child dies, the parents—and in particular, the mother—are likely to undergo extreme grief and may even develop mental illness. If a baby is stillborn or a miscarriage has occurred, then a couple may want to try again for another baby after two or three months. The involvement and support of the partner is essential, as feelings of guilt and discontentment may often be harbored. Such feelings must be brought out and resolved before introducing another child into an unhappy home. In this case, another baby is not always the answer.

When a parent dies, there is always a degree of guilt and a sense of loss and waste felt by the bereaved offspring. There are feelings that one should have been kinder, more considerate, listened longer, and said nicer things. For most people these feelings pass in time and are replaced by warm memories.

If a parent of a very young child dies, there is no point in trying to hide the death. Children always need to know; they also require constant and continual reassurance that although the parent is now gone, they themselves were always loved and wanted. When they grow older, the knowledge that they were cared for and loved by that parent will help offset the natural sense of grief and loss.

Facing up to death
Facing death is difficult enough; having to make decisions about it is almost impossible. It is for this reason that so many otherwise sensible people die without making a will. It is never too early to think about this, to make sure that those who are left behind will suffer the minimum of stress and strain and that a person's wishes are carried out. A note should also be included as to which method of disposal is preferred.

Cremation—the most popular method today—is permanent and clean. The body is reduced to ashes, which can be kept in an urn and placed in a memorial garden or scattered in a chosen place. With burial, a plot has to be purchased or rented for a number of years, and the body is placed in a coffin about 6 ft (2 m) below the ground.

Dementia

The mental disabilities that are caused by dementia are very distressing, but its effects can be minimized. The progress of the condition can be halted by stimulating those faculties still unimpaired.

Q My great-grandfather went crazy in a mental hospital, and my mother says he was suffering from dementia. Is this a hereditary condition?

A One type of dementia is caused by a faulty gene, and a parent with this gene could pass on the condition to 50 percent of his or her children. But such occurrences are very rare. While other forms of dementia have some genetic influence, the majority are not caused by family transmission.

Q I am in my 50s and seem to be getting increasingly absent-minded. Could I be in the early stages of dementia?

A This is highly unlikely. Admittedly, one of the first signs of dementia in the elderly is a tendency to forget things, but that is all. Absent-mindedness is usually due to intense concentration in another direction, which can hardly be equated with the deterioration associated with dementia.

Q Can taking certain drugs bring on dementia? I have read somewhere that it can.

A Yes, this is so. Any chemical that produces brain damage, such as excessive alcohol, will cause dementia. On the other hand, there are many drugs (taken for either medical or recreational purposes) that have no effect on the brain at all, or if they do, they do not permanently damage and affect brain function.

Q Do you have to be senile to be demented?

A No. There are at least six causes of dementia—only one of these is old age. And many old people do not suffer from it.

Q I have just been diagnosed as being in the early stages of syphilis. Will I go crazy?

A Not so long ago this would have been a possibility. But new and effective treatment will clear up symptoms quickly and make the likelihood of dementia at a later stage very unlikely.

Keeping the mind active and enjoying the company of young people helps older people maintain their mental health.

Dementia is usually characterized by a progressive deterioration of a person's mental faculties, and it affects males and females alike. It often involves brain damage or atrophy (wasting away); both are irreversible. In certain cases, however, dementia can be delayed.

Types and causes

Of the many types of dementia, the most common has no proven cause at present. It is called senile dementia (Alzheimer's disease). It is most prevalent after the age of 65 and occurs equally in males and females. Arteriosclerotic dementia is caused by a thickening of the arteries in the brain, which starves it of blood and oxygen—and this condition can occur over the same age span. Dementia can also be caused by a tumor in the brain: either the tumor itself can trigger the condition, or the growth may press against the brain tissue.

Nutritional deficiencies due to a faulty metabolism (the body's life-supporting process) may also cause dementia, as may poisoning by alcohol or the various toxic substances produced in vehicle exhaust fumes. However, the damage is only done after a period of long and massive exposure to these poisons.

Finally, dementia can be caused by a severe physical injury. Not every blow or loss of consciousness contributes to the condition, but if there is brain damage associated with a physical injury, a degree of dementia might occur.

Symptoms

One of the first signs of dementia is an impairment of memory. The recollection of recent events is initially affected. Judgment and reasoning become confused: the person fails to grasp what is going on and is unable to act appropriately. There is emotional instability, and moods may often change for no reason at all. Sometimes sufferers may not know where they are; they may also wander.

A patient may also commit irrational acts such as turning on the stove or water for no purpose. He or she may also suffer from delusions, together with an increasing lack of self-interest and awareness, leading to physical neglect. Those in an advanced state of dementia often have to be watched very carefully, for everybody's sake.

Treatment

Where brain damage or atrophy are concerned, there is little hope for improvement. The best that can be done is to try and halt the progress of the condition by stimulating the mental faculties remaining. Watching television, talking, or walking are better than doing nothing. In the case of dementia caused by metabolic defect, resulting from poor diet or poisoning, once this has been detected, the progress of the condition can be halted.

Dental care

Q My dentist's two children have beautiful teeth. Why should this be?

A Statistics have shown that children of dentists have much better teeth than the rest of us —something like one-tenth of the dental decay of the rest of the population. The main reason for this dramatic difference is that dentists are aware of the dangers of sugar, and they often manage to discourage their young children from developing a sweet tooth.

Q I sometimes have bad breath. What is the cause?

A Apart from occasional bad breath caused, for example, by too much garlic, the usual reason for unpleasant-smelling breath is a dental problem. Badly brushed teeth, tooth decay, and gum disease can all cause bad breath. So anyone with persistent bad breath should take better care of their teeth. If bad breath still doesn't go away, a dentist should be consulted for more advice.

Q I am a smoker. How can I keep my teeth clean?

A One of the side bad effects of smoking is yellow, nicotine-stained teeth. Of course the healthiest thing to do is to kick the habit. Otherwise you should be able to keep your teeth white by proper brushing. Special smokers' toothpaste is not recommended by most dentists, because it is too abrasive. But if you can't get your teeth white by simple, but thorough, brushing, then go to your dentist for a proper cleaning. Once they are white again, you should be able to keep them gleaming with regular, twice-daily brushing.

Q I have a very sweet tooth. How can I cut my sugar consumption?

A If you gradually reduce the amount of sugar in tea or coffee (down from three to two spoonfuls; then later down to one), you will hardly notice the difference. Avoid eating sweets between meals. Try savory snacks such as crackers or carrot sticks instead.

A smile revealing white teeth is universally admired. But teeth have to be very carefully cleaned and cared for if they are to last throughout a person's life.

Regular cleaning is vital for healthy teeth and gums, and for fresh-smelling breath. Without it unpleasant substances develop in the mouth, which cause tooth decay and gum disease. Of these the most dangerous is plaque. This is an almost invisible layer of yellowish-white sticky material composed of bacteria, saliva, and microscopic bits of food. It spreads and clings to the teeth, breaking down sugar into acids that attack the enamel surface of the tooth. This is the start of tooth decay, and once it is established, it slowly moves deeper into the tooth, and a hole—or cavity—appears.

Because plaque is such a sticky substance, it is vital to brush the teeth thoroughly twice a day to get rid of it. In fact, how thoroughly the teeth are brushed is much more important than how often they are cleaned. On average it takes at least three minutes of correct brushing to remove all the plaque. Brushing the teeth quickly several times a day is not as effective as a really good cleaning after breakfast and then before going to bed.

Work steadily around the outside of all the teeth, and then clean the inside surfaces. Moving the brush around and around in small circles is the most effective method, because it cleans the teeth without damaging the gums. The mouth should be rinsed thoroughly afterward.

Cleaning aids
Clean teeth also depend on a good toothbrush. A frayed brush will not be so effective, so buy a new toothbrush about every three months.

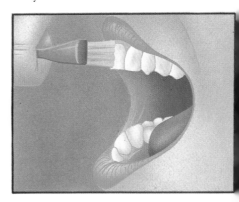

Using a flat-headed toothbrush, brush upper teeth downward from the gums and lower teeth upward from the gums.

Most dentists recommend a flat-headed, nylon toothbrush with a short, straight handle for reaching the awkward corners of the mouth. Hardness of bristle is a personal choice, but an extra soft brush is not a good idea for an adult, and a very hard one may hurt the gums.

Toothpaste is available with or without fluoride. An amount the size of a pea is ample for each brushing.

Dental floss is useful for cleaning the spaces between the teeth, where plaque can become trapped. Floss is a thin, silky yarn and may be waxed or unwaxed. Both are equally effective. The waxed kind of floss feels smoother but may cause inflammation if the wax coating is driven into the gums.

Interdental cleaners are an alternative to floss. They are flat, wooden sticks that are put between the teeth and pulled gently back and forth. They are not toothpicks, of which most dentists definitely do not approve.

A stimulator—a metal or plastic rod with a pointed rubber tip—is often recommended to massage the gums around the base of each tooth. A water pick is useful for dislodging any food particles caught between the teeth.

Care of gums

Healthy gums are pink and firm. They should not be swollen or reddened around the edges and should never bleed, even if they are brushed hard. Careful, daily brushing will keep them healthy. If the gums bleed or are inflamed, the dentist should be told and advice requested.

Gum disease starts when plaque accumulates around, and just under, the edge of the gums. If the gum tissue alone is affected, this is known as gingivitis. The gums should be massaged with daily, gentle brushing, but the dentist should also be consulted, since he or she can remove the plaque easily.

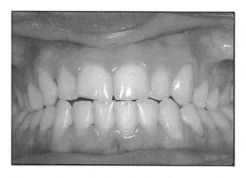

These apparently clean teeth, when coated with a special disclosing agent, soon reveal an accumulation of plaque. This can either

In advanced stages of gum disease—called periodontal disease—the deeper tissue, including the bone, is affected. This is much more difficult to cure: the gums recede, the teeth may be permanently loosened, and it is possible that they may eventually be lost.

It is particularly important to get into the habit of visiting the dentist regularly—every six months or so—even if the teeth seem healthy. In addition to performing any necessary treatment, he or she can also advise the patient on how to clean the teeth properly, how to plan a diet that is kind to teeth, how to detect damaging plaque and brush it off, and the correct use of dental floss.

Fluoride

Dentists believe that the best method of preventing tooth decay, especially in children, is to brush teeth regularly with fluoride toothpaste and to take it in other forms. It is also thought to help repair enamel after it has been attacked by acids and to have an antibacterial effect.

Fluoride is available from the drugstore in tablet, drop, or mouthwash form. In addition, fluoride is added to normal tap water in many places, both in the United States and abroad.

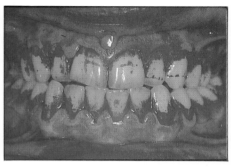

be done by the dentist as part of a check-up, or chewable tablets can be bought from the drugstore to use at home.

Opponents to fluoride claim that it can cause diseases, although there is no firm evidence of this. There is also the fear that too much fluoride is poisonous. It is possible to find out about the levels of fluoride in the local water supply from the dentist or water authority.

Diet

Cane and beet sugar not only interact with plaque to produce dangerous acids, but also actually increase the amount of plaque on the teeth. If a person tries to avoid, or keep to a minimum, foods like chocolates, toffees, candies, pastries, cake, jam, sugar in tea and coffee, cookies, and ice cream, he or she can greatly reduce the rate of decay in the teeth.

Fibrous foods are better for the teeth than soft foods, which collect on the teeth, particularly along the line where the gums join the teeth. Soft foods also tend to lodge between the teeth, leading to the development of plaque.

Foods such as green vegetables, salads, celery, raw carrots, nuts, and apples not only give the teeth work to do, but also keep them tough and firm. Since healthy teeth are, to a large degree, dependent on a healthy lifestyle in general, a balanced diet is most important.

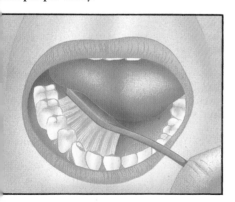

The inner surfaces of the teeth are just as important as the outer ones. Brush all around these upper and lower surfaces.

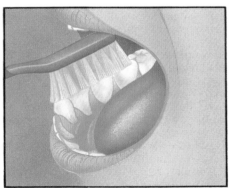

The back teeth have flat tops for chewing food. Brush backward and forward on these upper and lower surfaces.

Dental floss cleans between the teeth. Cut a short length and wind around the pointer fingers. Gently ease up and down, all around.

Venner Artists

Dentures, crowns, and bridges

Q I've just had a crown fitted, and I'm worried about breaking it when eating. Is there any way this could happen?

A Crowned teeth should be able to withstand the normal stresses and strains of eating, but they can be broken if used to bite on something exceptionally hard.

Q My dentist tells me that my 12-year-old daughter is too young to have her broken front tooth capped. Why is this?

A Capping involves trimming down the tooth so that it is not made too large by the cap. Children's pulp cavities (containing the soft tissue at the center of the teeth) tend to be especially large, and they are easily damaged if crown preparation is attempted. When your daughter is older, the pulp chamber will be smaller, and this makes crown preparation safer.

Q Is constructing a crown the only way of treating my broken front tooth?

A No. Where only a small piece is missing, it is now possible to use an adhesive filling material to replace it. This material is bonded to the tooth and lasts several years. A crown is, however, a more permanent solution.

Q My denture fitting is loose. Is there any way I can make it stay in place more firmly?

A There are a number of adhesives available, but these are not a satisfactory solution. You should discuss the problem with your dentist, who may either reline the denture to improve its fit or extend it at the edges to gain better suction.

Q As I get older, my dentures seem to become more uncomfortable. Is there anything I can do about this?

A After teeth have been lost, the bones that used to support them gradually become flatter, and this means dentures don't fit as well. Generally dentures need to be replaced every five years.

Dentures, crowns, and bridges are not just replacements for lost or damaged teeth. They are also important in restoring the correct shape to the wearer's face and insuring that the remaining teeth do not grow abnormally.

Dentures are artificial teeth. They replace teeth that have been removed as a result of decay, gum disease, or injury, or that have failed to develop in childhood. In many countries, about half the adult population wear dentures.

Advantages of dentures
If someone loses all their teeth, they also lose support for the lips and cheeks. This makes them look hollow-cheeked and older than their age. It also causes overclosing of the mouth, since there are no teeth to provide a "stop" against further closing. Replacing the missing teeth with dentures can overcome these problems.

The loss of a few teeth may, in addition, make neighboring teeth grow at the wrong angle, and this in turn can cause gum disease. A tooth that used to bite against one that has been lost tends to overerupt—that is, grow higher above

Well-made dentures can greatly enhance the appearance—dentists take great care to insure that the color and shape of replacement teeth look natural, as here.

the gum than its normal level. Fitting dentures can prevent both problems. Finally, of course, dentures enable the wearer to chew and to speak more easily than before. Therefore, although having dentures is never as good as the real thing, they do have many advantages.

Making dentures
False teeth have to fit the shape of the patient's mouth accurately, and they are therefore built on exact models of the patient's jaw. These models are made by taking a mold of both the upper and lower jaw, by means of a soft material that records the shape. Plaster is then poured into the resulting mold and allowed to set.

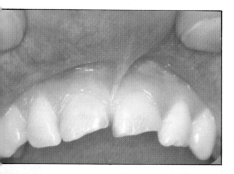

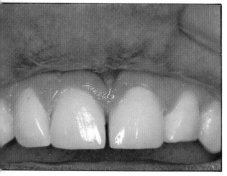

Before and after: these front teeth (top left) were broken in an accident. Two porcelain jacket crowns were made (bottom left) to restore their previous appearance. The original midline gap between the teeth was kept, so that the teeth look as they did before they were broken.

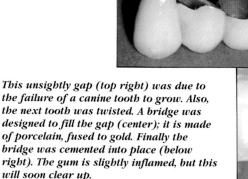

This unsightly gap (top right) was due to the failure of a canine tooth to grow. Also, the next tooth was twisted. A bridge was designed to fill the gap (center); it is made of porcelain, fused to gold. Finally the bridge was cemented into place (below right). The gum is slightly inflamed, but this will soon clear up.

Patients who only need a few new teeth are given partial dentures, which are positioned so as to be in line with the remaining natural teeth.

Those who have lost all their teeth receive a full set of dentures. These are carefully designed so that they are in the correct position in the mouth in relation to the tongue, the lips, and the cheeks. The distance between the upper and lower jaw is also carefully measured so that the replacement teeth will be the right length. This is done by means of a block of wax, which is placed in the patient's mouth. The patient is then asked to close the jaws together to give an impression of the mouth—this process is known as "taking the bite." Finally, the correct color and shape of the denture teeth are selected.

Construction of the dentures is carried out in a laboratory. The dentist will usually try out a wax replica of the dentures in the patient's mouth before the final fitting, so that any small adjustments can be made. This means that getting fixed up with dentures can take several weeks.

After the fitting

Once dentures are fitted, it takes about a month for the patient to get used to them, especially if he or she has been without natural teeth for some time.

There may be a few initial problems with talking, but this gradually improves as the patient learns how to adapt to having the dentures in his or her mouth.

Although eating with dentures in position can be rather awkward to start with, most people manage to adjust quite quickly. In the majority of cases, people take to dentures easily. Occasionally part of the jaw on which a denture rests may become sore, but this is easily soothed by minor adjustment.

Dentures should be removed from the mouth at night and kept moist. It is also important to clean them with a brush to prevent staining. If stains do form, they can be removed by one of the commonly available preparations.

It is advisable for dentures to be checked by the dentist if any discomfort occurs and, otherwise, at yearly intervals. Eventually dentures may need to be relined or replaced, since the shape of the jaw does gradually change.

Crowns

A crown is an artificial replacement of the visible part of a tooth. It is most often used as a means of restoring the shape and appearance of a tooth that has become decayed or has been broken beyond the point at which it can be built up with filling material.

Types of crown

Where a sufficient amount of the tooth is still left, a crown is constructed to fit around the outside of the tooth. This is called a jacket crown.

Where so much tooth has been lost that there is no sound base for a crown, support may be provided by inserting a metal post into the root. The fitting is then described as a post crown. In some cases a post can be avoided if the middle of the tooth is built up with filling retained by steel pins.

Construction of a jacket crown

A local anesthetic is given, and then the tooth is reduced in diameter and height by drilling in such a way as to leave a suitably shaped base on which the crown can fit. Once this has been done, an impression of the stump is taken and the color for the crown is selected.

A well-made crown can last indefinitely, but it is normally checked at each dental examination to make sure that it is intact, secure, and that the adjacent margins of the tooth are free from decay.

A crown can be expected to stand up to normal chewing and biting, but it is unwise to subject it to the pressure of cracking nuts.

Bridges

A bridge is an artificial replacement of a missing tooth, but unlike a denture, it is permanently fixed in the mouth to teeth either side of the gap. Bridges are therefore only advisable when there are sound adjacent teeth in healthy gums.

The most permanent form of bridge is cemented to the adjacent teeth, which have to be prepared by removing the outer layers (as for crowning). However, there are also less permanent forms of bridges available that do not involve filing down the adjacent teeth.

The first step in any bridgework is for the dentist to take an impression. The missing tooth may be matched to the corresponding tooth above or below, or on the other side of the jaw. The bridge is then constructed in the laboratory. Finally the bridge is fitted in the patient's mouth by the dentist.

Depression

Q My son's girlfriend has just died in a car accident. I know he is broken-hearted about this, but he won't let it show. Is it better to suppress grief or to let it out?

A The take-it-like-a-man approach has no place in grief, in either sex—in every case it is better to let it out. The suppression of grief, conventionally advocated as a means of showing emotional strength, can actually lead to psychological problems later. The real reason why people advise this is that they get upset by the sight of natural grief in others—their motives are self-centered.

Q During family arguments, my teenage son has often said, "I'll just die, and then you'll be happy." Is there a real risk of him committing suicide because he is depressed?

A What your son may be asking is for you to tell him that you would be very unhappy if he died because you love him, even if you do occasionally argue. If he does seem to have more dark moods than most adolescents suffer, you should watch out for other signs. Teenagers do not have to be as deeply depressed as adults do before they attempt suicide.

Q My friend takes prescribed drugs for her depression. Are these habit-forming?

A The amphetamine drugs can be habit-forming if taken in large quantities over a period of time. For this reason they are now only prescribed under strict medical supervision, or they are avoided altogether. Other antidepressants are safe enough and will be nonhabit-forming if the doctor's instructions are followed exactly.

Q Is there any specific age when people are most likely to be depressed?

A Depression can start at any age, but serious depression peaks at about 60 years old for males and 55 for females. For milder cases, the peak age is 50 for males and 45 for females.

Depression can be conquered—but it sometimes needs skilled medical and psychological help, in addition to support and understanding from family and friends.

Many people feel down from time to time, but these feelings are usually passing phases. In wondering where such moods end and real depression begins, it should be remembered that depression is not a simple condition. It can show itself in various ways and have a number of causes. Neither does it respect sex or occupation and can strike at any time from the teens to middle age, when it claims the greatest number of victims.

Early warning signals

If a person suspects that a spouse, parent, child, or friend is suffering from depression, there are ways of detecting the signs of serious trouble. Perhaps the most significant fact is that the victim loses interest and enjoyment in every aspect of life. Such a change is quickly noticeable to other people.

This can apply to work, school, the home, the family, food and drinks, hobbies, sports, and the desire for sex, and may extend to personal appearance and hygiene. Then the complaints begin—about all kinds of physical problems—

Going to a doctor to talk about your problems is not an easy thing to do when you are depressed, but he or she is trained to give sympathetic and practical help.

headaches, back pains, stomach troubles, tightening in the chest, dizziness, constipation, or blurred vision. The depressed are also so apathetic that they are often unable to ask for professional help. Therefore, it is up to others to seek medical or psychiatric advice for them.

The many faces of depression

Not all the symptoms of depression are shown by every patient—two people behaving in completely different ways can both be considered depressed. What makes the picture even more complicated is that the condition can be accompanied by acute anxiety or by bouts of mania—a mood of almost forced gaiety, talkativeness, and compulsive activity, leading to the term *manic-depressive*.

In general depression, moods may vary from slight sadness to intense despair and a feeling of utter worthlessness. Strangely, people with this condition seldom talk of these feelings to their doctor; instead they may complain about little aches and pains, tiredness, or loss of weight. They may even find it difficult to speak to anyone; to them, other people may seem to chatter constantly.

Compulsive chattering or virtual silence often occur as a result of thought difficulties. Patients often complain of

not being able to think clearly, concentrate, or make decisions—they know that something is amiss. This ability to realize their own unhappy state, without being able to do anything about it, affects depressives in another way. They tend to be preoccupied with themselves and seem completely unable to count their blessings. Instead they magnify the mishaps of the past and tend to blow them up into major disasters, always regarding themselves as totally to blame for these misfortunes.

The habit of distorting events affects sleep patterns, which may already be disturbed by the illness itself. Depressives lie awake worrying about the past, and the future. A vicious circle easily sets in, with worries about the inability to sleep added to all the others.

As if all this were not enough, the depression itself can cause early-morning waking. Small wonder, then, that for many such people the beginning of the day is the most miserable time of all.

When depression is accompanied by anxiety, the sufferer is nearly always restless and has a nervous way of talking; this is in marked contrast to the apathy of other depressives, who tend to hide their worries from others.

Postpartum depression
The particular state arising in a small number of women soon after they have given birth is called postpartum depression. It was once thought of as little more than a mood caused by the exhaustion of labor and the unaccustomed strain of

Brian Nash

A "depression cocktail" of contributory factors

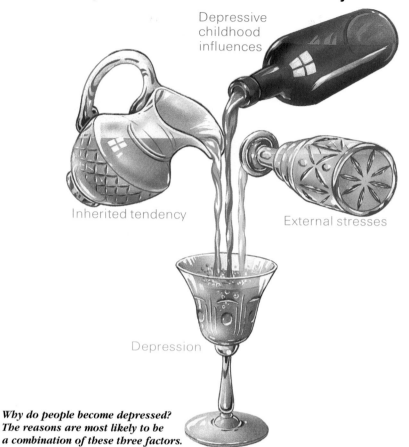

Depressive childhood influences

Inherited tendency

External stresses

Depression

Terry Allen Designs

Why do people become depressed? The reasons are most likely to be a combination of these three factors.

looking after the new arrival. However, it is now recognized as a definite illness, and symptoms include a surprising hostility toward the baby, with consequent feelings of guilt or indifference.

All of this can cause serious neglect of the child and of the home, and a feeling of being unable to cope with the situation. The result is often a weakening of both marital and family relationships. In serious cases it may even lead to suicide.

There is evidence now that the real cause of all these problems is a disturbance of the mother's hormonal system, which is a side effect of pregnancy and birth. Treatment must include the restoration of this hormone balance.

Heredity and environment
To some extent depression is thought to run in families; but this influence is one of increased liability to the condition, rather than actually producing it. In fact, there is nearly always a definite stressful event, or series of events, that brings on the depressive state.

Another way in which these symptoms can be "transmitted" is that the parent who suffers from depression invariably acts out their condition to others in

How to help with postpartum depression
- Ask the doctor's advice: treatment may be needed to restore the mother's hormonal balance
- Psychotherapy might also be necessary, or even a stay in the hospital
- Take over care, or help with care, of the baby to allow the mother to rest and have undisturbed nights. The baby can be taken care of by the partner, a close relative, or even a professional helper, if necessary
- Help with, or take over, domestic chores such as cooking, shopping, laundry, and cleaning
- Be tolerant, understanding, and patient. The mother has very little control over her state of mind, and the more the pressure is taken off her, together with medical or psychological treatment, the quicker she will be able to make a complete recovery

Incidence of first-case depressive illness in three major hospitals in one year

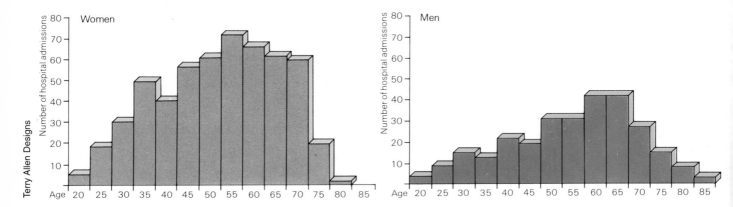

the household. The children then tend to copy this form of behavior themselves later in life, if they also feel depressed. Because they have had this role model, they adopt depressive behavior much more easily than would be the case if they had had no such model to copy.

When there is no family history of this condition, it is virtually always triggered by powerful patterns of outside events that affect the victim deeply. In such cases the chance of recovery from the depression is somewhat better.

The effects of grief
A temporary, but very real, depression can be caused by bereavement. When the death of a loved one is experienced, it is normal to express grief (see Grief). To attempt to suppress this feeling because it is painful, because it is felt that the person is being silly, or because the deceased person "wouldn't want me to be sad" is never helpful; it tends to prolong the grieving period.

Besides the usual reactions of distress, there are often feelings of guilt, irritability, and lack of affection toward others. Sometimes there is an unnerving habit of taking on the personality traits or mannerisms of the dead person.

People in this state may also have problems with their relationships with other members of the family and with friends. They may show intense feelings of anger toward doctors, hospital authorities, or "uncaring" relatives.

Alternatively there may be a complete lack of apparent signs of grief, accompanied by periods of restlessness and virtually pointless activity, which are justified as "keeping the mind busy," but which do nothing of the kind. In any of these situations, the bereaved person should be encouraged to let out their feelings of grief and to talk about their loss with friends, relatives, or even with a family doctor or therapist.

Treatment
Many people find it hard to appreciate the depths of despair that can affect the severely depressed person. In fact, about one in six cases of severe depression results in suicide. It is thought that this rate would be even higher were it not for the fact that the sufferer is often too apathetic to go through with a suicide attempt.

The use of drugs for the treatment of depression is less favorable than it used to be, possibly because psychological methods may better equip the patient for coping with the stresses or situations that contributed to their condition. However, drugs have their place, especially where inherited factors are concerned, because they are simpler to administer and do not involve extended visits to a specialist.

Stimulants such as amphetamines may be prescribed if the depression is not severe. More often used are the so-called tricyclic antidepressants, or serotonin uptake inhibitors, which lift the mood successfully by altering the brain's chemistry. Tranquilizing drugs may also be used in order to relieve anxiety, stress, and tension.

Psychological methods, such as learning to examine thoughts or self-assertion (classes may be held at certain clinics and therapy centers), in addition to behavioral therapy techniques, can work well. Even thinking about making the choice to use psychological methods has a certain power to lift depression.

Living with depression
Psychological treatment can help sufferers change their way of thinking about themselves and the world. But when living with a depressed person, it is best not to expect too much too soon. What is needed is continual friendliness, interest, and support—even if it does not seem to be having much effect. Often, a positive approach is much appreciated by the

depressed person, even if he or she cannot respond, and it will be remembered with gratitude later.

Strangely enough, the technique of not doing too much at once also applies to relaxation. Vacations can lead to additional anxiety for the patient and should be reserved for the time when he or she is well on the road to recovery, when everyone concerned will benefit more.

Hospital treatment
In severe cases of depression, home care may become impossible. Then the patient may have to spend some time in a hospital for continuous care and therapy. Electroconvulsive therapy (ECT) may be given. Carefully controlled electric discharges are passed through certain parts of the brain while the patient is anesthetized. The current induces a convulsion in the patient's brain and body. This is not felt, but it often produces a considerable improvement in the patient's condition—as few as two or three treatments may be enough to produce a complete recovery. Although some temporary forgetfulness of recent events may result, many depressives believe that this is a small price to pay for the dramatic relief that ECT can provide. However, it is a technique that some doctors and psychiatrists question, since its results, in some cases, may be only short-term.

Outlook
In spite of the large number of people who are afflicted with depressive illness, and the severity of some cases, the outlook is reasonably good. It has been estimated that of all those with a clear-cut, depressive illness, about 95 percent will probably recover, and only 4 percent will remain in a state of chronic illness. Of those that do recover, perhaps half may have another phase of depression at some time—but for most people the recovery rate is high.

Dermatitis

Q My best friend has dermatitis. I'm afraid that I will catch it from her and that it might leave me with scars. Is there anything I should do?

A Don't worry. Dermatitis does not cause scarring, and because it is not infectious, you will not catch it from your friend.

Q My neighbor's eczema was cleared up by the use of a hydrocortisone cream, which was prescribed by the doctor. Would there be any harm in my using the cream she has left over to treat my eczema?

A It is a very bad idea to use any medicine that is passed on to you by someone else. Hydrocortisone and the other steroids are powerful medicines that do not suit everyone and have to be used sparingly. And if they have been stored in a hot, steamy kitchen or bathroom, it is likely that they have deteriorated anyway.

Q I just bought a lovely ring, but it seems to bring out a rash. What would have caused this reaction?

A You may be allergic to the metal in your ring. Chrome and nickel commonly cause allergies, and they are often used in costume jewelry. Leave the ring off for two weeks and see if your skin gets any better.

Q I seem to know more females than males who have suffered from contact dermatitis. Does it affect females differently from males?

A Not really, though some contact allergies are more common in one sex because members of that sex tend to be more exposed to the allergen. For example, more females than males develop an allergy to nickel, which can cause dermatitis. This is because nickel is used in the fasteners on underwear for females. But chrome allergy dermatitis is more common in males because chrome is found in cement, which males handle more than females.

Most people have dermatitis—a skin inflammation—at some time in their lives. Identifying the cause is usually quite simple, and a wide range of remedies are available to treat the problem and reduce discomfort to a minimum.

Dermatitis is a red, itching inflammation of the skin. The term actually covers a wide variety of skin complaints, many of which result from the skin becoming oversensitive to some normally harmless substance. But while the symptoms of each type are similar, the causes can be very different.

The most common forms—eczema and contact dermatitis—are widespread, affecting people of all ages. Although uncomfortable and unattractive, most types of dermatitis are temporary, not dangerous, and not contagious.

Allergic reaction

Eczema (see Eczema), or atopic dermatitis, is largely caused by allergies, though it can be brought on or aggravated by other factors, especially stress or anxiety. The main symptom is itchy skin, accompanied by a patchy rash, especially in the creases of the arms, legs, and hands. The affected skin may be cracked and dry—or it can be wet and weeping, though this is

Construction workers are in constant contact with cement, which can cause the form of dermatitis shown (inset) on this man's fingers.

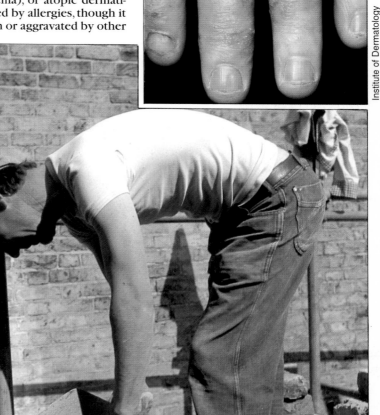

Institute of Dermatology

Sally and Richard Greenhill

Allergens commonly causing dermatitis

Once the allergen has been determined by your doctor, it is important to avoid it or to protect yourself against it to prevent dermatitis from recurring.

Eczema
Milk
Eggs
Other protein-rich foods from animals
Animal dander (fluff)
Pollens

Contact dermatitis
Rubber
Perfumes
Drugs
Synthetic resins, such as epoxy solvents
Lubricating oils
Metals, such as chrome and nickel
Chromate, found in cement
Certain plants, such as poison ivy, oak, or sumac
Wood oils and resins

Di Lewis

often caused by repeated scratching of the affected skin.

Common causes

Closely related to hay fever and asthma, eczema is frequently caused by an allergic reaction to pollen or animal dander (fluff and scales). Many different substances can cause allergies—and almost any of them can bring on eczema.

In young children eczema is commonly caused by an allergy to milk, eggs, or other protein-rich animal foods. Some allergens, or substances that trigger an allergic reaction, can pass through a nursing mother's milk, so a baby's eczema can be caused by something the mother happened to eat. Babies often grow out of these allergies, though they may develop other kinds of allergies later in life.

Direct contact

The other common type of dermatitis is called contact dermatitis. Its symptoms are similar to eczema—inflammation and irritation—but the causes are rather different. This type of dermatitis is also an allergic complaint, but unlike eczema, it is confined to those parts of the body that come into direct contact with the allergen. Metals, especially nickel and chrome, are often to blame, though in fact the list of these contact allergens, as they are called, is almost endless.

Contact dermatitis most often affects the hands, because they are so frequently exposed to contact allergens. But a rubber allergy would most likely show up on the parts of the body exposed to the rubber elastic in underwear. Similarly a perfume allergy would show up as dermatitis on the parts of the body where the perfume was applied.

Although allergies do tend to run in families, contact dermatitis is believed to be due more to regular and prolonged exposure to the substance. Contact dermatitis has been called a 20th-century industrial disease, because modern industry—and its products—exposes workers, in addition to consumers, to so many potential allergens.

Dermatitis of the scalp

Another common type of dermatitis is seborrhea, or seborrheic dermatitis. This is a condition that affects the hairy areas of the skin, particularly the scalp. It may be itchy and inflamed, with peeling of the skin and severe dandruff. Seborrhea is not caused by an allergy. It is thought that the condition is caused by the overactivity of the skin's oil, or sebaceous, glands.

Sensitivity to light

There is a type of dermatitis, called solar or photodermatitis, that is brought on by exposure to sunlight. In most cases the sun alone is not to blame, but sunlight can bring out another allergy that has not been strong enough to produce symptoms by itself. Certain drugs, such as the antibiotic tetracycline, can increase the skin's sensitivity to light.

Treatment

Though there are no real cures for the various kinds of dermatitis, they can be relieved and controlled. The most important treatment is to keep the affected area clean and to avoid scratching it. This allows the skin to heal naturally and reduces the risk of infections. There is a wide range of ointments, creams, pastes, and lotions that are prescribed by doctors or can be bought directly over the counter at a drugstore.

Dry and flaking inflammations can be soothed and protected with oily preparations such as lanolin or petroleum jelly; while wet, weeping inflammations are better treated with gum- or starch-based applications or with some form of astringent to dry the skin.

Some of the most potent medicines are steroids such as hydrocortisone. They are anti-inflammatory and are made into preparations for skin conditions that are available only on prescription.

Though undeniably effective, these drugs have their drawbacks. If used for long periods on the same area of skin, they can damage its underlying layers. And if they are abruptly abandoned after being used for a long time, the dermatitis may suddenly recur. Nor are they cures. If the dermatitis is due to an allergy, steroids may suppress the symptoms but will not stop them returning once the use of the cream has stopped.

The root of the problem

The only permanent cure for dermatitis is to remove the cause. If an allergy is at the root of the trouble, the allergen should be identified and then avoided. This may not be easy, for sometimes the dermatitis only shows up a few days after the exposure to the allergen.

People who are allergy-prone need to watch out for potential allergens from unsuspected sources—e.g., milk or eggs. To help isolate the substance responsible, dermatology departments in hospitals keep stocks of all the major allergens, which can be tested on the patient.

Avoiding irritation

People with sensitive skin should use unperfumed, hypoallergenic (i.e. non-allergenic) soaps, bath products, and cosmetics, since ordinary types usually contain perfumes and additives that can cause contact dermatitis.

Barrier creams and sprays can protect the skin against irritating substances, and sunscreens filter out some of the sun's ultraviolet rays, which can cause solar dermatitis. Contact with some industrial allergens can be reduced by wearing gloves, a face mask, or other types of protective clothing.

Diabetes

Q Will eating too much candy make my child likely to develop diabetes—either now or later in life?

A No. If a child is going to get diabetes, it will be the type caused by failure to produce insulin (a hormone produced in the pancreas). Being overweight or eating sweet things has nothing to do with whether the insulin-producing cells in the pancreas are functioning properly or not.

Q Is there any age when diabetes is more likely to develop?

A It can start at any age, but it is unusual before a child reaches five years. If the disease does come on in early life, it is most likely to do so at puberty or in the late teens or early 20s. After that there is no particular age at which it is more or less likely.

Q My husband has been diagnosed as a diabetic, and I am afraid the illness may change his personality, for example, by making him bad-tempered. Am I right to worry about this?

A Not really. Obviously diabetes, like any illness, can put the patient under a degree of strain, but it does not cause personality changes. There is certainly nothing to suggest that diabetic children develop inadequate personalities as they grow up because of their diabetes.

Q Is it safe for a diabetic person to drive a car or ride a motorcycle?

A Generally, yes. The only danger is that the insulin-controlled diabetic might suffer sudden loss of consciousness as a direct result of a hypoglycemic attack—which happens when the blood sugar level falls too low as a result of the insulin dose getting out of balance.
Diabetics have to declare that they suffer from the disease when applying for a license to drive any kind of vehicle.

Diabetes is no longer feared as it was before treatment was discovered in the 1920s, and current research is constantly improving the outlook for diabetics.

Diabetes is a condition where there is an abnormally high level of sugar in the blood. The disease, and its symptoms, have been recognized for hundreds of years. Affected people pass abnormally large quantities of urine as a result developing an abnormal thirst and losing a great deal of weight.

In the 17th century, when diabetes was known as "the pissing evil," it was noticed that the urine of most sufferers was especially sweet. In a few cases, however, it was insipid—that is, it was not sweet.

The first type had diabetes mellitus (*mellitus* means "like honey"), and this is the disease we know today as plain diabetes. The second type of the disease, diabetes insipidus, is extremely rare and results from a failure of the pituitary gland in the skull.

A common condition
Thousands of people in every country suffer from diabetes mellitus. In the United States, 2 to 4 percent of the population are diagnosed diabetics. One in six hundred school children requires insulin.

Diabetes results from a failure in the production of insulin, one of the body's hormones or chemical messengers. Its job is to keep the blood's sugar content under control by directing it into the cells, where it can be put to its proper use—as fuel to produce energy.

Without insulin the body's cells become starved of sugar, despite the high level in the blood.

How diabetes starts
In most diabetes sufferers, the lack of insulin is due to a failure of the part of the body responsible for producing insulin. This is the pancreas, and the failure is caused by the destruction of its insulin-producing cells. No one knows exactly how the destruction occurs, but it is the subject of much research. It seems that some people are more likely to develop diabetes and that some event—possibly an infection—may trigger the onset of the disease.

The sort of diabetes that develops suddenly, due to a complete or serious failure of insulin, tends to afflict young people and children, and it is often called juvenile diabetes. Luckily it can be treated with injections of insulin from cattle or pigs, or from genetically engineered "human" insulin.

The treatment for juvenile diabetes is a strict diet combined with regular injections of insulin. Here a nurse shows a young diabetic how to give herself an injection.

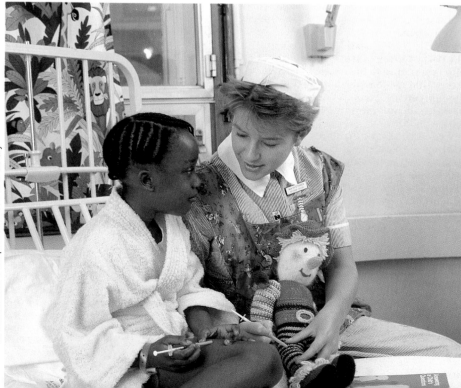

St. Bartholomew's Hospital/Science Photo Library

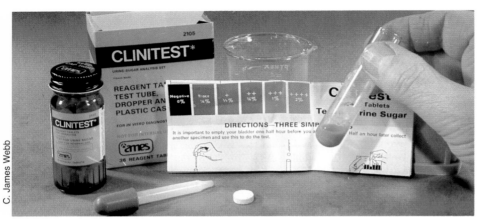

Identification disc

Diabetics check the sugar level in their urine against a color chart. If the level rises too high, insulin intake is likely to need adjusting.

Older diabetics

The majority of diabetics, however, suffer from what is called maturity onset diabetes. In this case the pancreas does produce insulin, often in normal amounts, but the tissues of the body are insensitive to its action—and this produces the high blood-sugar level.

The condition often goes hand in hand with being overweight, and the problem is treated by dieting. Therefore the diet is usually supplemented with tablets that stimulate the pancreas so that it produces more insulin.

However, this picture of two separate sorts of diabetes is too simple. In reality the two types tend to merge into each other. Some younger people, and even children, seem to have the maturity onset type, while some elderly patients may require insulin to keep their blood-sugar level down.

How serious is diabetes?

The disease may be serious for two reasons. First, without insulin injections, the young diabetic simply continues to lose weight and may eventually lapse into a coma and die.

Second, diabetics can develop complications—in other words, additional complaints that are brought on as a result of their condition. Generally speaking, the better the level of blood sugar is controlled, the less likely complications are to occur.

The most serious complications concern the eyes and the kidneys and are caused by the disease's effect on the blood vessels. It is usually possible to see changes to the blood vessels in the back of the eye of any long-standing diabetic; in very few cases, this worsens progressively to the extent that the patient eventually loses the sight of one or both of his or her eyes.

In addition diabetics may also develop abnormalities in their nerves and this, among other problems, can lead to a loss of feeling in the hands and feet.

Finally, the diabetic has, unfortunately, a tendency to develop artery trouble, which in turn causes strokes and heart attacks. For this reason, anyone suffering from diabetes will be strongly encouraged not to smoke, since it is well known that smoking also increases the likelihood of arterial disease.

The role of insulin

- Insulin
- Glucose
- Acid

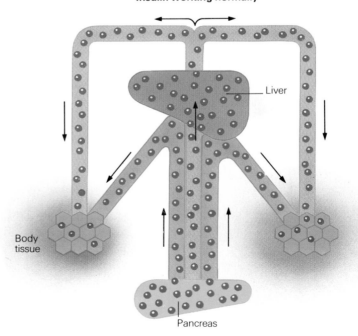

Insulin working normally

Liver

Body tissue

Pancreas

When insulin is being made normally by the pancreas, it enables glucose—which the body cells need to burn to produce energy—to be stored in the liver. Then, when the body cells need more energy, and therefore more glucose to make it, the glucose will be released from the liver, and insulin from the pancreas enables it to be used by the body cells.

How insulin works

In general, it is the patient whose diabetes comes on early in life who needs insulin, although a fair proportion of those whose diabetes starts later in life will also eventually need it.

The hormone is given by injection, usually under the skin of the thigh. Diabetics are instructed how to draw their own insulin up into a syringe and give themselves the injections. This usually has to be done twice daily, and often different formulations of insulin are used to try to spread the total effect out throughout the course of the day.

Once a diabetic has taken insulin, his or her blood-sugar level will start to fall, but this is not, however, the end of the problem. Sometimes the sugar level falls too far as a result of taking the insulin. Sugar is an essential food, not only for the body's tissues in general, but particularly for the brain. If the sugar falls too low, the brain ceases to function properly, and the patient becomes unconscious.

Luckily diabetics can learn to recognize the early symptoms of a falling blood-sugar level. These are shakiness, sweating, tingling around the mouth, and often a feeling of being rather muddled. The treatment for these symptoms, called hypoglycemia (which means low blood-sugar level), is to take some form of sugar by mouth immediately.

Balancing the insulin

Because of the risk of "hypo" attacks, it is important for diabetics to try and balance their food intake with their insulin injections, so that the sugar level is kept somewhere near the normal range, without too much soaring up and down.

This means eating regular meals containing similar amounts of carbohydrates (foods that are broken down to sugar in the blood). All diabetics, whether insulin-treated or not, should avoid sugar itself or foods that contain sugar, such as jam, candy, cakes, and fruit drinks. (Sugar is absorbed rapidly in the stomach to produce brisk increases in the blood-sugar level.) But clearly, the use of sugar to halt a "hypo" attack is an exception to this general rule.

Measuring techniques

As well as carefully planned insulin injections and a regulated intake of carbohydrates, most diabetics use some form of measuring technique to keep a check on their blood-sugar level.

The traditional way of doing this is to measure the amount of sugar in the urine, which gives an idea of the amount of sugar in the blood.

However, diabetics are making increasing use of special testing sticks to measure the blood-sugar level directly. The sticks contain sugar-sensitive chemicals, and blood is taken from a small prick in the finger.

What causes a coma?

Diabetics may suffer from two types of coma. The diabetic coma is different from the one caused by hypoglycemia, when a low blood-sugar level results in a loss of consciousness. In a diabetic coma the diabetic develops a high blood-sugar level, and this leads to complications.

Clearly the two conditions are different, although some people may confuse them. A "hypo" attack can develop in a matter of minutes and is easily stopped by taking sugar.

A high blood-sugar level, on the other hand, takes hours, or even days, to develop and may take hours to cure.

As the sugar level rises, due to lack of insulin, the cells are starved of fuel. They have to burn something to keep alive, and so they start burning fat instead. Used-up fat produces waste products called ketones, and the presence of excess ketones produces high blood-acid levels. If this is not corrected with insulin, coma and death can result.

The future for diabetics

Apart from research into the basic cause of the disease, there have been a number of helpful improvements in the treatment of diabetes.

Insulin is steadily becoming more highly purified, and thanks to the technique of genetic engineering, insulin that is identical to the insulin produced by the human pancreas can be used instead of the animal insulin that was used in the past.

Techniques for taking insulin are, in addition, becoming more refined. The twice-daily injections may be replaced, for some patients, by a constant delivery of insulin from a special pump. This is worn, possibly from a belt, and is only about 6 in (15 cm) in length. The insulin enters by a needle inserted in the skin of the abdomen. Finally the treatment of eye problems caused by diabetes has advanced tremendously because of the introduction of lasers to treat abnormalities at the back of the eye.

How lack of insulin causes a diabetic coma

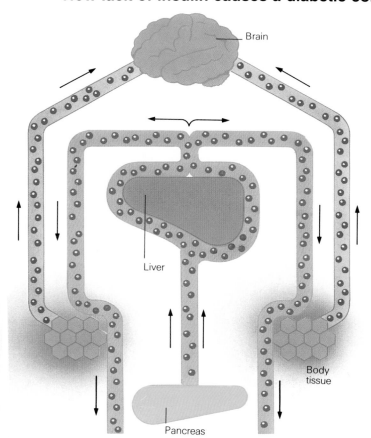

If there is no insulin, glucose cannot be stored or utilized. The result is a great deal of urine with a high glucose content. In place of the lost glucose, the cells produce energy by burning up fats, but these cannot be burnt properly without glucose and therefore produce high acid in the blood. If untreated, a diabetic coma will result.

Diagnosis

Q Why does my doctor always ask me so many questions about my relatives?

A The doctor does this to help make the diagnosis and also to assess the possible course and best treatment for your illness. Some diseases, like diabetes, tend to run in families, and if a relative has suffered from one of these, your doctor needs to know this.

Q My doctor described my high blood pressure as "essential." What does this mean in medical terms?

A The word *essential* means that, although the doctor can identify and treat your symptoms, the problem seems to have started of its own accord for some unknown reason. Doctors use other words, such as *idiopathic* and *primary*, to describe a disease without an obvious cause.

Q I feel completely healthy, but my doctor has suggested a general medical examination. Does he suspect something is wrong?

A Not necessarily. Doctors believe it is wise to have regular medical checkups because checkups involve tests that may reveal a serious illness before the patient feels that something is not right. General medical examinations are particularly useful for certain diseases, such as cervical cancer, that can be cured if they are diagnosed early.

Q Why does the doctor use his stethoscope on my back as well as on my chest?

A By putting his stethoscope on your back, a doctor can hear the noises made by your lungs. He will not only be able to listen to the back part of the lungs but also be able to distinguish these sounds without getting interference from the heartbeat, which occurs when he listens at the front. If the lungs are diseased, he will hear a typical squeaking, crackling, or bubbling sound through the stethoscope. Each of these sounds is caused by a particular type of lung disorder.

To a patient, diagnosis may sometimes appear to be a matter of guesswork. In fact, it requires considerable skill and is a systematic procedure followed by doctors to enable them to identify their patients' health problems.

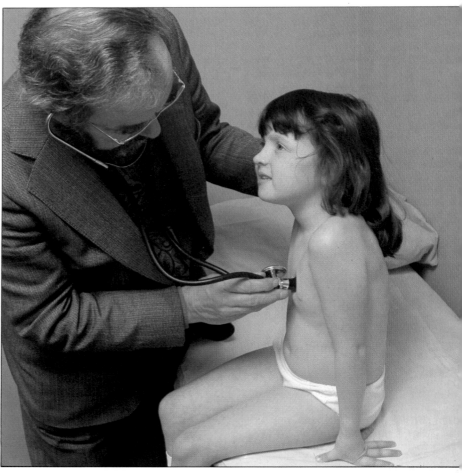

Usually a family doctor will be able to diagnose common illnesses in his or her office, but where additional knowledge is needed, the patient may be sent to see a specialist, who will run further tests.

How a diagnosis is made

To make a diagnosis, a doctor calls on a number of different diagnostic aids. These include his or her senses, training, experience, and a wide range of instruments, all of which provide information about what is going on inside the patient's body. He or she will also ask a series of questions and carry out tests to detect abnormalities and, at the same time, eliminate various possibilities.

Not only will a doctor attempt to find out what is wrong, he or she will also try to assess how far a disease has progressed, what course it may take, and what treat-

Almost a medical symbol, the stethoscope is one of the best-known diagnostic instruments. It is used to listen to the sounds made by the heart and lungs and helps in the diagnosis of many conditions.

ment and advice the patient needs in both the long- and short-term.

Questioning the patient

To obtain a full picture of the patient's condition, a doctor will seek out the signs and symptoms of disease. The symptoms are the feelings experienced by the patient, while the signs are such findings as pulse rate, temperature, blood pressure, the results of X rays, and blood and urine tests.

The doctor usually begins by asking about the patient's symptoms: what they are, how and when they started, and whether they have occurred before. Next, the doctor may ask if any relative has suffered from the same or a similar ailment. He or she will also inquire about the patient's diet, alcohol intake, cigarette consumption, their work and home life, and leisure activities. All the replies will help give the doctor a broader picture of the patient and indicate the likelihood of a particular illness.

When diagnosing illness in a young child, the doctor relies on the parents' answers to these questions. He or she might also ask about the mother's pregnancy and delivery, and about important milestones in the child's life, such as the age he or she started walking or talking. Difficulties can arise when a parent tries to interpret a very young child's symptoms; and when a child is old enough to give a description, it may not be accurate since children find it very hard to identify sites of pain precisely. So parents should try to give as full and accurate a statement as possible in order to help with the diagnosis.

Examining the patient

Following this initial questioning, the doctor will perform a physical examination. First, he or she will take a closer look at the outside of the patient's body, examining the skin, tongue, eyes, and general condition, all of which often reflect a person's state of health. Next, the doctor may press the tongue down with a spatula to look at the throat and tonsils. Then the patient's temperature will be taken. For adults, the thermometer is placed under the tongue, but in babies and young children, the temperature is taken by putting the thermometer in the rectum or under the armpit.

A patient who is obese or underweight may be weighed and measured; the same checks are done on children to assess their progress.

Detailed tests

This general examination is now followed by more detailed tests. To investigate the circulatory system, the doctor will take the pulse and blood pressure and then look at the blood vessels of the eye by pulling down the lower lid. Examination of the vessels on the retina is done with an instrument called an ophthalmoscope. Diseases of the blood or circulation often reveal themselves during such eye examinations. Finally the doctor will listen to the heart with a stethoscope and note any abnormal sounds.

The doctor will assess the respiratory system by tapping on the patient's chest and listening to the sound produced. The patient will be asked to breathe in and out deeply while the doctor uses the

Instruments used in diagnosis

Instrument/test	Use	Conditions that may be revealed
Clinical thermometer	To test body temperature	Raised temperature—a sign of inflammation in some area
Percussion	Tapping of patient's chest or abdomen to feel the solidity or hollowness of underlying organs	Solid or fluid areas, perhaps unexpected and abnormal, can be identified
Stethoscope	To listen to sounds made by heart, lungs, and occasionally intestines	Malfunction of heart, heard as abnormal sound quality or timing. Disease in air passages of lungs, heard as abnormal sounds
Otoscope	To look at ear canal and eardrum	Wax, foreign bodies, inflammation, and condition of eardrum can be seen
Ophthalmoscope	To look at the retina at the back of the eye	State of retina and its blood vessels indicate various diseases of the circulatory and nervous systems and of the eye itself
Sphygmomanometer	To measure blood pressure	High blood pressure
Electrocardiogram (ECG)	Electrical device used to obtain a trace of the heartbeat	Abnormal patterns of heart action show up on tracing and indicate type of heart disease and its likely site
Rubber hammer (patella hammer)	Used to test reflexes; for example, a knee jerk	Slow or absent reflexes may indicate damage to nerves
Blood test	Blood removed from a vein, chemically examined, and examined under a microscope	Vast range of tests possible. Too few red blood cells indicate simple anemia. Too much uric acid in blood is an indication of gout
Urine test	Chemical tests and microscopic examination of urine	Many tests possible: for example, diabetes mellitus shows up as high blood-sugar level in urine

Hospital and laboratory tests

Other tests include: many types of X-ray examination; plain X rays to diagnose bone fractures or disorders; the barium meal, in which barium sulfate is swallowed so the alimentary canal can be examined for abnormalities; the barium enema, to detect conditions of the bowel and lower intestine; the intravenous pyelogram, in which radiopaque dye is injected into the bloodstream and excreted through the kidneys, to show possible kidney damage; and the angiogram, to examine blood vessels.

Electrical devices for diagnosis include the electroencephalogram (EEG), which shows traces of electrical activity in the brain and is used to assess epilepsy and other brain disorders. Laboratory tests include serology, the study of blood serum, in which a vast range of diseases show up as specific antibody reactions. Body tissues are also examined in a biopsy, to check for cancerous cells; and in a lumbar puncture, fluid from around the spinal cord is examined to detect, for example, meningitis.

DIAGNOSIS

Brian Nash

With the otoscope, the doctor is able to look inside the patient's ears to see the state of the eardrums.

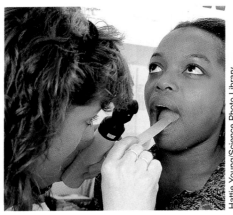

To examine the throat and the tonsils, a light is shone inside the mouth, and the tongue is depressed with a spatula.

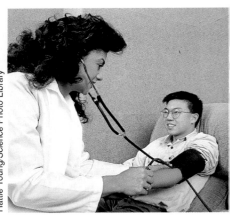

Hattie Young/Science Photo Library

Blood pressure is measured using a sphygmomanometer and can give valuable clues to the patient's general state of health.

stethoscope to listen to the lungs, first at the front of the body and then at the back. As with the heart, abnormal sounds can help in diagnosis.

In addition to looking at the mouth and teeth, and examining the anal area, the doctor may examine the alimentary system and the internal organs by feeling them through the anal canal or, in females, via the vagina, and by pressing carefully and systematically on the abdominal wall. Experience will tell the doctor how to interpret what he or she can feel, as well as the significance of pain felt by the patient during the examination.

Problems of the muscular system usually result in discomfort or pain on movement. The doctor will check to find out exactly which movements cause pain by, for example, bending the patient's knee into different positions. Any suspect part will be put through its normal range of movements, and the results will be noted.

To test the central nervous system, the patient will be asked to sit in a relaxed state with the legs swinging loosely. The doctor taps below the knee of one leg with a small rubber hammer. This should elicit a jerking reflex response. A similar process is used to test other reflexes.

To check the sense organs, the doctor will examine the eyes with an ophthalmoscope for signs of damage or disease. An otoscope is used to look into the ears. This instrument detects any signs of damage or infection in the middle ear or eardrum. A wide range of tests will also be done to make sure that the senses of touch, pain, temperature, movement, and balance are all in good order.

Prescribing treatment

Having completed the examination, the doctor can now make a diagnosis and prescribe treatment. He or she will take into consideration not only the answers

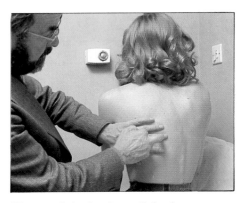

The sounds in the chest tell the doctor a great deal about the health of the lungs and respiratory system.

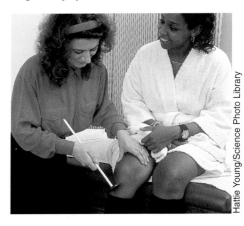

Hattie Young/Science Photo Library

The knee-jerk test, shown above, is designed to test the reflexes of the central nervous system; a special type of hammer is used.

to the questions asked and the findings of the examination, but also the information gained about the patient's mental health and general physical condition.

The doctor may conclude, for example, that while the patient has high blood

pressure, which needs treatment with drugs, they should also be advised to lose weight, to seek help with emotional problems, or to stop pushing themselves so hard at work. Similarly the doctor may conclude that the patient has underlying problems such as loneliness, obsession with illness, or a reluctance to work.

The ease or difficulty of diagnosis depends upon the illness itself. Many childhood infections, such as measles, mumps, and chicken pox, have such distinctive symptoms that it would be hard to mistake them for anything else. Many diseases of adulthood present themselves just as clearly. Sometimes the diagnosis is so obvious to the doctor that the full examination is unnecessary. However, other illnesses are more complicated and can be harder to detect, and further tests may be required.

When further tests are required

When a complete diagnosis proves impossible, or when a doctor seeks to confirm a diagnosis, he or she will send the patient for additional tests at a hospital where equipment and special knowledge are available.

The role of the hospital in diagnosis ranges from taking X rays and conducting chemical and microscopic examinations of blood and urine to operations conducted under general anesthetic, in which the interior of the body is examined with a lit tube called an endoscope. Technicians will very often carry out the tests, and the results will be interpreted by specialists.

Diagnosing by computer

In computer diagnosis the patient's symptoms and the results of any other tests are fed into a computer that then punches out its conclusions. This is useful in the case of a rare disease.

CLARKSTON